PASSPORT TO NEVAEH

*The Universal Ruler of all Nations in 2001 - The Sole Spiritual Head of the Universe:*

 **O**lumba **O**lumba **O**bu

*"I Am Before You And Behind You!"*

**BCS:** **B**rotherhood of the **C**ross and **S**tar - *The New Kingdom of God on Earth.*

# Passport To Heaven 2001

### By W.B. Smith

**Spiritual Chorus**: *"From the year 2001 every lip shall praise Olumba, every church will be Olumba."*

**Everlasting Gospel:** *"The Universal Ruler in the Year 2001 is Born of a Woman."*

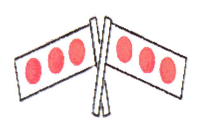

© WBS Reproductions 2000. All rights reserved.
ISBN 0 9522022 5 5

No part of this publication may be
reproduced, stored in a retrieval
system or transmitted in any
form for commercial purposes
without the prior written permission
of WBS Reproductions.

Published and Distributed by:
WBS Reproduction of BCS Gospels,
6 Stokenchurch Place, Milton Keynes,
MK13 8AW, England, Tel. 01908 606279.
E-Mail: pass38@passporttoheaven2001.com
WEBSITE: www.passporttoheaven2001.com
Printed by Polaprint of Bedford. Tel:01234 213885

British Library Cataloguing-in-Publication Data.
A catalogue record for this book is available from
the British Library.

*The entire Net Sales Proceeds of this book is donated to Third World Poverty Relief.*

# Contents

| | |
|---|---|
| Introduction | i |
| Acknowledgements | iv |
| Dedication | v |

Chapters :

| | | |
|---|---|---|
| 1. | Human Beings | 1 |
| 2. | The Holy Trinity: God Is One | 5 |
| 3. | What Is Brotherhood Of The Cross And Star? | 12 |
| 4. | Christ Was Not Crucified On Friday | 17 |
| 5. | Veganism | 20 |
| 6. | Celibacy: It's Religious Support | 27 |
| 7. | A Woman Must Not Rule Over A Man | 30 |
| 8. | When Man Fights Against God | 32 |
| 9. | The Steps To God And His Kingdom | 34 |
| 10. | Those Who Will Go To Heaven | 47 |
| 11. | Those Who Will Go To Hell | 65 |
| 12. | Incarnation, De-Carnation and Re-Incarnation | 88 |
| 13. | After 1999 Something Spectacular Will Happen | 97 |
| 14. | The Universal Leader In The Year 2001 Is Born Of A Woman | 105 |
| 15. | When God Becomes Man He Is Water, Blood And Spirit | 116 |
| 16. | Whosoever Wants To Be Great Must First Be A Servant | 125 |
| 17. | Murder | 135 |
| 18. | An Open Letter To The World | 141 |
| 19. | Prayer For The World | 144 |
| 20. | The Power Of The Spoken Word | 147 |
| 21. | One Government: One Currency | 154 |
| 22. | My Words: Your Watchwords | 160 |
| 23. | Theology, Hypocrisy And Our Lord Jesus Christ | 163 |
| 24. | The Creator Is On Earth | 166 |

*Contents*

| | |
|---|---|
| 25. The Last Commandment | 175 |
| 26. The Reign Of Love By 2000 A.D. | 178 |
| Appendix 1  Addresses Of BCS Bethels | 183 |
| Appendix 2  God And The Internet | 185 |
| Appendix 3  Father's Phone Number Gospel | 186 |

**Photographs and Illustrations:**

Page vi: The Holy Father Leader Olumba Olumba Obu welcoming BCS UK Brethren during April 1988 Pentecostal Celebrations, Calabar, Nigeria..
*Photo reproduced by Elder W. B. Smith.*
Page 4: God's plan for the World from creation to the present era.
*Designed by Elder W.B. Smith.*
Page 9: The Holy Father Leader Olumba Olumba Obu.
*Photo reproduced be Elder W.B. Smith.*
Page 10: His Holiness R.O. Obu, King of Kings.
*Photo reproduced by Elder W.B. Smith.*
Page 11: Her Holiness I.O. Obu, the Holy Queen Mother.
*Photo reproduced by Elder W.B. Smith.*
Page 16: The Kingdoms Of The World vs The Kingdom of God and His Christ.
*Illustration designed by Elder W.B. Smith.*
Front Cover:  Top - The Holy Trinity and the Holy Insignia.
              Bottom: A section of the attendants at the annual BCS Pentecostal Assembly, Calabar, Nigeria.
*Designed and Reproduced by Elder W.B. Smith*
Covers: Designed by WBS Reproduction of BCS Gospels.

# Introduction

The Holy Bible contains God's plan for the world. It tells what has happened, what is happening and what will happen. But who can interpret the Bible except He Who comes direct from God or the Almighty Himself? This is exactly what is happening at this end of time to this lucky generation.

**1. St John 16 v 7 - 13**
" Neverthe less, I tell you the truth, It is expedient for you that I go away, for if I go not away the Comforter will not come unto you, but if I depart I will send Him unto you. And when He is come, He will reprove the world of sin, of righteousness, and of judgement. Of sin because they believe not in Me; of righteousness because I go to My Father and ye see Me no more; of judgement because the prince of this world is judged. I have yet many things to say unto you, but you cannot bear them now. Howbeit, when He the Spirit of Truth is come, He will guide you into all truth; for He shall not speak of Himself, but whatsoever He shall hear, that shall He speak, and He will show you things to come."

**2. St John 15 v 26**
"But the Comforter which is the Holy Ghost whom the Father will send in my name; He shall teach you all things and bring all things to your rememberance, whatsoever I have said unto you."

**3. Revelation 5 v 9**
"….. Thou art worthy to take the book and open the seals thereof for thou was slain and has redeemed us to God by thy blood….."

**4. Revelation 12 v 5**
" And she brought forth a man child who was to rule all nations with a rod of iron, and her child was caught up unto God and to His throne."

**5. Hebrews 1 v 6**
"And again when He bringeth in His First Begotten into the world, He said and let all the angels of God worship Him."

**6. Acts 1 v 11**
"Ye men of Gallilee why stand ye gazing up into heaven? This same Jesus which is taken up from you into heaven shall so come in like manner as ye have seen Him go into heaven."

The true interpretation of all these passages from the Bible is that our Lord Jesus Christ will come back on earth as a human being. Not to shed His blood again, nor to go preaching from place to place, but to remain in one place and assume His reign as the King of Kings and Lord of Lords. That book mentioned in Revelation Chapter 5 is the Holy Bible. There is no human being nor church denomination, that can interpret the Bible. It is only our Lord Jesus Christ that can open the Bible, break the seals thereof, and reveal its content to the world. On His second and final advent into the world, His main assignments are as follows:

    1. To open the Bible and teach the world of the ways of God.
    2. To reform sinners and bring them up to the standard required by God.
    3. To establish the kingdom of God on earth, so that the will of God is done on earth as it is done in heaven; thus fulfilling the words of our Lord's Prayer which said, "Our Father which art in heaven, hallowed be Thy name Thy kingdom come; Thy will be done in earth as it is in heaven……"
    4. To judge the world, and
    5. To rule all nations of the world.

Every word of God must be fulfilled. God said, "Heaven and earth will pass away, but My words will not pass away." The generation of our Lord Jesus Christ ends on 31 December 2000. The year 2001 will be the start of the 'New Age' in the 'New Heaven' and the 'New Earth' where only righteousness dwells. The six passages quoted from the Bible are now fulfilled in the Brotherhood of the Cross and Star (BCS); its world Headquarters situated at 34 Ambo Street, Calabar, Cross River State, Nigeria, West Africa. It is also the Headquarters of the Everlasting Gospel Centre and the Christ Universal Spiritual School of Practical Christianity. Brotherhood of the Cross and Star covers the entire universe and includes all things created by the Almighty God; Animate and Inanimate, Visible and Invisible. It is not a church, group, prayer house or secret society. **It is the " New Kingdom of God " on earth**. For over 30 years, from January 1st to December 31st, the Founder and Sole Spiritual Head of the Brotherhood of the Cross and Star- Leader Olumba Olumba Obu (OOO), has been preaching the New Gospels of Reformation and Reconstruction to the world; as promised by our Lord Jesus Christ.

The gospels delivered daily by Leader Obu has never been preached before, nor will they be preached by anyone again. These are the last gospels. His teachings and sermons goes further than those of our Lord Jesus Christ, thus fulfilling these words of our Lord Jesus Christ: " I have yet many things to say unto you but you cannot bear them now. Howbeit, when He the Spirit of Truth is come, He will guide you into all truth, for He shall not speak of Himself, but whatsoever He shall hear, that shall He speak, and He will show you things to come," and " Greater things than these shall ye do, because I go to My Father." You need only to read one of Leader Obu's gospels to be completely convinced. One can only obtain salvation by practising the teachings of our Lord Jesus Christ, and that is the reason why only the life and teachings of Christ ( Who is the Word of God ) are preached daily by Leader Obu. Our Lord Jesus Christ said, "False Prophets and false Christs shall rise, but you shall know them by their fruits. On His second advent, the CHRIST will not come with the old name "Jesus," but with a New Name. If He comes back with the old name "Jesus" then He is not the one; neither will He come back as a Spirit. No human being can see the Spirit, and no human being can withstand the Spirit. The Prophets of God prophesied about the birth of our Lord Jesus Christ, and these prophecies have been fulfilled and set aside. Our Lord Jesus Christ Himself spoke of His return to earth. He revealed to Paul, the Aposthes and John the Divine that He will return to earth in the flesh. Leader Olumba Olumba Obu is that promised Comforter, the Holy Spirit of Truth personified. He has come into the world as the Supernatural Teacher, to reveal God to the world and guide all mankind into the accurate wisdom of truth. The people of old continued to look up at the sky to see the promised Messiah flown down from the sky into the earth plane in glory and great splendour. They did not realise that the small child born to Mary in a stable was in fact the Christ. Until this day the vast majority of Jews do not accept that the Messiah has come. They are still waiting for the first coming of our Lord Jesus Christ. God has confounded the wisdom of human beings. God never work according to the interpretations and expectations of human beings. He works according to His own will. The town of Nazareth was an evil and notorious place. All kinds of attrocities and lawlessness were committed there; yet our Lord Jesus Christ was born there. That was why Nathaniel asked, "Can any good thing come out of Nazareth?" At this end of time, history has repeated itself. Today the people of the world are gazing up at the sky and waiting for our Lord Jesus Christ to emerge and fly down to earth with His angels to collect all christians and take them up to heaven. The promised Comforter, the Holy Spirit of Truth personified is now reigning at this end of time. He has been manifested in Africa, the land of slavery, poverty and famine; a rejected place. Today, like Nathaniel the peoples of the world are asking, "Can any good thing come out of Africa?"

# Introduction

The Almighty God has again confounded the wisdom, interpretations and expectations of the Church denominations, Secret Societies, and all the Nations of the world. At this closing of the age, there is a Great Phenomenon in our midst, and the world cannot comprehend. Jehovah God and His Christ, and all His heavenly hosts are now on earth. All the Patriarchs, Prophets, Kings, Saints, Apostles and other people of old from Adam onward, are here on earth today, awaiting the Judgement Day. All will be revealed soon. Who is a Christian? A Christian is any person who practise the teachings of our Lord Jesus Christ as recorded in the New Testament; particularly, St Matthew Chapters 5, 6 and 7; and St Luke Chapter 6. There is no church denomination and there is no human being in the world today who practise the teachings of our Lord Jesus Christ **precisely.** The worldly wisdom, and the interpretations of the so-called righteous people of today, is that a person only has to declare that he or she believe in God or Jesus; then get baptised and attend church regularly; after that they are sure to go to heaven; but they continue to commit all kinds of sins and vices, claiming that the Father sent His Son Jesus to shed His precious blood to wash away their sins. The question is, are those who claim to be rightious really rightious? Remember that there were millions of people in the world of Noah, but only eight persons were saved. There were also many people in the two cities of Sodom and Gomorrah, but only three persons were saved. The behaviour of the peoples of today's world, is worse than the people of old.

This book is not written as a result of worldly wisdom and worldly interpretations of the Bible. Neither is the writer seeking fame or financial reward. **All the writings in this book, comes from the recondite teachings and Everlasting Gospels which are delivered daily by the Supernatural Teacher and Sole Spiritual Head of BCS and the Universe and we have a Divine duty to disseminate these Gospels throughout the four corners of the earth before the end comes.** The peoples of the world today are very confused. There are those who are searching for God and want to know how to worship Him. There are those who interpret the scriptures to suit themselves and use their worldly wisdom and establish many churches, secret societies, sects and healing homes (some for personal fame and financial motives). There are those who claim that there is no God. There are those who claim to believe in God, but continue to commit all kinds of sins and vices. There are others who claim that God sent His Son Jesus to die for their sins, so they are free to curse, hate, fight, indulge in drunkeness, lawlessness and other sins and vices. The Lord God Almighty has long patience with human beings, but the long patience of God should not be regarded as stupidity. The only Passport to Heaven is to practise the Holy Gospels of Good Tidings now delivered by the Holy Spirit of Truth.

The sole intention of this book is to help us face that reality because the only Divine Law in the New Era which begins in 2001 is "**Love One Another.**" any other option will result to total elimination from the face of the earth. In this New Era, the Universal Ruler comes with a New Name ( OOO ), New Kingdom of God ( BCS ), New Everlasting Gospels, New Insignia and a New Universal Flag.

*May 2000*                                     *W.B. Smith.*

# Acknowledgements

All thanks, glory and praises to the Holy Spirit for His guidance and inspiration in the compilation of this Publication.

My sincere gratitude to Sister EmEm Ette and Brother Ola Ajayi for their contribution and for their organisation of BCS UK Internet Website from where some of the New Gospels of Good Tiding recorded in this book are extracted.

Finally, my thanks to Sister Paulette Atkins for supplying me with BCS Booklets, Tracts and CDs.

# Dedication

This Book is dedicated to the Holy Spirit of
Truth & Supernatural Teacher
Leader Olumba Olumba Obu, Sole Spiritual Head
of the Universe Who is daily delivering the
New Everlasting Gospels and Whose
instruction to His Disciples reads:

" *You are privilaged to have this TRUTH preach to you,*
**thus increasing your faith. You are now required to go
out with this TRUTH, and help others to share this same
Message, since you are now rich with the Message of Life.**"

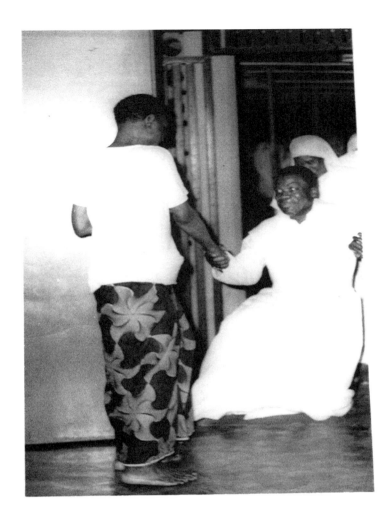

**Leader Olumba Olumba Obu**
He welcomes daily, thousands of Converts and Visitors (individually) from all around the World.

---

Godly Virtues in action: Humility, Meekness, Gentleness, Love, Patience, Mercy, Peace, Tolerance and Understanding displayed by the Sole Spiritual Head and Commander of the Universe, the Iron Rod Ruler, King of Kings and Lord of Lords. The powerful Holy Angels bow to Him and revere Him; but weak, puny and sinful human beings who can be tossed about by sickness and death, will ignore, reject and treat Him with scorn because of pride, arrogance, pomposity and conceitedness.

*"Behold the Tabernacle of God is with men, and He will dwell with them, and they shall be His people, and God Himself shall be with them and be their God" (Rev. 21 v 3).*

# CHAPTER 1

# HUMAN BEINGS:
## Where We Came From? Where Are We Now? Where Are We Going?
*Know the Truth, the whole Truth and nothing but the Truth; as revealed by the Holy Spirit of Truth.*

**( Holy Spirit of Truth's Revelations, Summarized by:    Elder W.B. Smith )**

Man is a Spiritual Spark from GOD or SOURCE. Man had existed as 'Spiritual Being' and is part and parcel with God our Father. The Spirit (Man) was materialised when God said "Let us make man in our image and likeness" (Gen. 1 v 25 - 29). So God created Adam and Eve (the Spirits embodied in flesh) and human beings became living Souls (Gen. 2 v 7). On earth Human Beings are the House of God because the Holy Spirit of God (the Doer and Teacher of all things) dwelth in Adam. Adam was the house built by God; the human body is the Temple of God ( 1 Cor. 3 v 16 - 17 ).
The Kingdom of God (the Garden of Eden) was then on earth because God Himself dwelth there. Human Beings, animals and all the creations of God lived there in love, peace and harmony; no quarrel, fighting, sickness or problems. God advised Adam and Eve that He would teach them everything, therefore they should take instructions only from the Holy Spirit and no one else. God also told Adam and Eve "Be fruitful and multiply and replenish the earth.....(Gen. 1 v 26 - 29); eat from every tree except the tree of knowledge, good and evil... (Gen. 2 v 16 - 17)." Eve heeded the advise of the Serpent; Adam succumbed to Eve's suggestion and both of them ate the forbidden fruit. As a result their eyes were opened and they had sexual intimacy (fornication); God's instructions were rejected and Man's lust and desires enthroned; and that is how all Human Beings behave until this day; but the God of righteousness will never allow such behaviour to continue, (especially after the crucifixion of our Lord Jesus Christ the Saviour and Redeemer of all mankind ). As a result God cursed Adam and Eve (and the Serpent); the Holy Spirit left them and they were expelled from the Garden of Eden - the original dwelling place of all Human Beings as ordained by God our Creator and Father (Gen. 3).

# PARADISE LOST

It was not God's plan that man and woman should be intimate with each other. Women were to bear Holy children exactly as the Virgin Mary who was not intimate with man, but was conceived by the Holy Spirit. If Adam and Eve had waited for God's further instructions, things would be different between man and woman. By disobeying God they defiled the temple of God, and so, every child born via sexual intimacy is unholy, impure, sinful and is under God's curse. This is the fate of the entire Human race - the descendants of Adam and Eve. Outside of the Garden of Eden, man experience suffering, tribulation, division, quarrelling, fighting, sickness and death. Man now has to fend for himself because the Holy Spirit had left him. Adam pleaded with God to return to Him, but God promised him that only when a Holy Blood is shed would He return to man and that the sign of His return would be Gold, Frankincense and Myrrh. Until this day all Human Beings continue to ignore and disobey God's injunctions and do their own thing; claiming that "God wants all to be happy, therefore whatever makes one happy, he or she should be allowed to do it even if it is sinful;" they call this 'freedom of choice' and these include diverse sexual habits, eating habits and other social and Spiritual habits not authorised by God. These actions of man resulted in the destruction of the world of Noah; but God remembered His promise to Adam and saved Noah and his family to continue the human race on earth so that the 'blood of the Holy One' could be shed as atonement for the sins of Adam and his offsprings; only then will the Holy Spirit return to man to teach him God's ways and reconstruct him to the standard required by God to inherit the lost Paradise. God promised Abraham that the Holy One would come from his family - the Israelites (Gen. 12 v 1 - 7 & Gen. 17 v 1 - 8).

# WHERE ARE WE NOW?

The Garden of Eden was the Kingdom of God on earth where righteousness dwells; love, joy, peace, happiness, patience, mercy, humility, honesty, good health, disipline and all the Godly Virtues were there because the Holy Spirit dwelt there. We are all outside of the Garden of Eden right now, therefore the entire Human Race is in hell (Gen. 3 v - 23 - 24). WHAT IS HELL? It is not a place where fire is stored and people or spirits are thrown in to be burnt. Hell is a condition of suffering, trials, tribulation, lawlessness, fighting, quarrel, killing, sickness, diseases, division, confusion, hatred, backbiting, falsehood, stealing, fornication, adultery, sexual perversion, drinking, drug taking, whoremongering, homosexuality, child abuse, abortion, killing and eating of animals, birds and fishes, blasphemy against God, idolatry, court actions, famine, food poisoning, pollution, greed, bribery, fear, discrimination, rioting, strikes, terrorism, smoking, pride, arrogance, pomposity, e.t.c. Are we not experiencing these conditions daily? Are we not in hell? These conditions are not ordained by God; they are man-made and self inflicted. We reap what we sow; God is not responsible for our problems; why blame Him? But at last there is hope, there is a way out of this hell.

# TO WHERE ARE WE GOING?

The world has no end because God has no begining and no end. Man cannot die because God cannot die. There is no death because the Spirit (God) in man cannot die; rather, it is transfered from the body to the Spiritual world and later return in another body (re-incarnation) to the mortal world to experience hell again, or, to repent, serve God and experience Salvation. This process or cycle goes on continuously from the time of Adam till today. The coming of the Holy One of God gave man hope and another chance to get back into the Garden of Eden (the Kingdom of God) and so put an end to the cycle of continuous suffering (Hell). That Holy One is our Lord Jesus Christ ( Matt. 1 v 23).
BUT WHO REALLY IS OUR LORD JESUS CHRIST? Would you send one of your sons or daughters to die for the sins committed by other people? You would not. "For as by one man's disobedience many were made sinners, so by the obedience of one shall many be made righteous." (Romans 5 v 19). Our Lord Jesus Christ in His first advent was Adam (Rom. 5 v 1 - end) and the Virgin Mary was Eve His wife. As Adam and Eve they disobeyed God's injunction and committed fornication (sexual intimacy). That is why He came as 'Jesus' to shed His precious blood to atone for His sin and the sins of the entire Human race. This time having learnt His lesson He had nothing to do with women and Mary (Eve re-incarnated) was now His mother instead of His wife. At His birth Gold, Frankincense and Myrrh were presented to Him, indicating that He was the Holy One sent by God in fulfilment of His Promise to Adam and Abraham.

### ABRAHAM'S DESCENDANTS: TWO NATIONS: Israelites and Gentiles

Abraham begat Ishmael and Isaac who was the chosen one to father the 'Holy One' promised by God. Isaac begat Esau and Jacob who was the chosen one to father the 'Holy One.' The birth of Esau and Jacob (twins) generated two nations - the Israelites and the Edomites (Gen. 25 v 21 - 24 & Gen 27 v 1 - 40), one stronger than the other and the elder to serve the younger. The elder sold his birthright to the younger and the younger stole the blessings of the elder by trickery. Jacob and the Israelites represents the White nation; Esau and the Edomites represents the Black nation. The Gentiles (that other nation) constitute the Edomites and other 'Non-Israelite' races of people. Having received the blessings, the Whites are richer, wiser and stronger than the Blacks who are their slaves; but for how long? ( Gen. 27 v 40 ).

## CHRIST THE SAVIOUR & REDEEMER FIRST CAME TO THE WHITES (St John Ch. 1)

The Jews rejected Him and His New Divine teachings. They derided Him, mocked Him and treated Him with scorn; finally they crucified Him; but can man kill God (John 10 v 17 - 18)? The Lord surrendered His life willingly to atone for the sins of the entire human race and redeem man to God, and He was resurrected after 3 days, thus conquering death. He made several pronouncements on the Jews because of their rejection and unbelief; i.e. "The Kingdom shall be taken from you and be given to a nation that bear much fruits" (Matt. 21 v 43), etc.

## CHRIST THE COMFORTER NOW COME TO THE BLACKS (St John 14 v 26)

Who is the 'other nation'? They are the Blacks (1 Peter 2 v 9 & John 10 v 16) - the Gentiles. Jacob had most of the blessings by trickery, but Esau did receive some blessing: ".....And it shall come to pass when thou shalt have the dominion, that thou shalt break his yoke from off thy neck." (Gen, 27 v 40). Esau (the Black Nation) now have the dominion because the Comforter and the New Kingdom of God is now on earth and have been germinated in black Africa.

## PARADISE REGAINED ( Rev. Ch. 21 & Rev. 19 v 11 - 16.)

Brotherhood of the Cross and Star (BCS) is the New Kingdom of God on earth and Leader Olumba Olumba Obu (OOC) the Sole Spiritual Head of the Universe is the promised Comforter and Holy Spirit of Truth (St. John 16 v 7 - 13). Brotherhood of the Cross and Star is the Garden of Eden (man's original position); Paradise Regained. The gates are now re-opened to admit human beings again. We can get there only via our Lord Jesus Christ (St John 14 v 6). We have to practise His teachings as recorded in the New Testament, and, the current New Teachings of the Comforter - the Holy Spirit of Truth. The Church Denominations teach people that when they die they go straight to heaven so long as you accept Jesus as your Saviour, baptise and attend Church regularly. That is erroneous and impossible. To inherit the Kingdom of God we have to return to man's original position in the Garden of Eden i.e., love one another, no fighting or killing of man and lower creatures, no eating of flesh (Gen. 1 v 29), no fornication, adultery, homosexuality, abortion, stealing, lying, division, etc. Then, there will be no sickness, sorrows, suffering and tribulations. So where do we want to go? It must either be to Heaven or Hell. It is either Brotherhood of the Cross and Star (the New Kingdom of God on Earth) or Hell (the kingdoms of the world). BCS is the New Heaven and New Earth where only righteousness dwells. WHERE IS HELL? It is in the world. WHERE IS HEAVEN? It is also in the world. If we accept Brotherhood of the Cross and Star we will experience heaven eternally wherever we reside in the world. If we reject Brotherhood of the Cross and Star we will experience hell eternally wherever we are in this life and the other lives to come. These are the TRUTH, the whole TRUTH and nothing but the TRUTH as revealed by the HOLY SPIRIT of TRUTH Who has come in Holy Trinity (OOO) to Judge and Rule all nations with an iron rod (Rev. 12 v 5 & Rev. 19 v 11 - 16). The Choice is ours.

## LOVE: The New Covenant; BCS: The New Kingdom of God.

Take note of the following quotes by the Sole Spiritual Head of the Universe:-

"In order to have good preservation, new wine should be put in a new wineskin. Brotherhood of the Cross and Star is the New Kingdom of God and the only known law is love. Everybody is implored to express love to one another. If you do not have love and express it to others, you would not have share in the kingdom. Should you take a critical look at the entire situation in the world and her inhabitants, you would discover that there is nobody who loves his brother . But God has now come with His kingdom to supplant all other worldly kingdoms. So the consequence for those who do not have love is complete extermination from the surface of the earth. When this mass elimination would be carried out, no consideration will be given to the Catholics, Presbyterians, Methodist, Buddhists, Eckists or Muslims. As a matter of fact, religious affiliation is not a criterion for salvation. The only key to salvation is love. If you possess love, the gate of the kingdom lies ever open to you.

Beloved, God has come into the world to reform mankind. You should count yourself most fortunate to be taught by Him. So you do not have time to waste, you should at once start expressing love to one another. Where you fail to do so, you will certainly face damnation. Let this sink into your marrow, blood and mind, the covenant of Moses is now obsolete and no more relevant to the new system; love is now the covenant. Therefore, if you refuse to exhibit love to everybody, you would not exist in the world by 2000 AD. The divine assurance is that love will permeate all realms, and control all planes of manifest by the close of this century. Let me resound this warning: whoever do not turn a new leaf by practising love shall be destroyed. There is no other law that shall exist at that time in the world apart from love. The deadline meant for everybody to possess love is 2000 AD. Anybody who has no love by this time shall face destruction. Love is the only law for all the children of God. It is only through love that you can be identified as a true child of God." End of quotes. For more details refer to the Everlasting Gospel "The Reign Of Love By 2000 AD" later in this book.

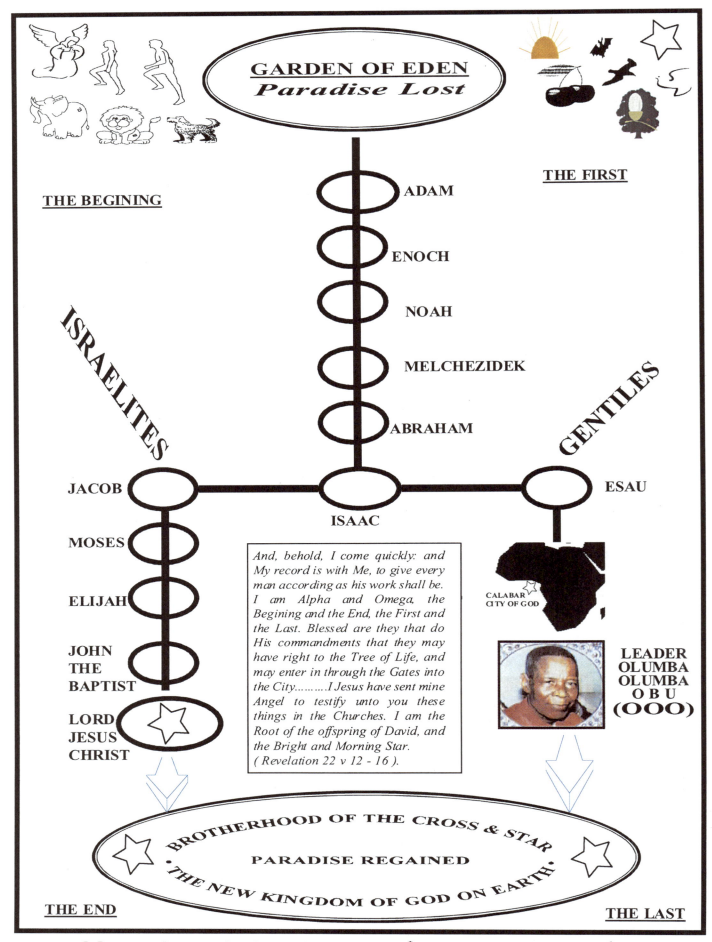

# CHAPTER 2

# THE HOLY TRINITY: GOD IS ONE
### ( Holy Spirit of Truth's Revelations )
#### Summarized by: Christ's Servant EmEm Ette

It is very hard and almost impossible to write on the individual character of the Holy Trinity ( no wonder some religion dont bother ); they are divine and inseparable and therefore are addressed as ALL and ONE; Alfa and Omega; all creation under one rulership of God (Galations 3:20). When our Lord Jesus Christ manifested as the Son of God to save mankind He was also the Father ( John 14 v 3 - 11) and the Holy Spirit. The Holy Trrinity is worth acknowledging and must be acknowledged, worshipped and honoured by all creations; especially man; because they (the Holy Trinity) unanimously created man in their likeness - Genesis 1 v 26 - 27 and Romans 1 v 20.

## The Holy <u>Word</u>, the Divine <u>Love</u> and Eternal <u>Life</u>

These three ( Word, Love and Life ) signify the Holy Trinity God and had existed before man was made. Out of the spoken Word of God was everything created; out of Love there exist Life, which is also Light and which is also everlasting. The Light is the Holy Spirit. There is no creation without the Holy Three. If these three are one and creation cannot do without them, how can man claim to prove the inexistence of the Holy Trinity, let alone do without them? How can man define Word, Love and Life or more so Godhead, when his knowledge is limited to the things he sees with his physical eyes? - John 20 v 25 & 29.

## WORD

The Holy Word was in the begining - John 1 v 1 - 3, He was the only tool that God needed to create the whole world and all the things therein. "YAK" meaning LET became the first manifestation of word in action, the creating tool and the power of invention - Hebrews 4 v 12. Hence all things are done with the power of the word, be it spiritually, mentally or physically, directly or indirectly. If Word is God, then all creation is God - Rev 1 v 16. Word is a two edged sword, on one side it is a consuming fire and on the other hand, peace and tranquility. Note that all creations are god, BUT all creations are not the Father. The Holy Spirit and the Holy Son are One with the Holy Father. They formed the Godhead or the Holy Trinity "the Everlasting Entity." Those who love, honour and obey our Lord Jesus Christ - the Holy Son and King of Kings; are one with the Holy Father also - John 14 v 6 - 7 and 17 v 25 - 26. The Holy Spirit is also the silent Listener and the positive Director, has always been, but at this end of time has also been personified as Christ promised. The Father, Son and Holy Spirit are One whether addressed as he or she. One must not try to separate them by any method, thoughts, acts or deeds; whatever is bound by the Father, Son or Holy Spirit is bound by the Trinity God; whatever is blessed by the Father, Son or Holy Spirit is blessed by the Holy Trinity automatically. It is a serious offence, and indeed an insult to think that the Holy Son - His Holiness the King of Kings and the Holy Spirit - Her Holiness the Holy Queen Mother does not know anything or worst still that they act on your advice or suggestions. The Father repeatedly said that the rulership of the whole universe has been handed over to the King of Kings.

If an ordinary King should know everything about his kingdom, how much more the King of Kings and Lord of Lords who existed before creation and who made man in His own image? That is why the Holy Bible - John 4 v 24, confirmed that God is Spirit, and those that worship Him MUST worship Him in Spirit and in truth. If you do not know the Holy Trinity God in Spirit, then you do not know them at all, even if you claim to be His right hand man, live with Him for many years of your life, dined with Him all the time or lied to Him and believe that you have got away with it: the wisdom of the the Trinity God is divine; beyond human imagination and comprehension.

## LOVE

God is Love - 1 John 4 v 8; man was made out of Love by the Holy Trinity God, hence he was made in the likeness of God and limited power was also given i.e. to have dominion over the fishes in the sea and NOT the sea; over birds of the air and NOT the air. Man has totally gone beyond his boundaries (sea and air pollution, deliberate poisoning, animal slavery and murder; to mention a few). God designed that man should cater for all animals, birds, fishes and all other living things; and that the fruits and the herbs should be used as food (Genesis 1 v 29 - 30) for man, animals, all creeping things and birds. As a leader of other creations man derailed and fell out of his glory by using animals as food without mercy. Every living things have lives of their own, and are fully aware of their mission. Man has completely fallen from his first love, by disobeying, fighting and insulting his Maker. Man suffered a great deal, but for the sake of the first love of the Holy Trinity God to man - John 10 v 11 and 17 v 1, Our Lord Jesus Christ agreed to come and save man by carrying all the sins of the world and nailed them to the cross thereby giving man a chance to reconcile with his Creator if he confesses and repents of his sins and accept baptism of the Holy Spirit and practices total perfection of goodness. Man must now hearken to this and return to his first love or remain in captivity ready to face the consequences; the work of grace finished on the cross of Calvary.

## LOVE IS MAN

Our Lord Jesus Christ is Love; life without love is either empty (which is lifeless) or full of mistakes, regrets, nightmares, fears, uncertainties, dissappointments, greed and difficulties. Love is the bond between God and man and between man and other creations; the growing part of all creation towards their Creator and is made manifest through the exemplary life of the Holy Son of God. Love was born out of word and life was made manifest through love - John 10 v 27 - 30. Yet everything that exist in the world today existed in the Spiritual world long before the Holy Word (God) made them into manifestation for the physical eyes - Romans 1 v 20, a sort of "copy and paste." All things come from the spiritual world and return to the spiritual world after its duration. Man, animals, fishes, trees and all creations are strangers or mere visitors on this earth plane. That is why they are temporary because they all have to return at the end of their services. The way of life while on earth determines the next level of elevation or demotion. Any man who claims ownership of land, water, children, wife, husband, e.t.c., is a thief, liar and a disobedient child and will be judged. The Holy Trinity God rules the four corners of the world: heaven, ocean, earth and the hades - Rev. 5 v 13 and Colossians 2 v 9 - 10. The Holy Bible reveals that our Lord Jesus Christ rules in heaven - Rev. 7 v 12. He fought and conquered His opposers; the devil and his angels were all dropped to the earth and to the sea. Our Lord Jesus Christ came to the earth and conquered through His priceless blood, and through death He went to the hades and conquered.

The King of Kings is the Love who came down as our Lord Jesus Christ and made Love perfect by demonstrating the highest form of love- John 15 v 13. A shameful, slow and painful death on the cross of Calvary for the very man He made and also came to save. He knew the ignorance of man, and His mission, and so He begged the Father to forgive men for they know not what they were doing. Ignorance or preteence has always been man's sickness, yet the inability to listen, reason, understand and learn from previous experience proved even more deadly. Man must regret and apologise and be cleansed through baptism of the Holy Spirit before he could return to his Creator and become one with Him - Mark 16 v 16 and Matt. 3 v 11.

Our Lord Jesus Christ the Love came, and love was made perfect through His precious blood on the cross. He then returned to the Father, but before He left, seeing the sadness in the heart of His dicsiples, He made three promises:
1. That He was going to prepare a place for them; after that He will return again, NOT from the sky and He will receive them unto Himself and they will be with Him wherever He goes - John 14 v 3 - 4. An Angel confirmed His return just after His ascension, that He will return in like manner, not crash landing - Acts 1 v 11.
2. John 14 v 26 "But the Comforter which is the Holy Ghost, whom the Father will send in my name, He shall teach you all things and bring all things to rememberance, whatsoever I have said unto you." He the promised Comforter, which is the Holy Spirit (female) whom the Father will send in His name (the female is merged into the Father) - John 16 v 7 - 8. Just as our Lord Jesus Christ said "I and My Father are One." The Father who is the Word is the voice and the first physical manifestation although the Holy Three have always been.
3. Our Lord Jesus Christ testified about the truth; and promised the coming of the Spirit of Truth, who will speak of Him and also guide man to the truth and reveal things which have never been revealed by Him nor anyone - John 16 v 13 - 14. This Spirit of Truth is the Holy Father and the Perfect Man as St Paul described in 1st Corinthians 13 v 10 and 12: "But when that which is perfect is come, then that which is in part shall be done away with. For now we see through a glass darkly, but then face to face: now I know in part; but then shall I know even as also I am known." The promise of our Lord Jesus Christ reveals the manifestation and reign of the Holy Trinity God and His Christ, Rev 7 v 12 - 17.

## LIFE

Life was brought as an outcome of Love - John 10 v 10 "The thief cometh not but to steal, and to kill and to destroy: I am come that they might have life, and that they might have it more abundantly;" John 1 v 4 "In Him was life, and the life was the light of men." Life or light is the Holy Spirit which darkness cannot comprehend. With the presence of the Holy Spirit there is nothing secret under the sun from one man to another. Life to man is the most wonderful gift of all, but why can man not value and treasure it? Is it because life is not priced and bought with man made money? Or because man is used to learning from personal experience? Whatever the case blessing could be a single or a relay race, but salvation is purely an individual race. If you abuse word and ignore love, life could help to build back word and love; but if you abuse and ignore life then there is no hope of a second chance because life cannot be duplicated; and so is the Holy Spirit if you abuse Her - Matt. 12 v 31 - 32. But the Father, Son and the Holy Spirit are One.

# OOO

**Omnipotent**: All Powerful and authoritative, Olumba
**Omnipresent**: All over at the same time, Olumba
**Omniscient:** All Knowledgeable and wise, Obu

## THE HOLY TRINITY AND MAN

**OOO** is the three profound identification of the Holy Trinity and, one cannot exist without the other. But from the time Adam ate the forbidden fruit, man started from that moment to claim equality with God, "O" Omniscience - Genesis 3 v 7. The punishment that followed was severe and still is. Man became an outcast, only hanging on a thread of rope waiting to be rescued or disposed of. Man went forth and claimed Omnipotence from the moment Cain rose up against his brother Abel and killed him - Genesis 4 v 8 "And Cain talk with Abel his brother; and it came to pass, when they were in the field, that Cain rose up against Abel his brother and slew him." Another heap of punishment on man by his Maker followed in Genesis 4 v 12; this particular sin by Cain brought divisions, created boundaries and gave way to division and enmity among men: fear, insecurity and lack of trust as a result was born among men. This is totally the knowledge and the power of man, which is still prevalent today - Romans 1 v 21 - 23. The scientists for example, are using all their false and unrealistic knowledge to undo the punishment of man caused obviously as a result of man's claims. The result is more devastation, titled; "the after effect" and these they always try to cover up.

To be Omnipresent has proved unthinkable, and to attempt is like a fish trying to climb an Iroko tree. It is a mission impossible to man. As the head of a man is above his neck and body, so is the wisdom and power of the Trinity God above man and angel, and so shall it be, Amen.

*The Holy Trinity: God is One*

## OOO

**Behold The Holy Father - Leader OLUMBA OLUMBA OBU**

## The Sole Spiritual Head Of The Universe

This is the promised *Comforter, the One in Red, the Iron Rod Ruler,* the one that has come with the entire hosts of Heavens and has taken over the rulership and control of this Earthplane of manifest. He is the Omnipotent, Omnipresent and Omniscient God who has come at this end of time to teach and lead man to the accurate knowledge of truth and to judge the world. Those who stood against Him testify of His might. He is the house of power and light and the fountain of life where love, peace and righteousness radiates from. He has the answers to the mysteries of the world. His name is the only name that subdue Satan. All creation hear and obey Him except man but the time of mercy is fast running out for man. Man must either recognise and worship Him or face the calamities that will befall the earth in a very short time such that has never happened before ( Luke 28 ).

# OOO

### *His Holiness, The King of Kings: King R.O. Obu*

All Hail <u>The King of Kings!</u> Hosanah in the highest, for the return <u>of the Holy Son of God!</u> *John* 14: 3-4,. *Matt* 16: 27-28. Blessed is He who had achieved the greatest and the highest level of love - *John* 15: 13, 10: 11; by shedding His precious and priceless blood on the cross of Calvary about 2000years ago; so that we might have eternal life - *John* 10: 28.

He has come with the glory which He had before the world was, *John* 17:5; <u>His Holiness the King of Kings - The Iron Rod Ruler -</u> *Rev.* 12:5, and to dwell with His children and reign forever, *Rev* 21: 3-5. This is the age of Christocracy. Now is the time for all the Head of states and Governors, Prime Ministers and Ministers, Presidents and Senators, kings and Queens, Emperors and all those in the corridors of power to pay homage to the King of kings and indeed the Holy Trinity, so as to rule in peace with Him now and in the new world. First you must repent and follow the King's footsteps. You must obey the universal injunctions of "love one another and practical Christianity" and accept the baptism of the Holy Spirit now before the dooms-day. *Luke* 19:27, 2 *Peter 3:10, Jude* 1:14-15, *Joel* 2:2-13.

*The Holy Trinity: God is One*

# OOO

## Her Holiness, The Holy Queen Mother: Queen I.O. Obu

Receive oh earth with a clean heart; **Her Holiness. The Holy Queen Mother**.

Rejoice ye children for your Mother is here; wipe your tears and sing thanksgiving songs for the manifestation of the Holy Spirit. **The universal Queen, the Mother of God. and the feminine** part of the Holy Trinity, 1st John 5:7, *Isaiah* 7: 14, has brought freedom, liberation and great joy for children, mothers, slaves and all creation.

# CHAPTER 3

## WHAT IS BROTHERHOOD OF THE CROSS AND STAR?

Sermon delivered by Leader Olumba Olumba Obu
Sole Spiritual Head of the Universe.

**FIRST LESSON:** St John 20 v 17
**SECOND LESSON:** Ephesians 4 v 4 - 6
**GOLDEN TEXT:** 1 Peter 2 v 17

"Dear brethren, we want to reveal an important thing to you today. The three lessons will give you an idea of what we are going to reveal. So please brethren, be attentive. You may say that you know what Brotherhood means, but we know from our heart to hearts that no one knows what Brotherhood means. People have given it many meanings. It is as a result of these misconceptions that we have decided to take this opportunity to preach this gospel. Therefore today will go down in history as a great day, a day that Brotherhood was revealed to the world.

Professors in history from many universities, have from time to time been coming to us to tell them the meaning of Brotherhood. We have in each case laughed at the limitation of their wisdom, and have asked them to go and love one another. Anybody on the surface of the globe who tells you that he has known the foundation of Brotherhood is a liar. In this gospel, we are not including the words "Cross and Star," but Brotherhood only. Search yourselves, you who say that you are Brotherhood, whether you are Brotherhood. Search yourselves, you who say that you are not Brotherhood, whether you are not Brotherhood. What is the meaning of Brotherhood? It means God, Christ and the Angels. It means the people in the world, the fishes in the water, the trees in the forest, the grasses that grow in the field. It means the ground on which we walk. Brotherhood means the sky, the moon, the sun, the stars. It means the worms, the ants, the birds. Brotherhood means every four footed animals, and every creeping thing. In short, Brotherhood means everything created by God. Brotherhood means oneness. God and everything created by Him put together are Brotherhood. Who owns Brotherhood? It is God who owns it, rules and leads it, but Christ take charge. What are the duties of Angels? They are servants in Brotherhood. What are the duties of the people? They too are workers in Brotherhood. The stars, moon, fishes, animals, birds of the air, etc. are workers in Brotherhood.

Brotherhood does not mean two things, it means oneness. It is the Word. It is the Truth. What is the Word? It is God, Christ, human beings. It is everything in the whole world. Brotherhood is the Word of God. Why is it that the peoples of this world, do not know what Brotherhood means? It is because it is not given to them to understand. Brotherhood is not a society, it is not a cult, it is the Spirit of Love. I am Brotherhood, you are Brotherhood. You do not need to say, "I want to be Brotherhood." You are Brotherhood whether you like it or not. Everybody is Brotherhood. To those who wants to know its origin, we say Brotherhood has no origin. It has no beginning, it has no end. Except such a person wants to know the origin of God. Brotherhood was not founded by Christ, Angels or man. It was founded by God Himself. God the Founder of Brotherhood is Love. Brotherhood means love, it is truth, it is good manners, mercy, patience. It is humility, meekness, unity, it is oneness. It is One thought, One mind, One Spirit, One faith, One hope. There is no division in Brotherhood. From the smallest child in the cradle to the oldest man; from the smallest village to the largest one; all the countries in the world put together are Brotherhood.

## WHAT IS CROSS?

Anybody who wants to follow Me, but does not want to take up the Cross after Me, cannot be my follower. This afternoon brethren, our gospel is about Cross. After that celebrated gospel on "What is Brotherhood?" during the Pentecostal Convention, many had thought that gospels on Cross and Star would follow. But since the Father did not signal throughout the Convention that I should do so, I could not do anything more than to let His will prevail. This afternoon brethren, it has pleased Him, and He has given Me the signal that I should do so. Therefore I would be failing in my duty as His Mouthpiece, if I should fail to give you the gospel on Cross today.

### DOES CROSS MEANS ALMS GIVING?

Some people think that to give alms means carrying the Cross; others think that to heal the sick by praying means carrying the Cross; yet another class of people think that to pay tithes, free will offering and charity means carrying the Cross. Cross has been made into different forms. Some carry it around their necks, some hang it on their doors. Do all these make up the Cross that Christ say we must carry? We all know that Christ fell down with the Cross when He was carrying it to Calvary. Does carrying the Cross then means the piece of wood He carried? Without the Cross the world would not have been saved. The Cross is light and it is heavy. For the world to be in perfect peace, each of us must agree to carry the Cross.

By what means does one convert a smoker, a snuffer, a thief, a fornicator, a murderer, a backbiter, a liar? It is by carrying the Cross. If we all should decide today to take up the Cross, the sins of the world would vanish immediately. Then what is the Cross? Is it vision and prophecy, building house for people or buying dresses to clothes people? If Jesus had only healed and prophecied without carrying the Cross, His work would have come to nothing. **Cross means bearing one another's burden.** If you hire bicycles for brethren going on ministry work to make their jobs less difficult, you are not carrying the Cross. Cross is not huge as you might imagined. It is very small, it is light but it is very heavy. Cross means bearing one another's burden without complaining; tolerating all kind of sinners; the murderers, the thieves, the backbiters, etc. If one accuses you falsely, yet you stand firm with Christ; if you are spat on, jeered at, disgraced without a cause; if you are insulted without just cause, yet you tolerate such a person wholeheartedly. If you are informed that someone has planned to shoot you, and you fail to run away when he aims at you to shoot, then you are carrying the Cross. To carry the Cross does not cost anything. To be able to carry the Cross, you must resign yourself completely to God. You must be loving, humble; you must have patience; you must be forgiving; you must see another man better than yourself, you must not be envious. If Jesus did not possess all these qualities, He could not have carried the Cross. If you can remain with a cunning man without hurting his feelings for being trickish and crafty; if you can stay with a notorious liar happily, without stirring up his anger when he tells you a lie; when one persecutes you falsely and seeks to destroy your life by all means, yet you tolerate him wholeheartedly, you are carrying the real Cross.

## WHAT IS STAR ?

You have been reading in the Scriptures about a Secret Name. That Secret Name is the Star. The Star is Christ. The Star is the glory of God and it is also the glory of Christ. The Star is the revelation of God. It is the hidden name to the people of the world. The Star indicates the reign and glory of Christ. The Star does not refer to the whole constellation above. The Star means the brightness of God and the power of His reign. The Star is the peace of the Almighty God that governs the universe. There is no other monarch than Christ the Star. From His birth, the Great Light has been shining over His head. It is the only Light that shines the world over. Therefore, it is not just enough for anyone to be a Brotherhood only, or carry the Cross only. To be worthy children of the Kingdom of God, we must be of the Brotherhood of the Cross and Star.

The Star indicates those who will rule and are ruling with Him. The Ruler of the Brotherhood of the Cross and Star is the Star. That is Christ, and Christ is not alone. He is in the Father, and Christ is the City of which we are told that no light is needed, because He shines there, and because the Father and the Son also shines to eternity. The name Star is known to Christ alone, and not to any other human beings. We worship the Star which is Christ, and not the cross that exists in the world. The Star is the glory that reigns over the whole world. In His first coming, Christ passed through pains and tribulations. The primary aim of His second coming is to rule in glory. It is the glory indicative of His reign. He is coming to take up His Kingdom to rule.

His Kingdom is down here on earth. The Star means Christ, His glory and that of the Father. He has arrived with the Father to live with men on earth. He comes in glory to rule the whole world, not to serve, suffer and die, as He did in His first coming. Each time the Almighty Father sends His Son out, He gives Him a New Name. His disciples were also given different names. When He departed from the world, His disciples were called Christians. When He worked among men, He was called Jesus. When He asked His disciples, "Who do men sat that I .am?" He was told that He was the Christ. He warned them against their untimely calling Him that name, and He advised them that they should keep it as a secret among themselves. God knows best why His Son should be given a New Name each time He is sent out. When you hear the name Christ, you cannot tell whether it is white, great or small. When He is called Star, you cannot distinguish one from the other. The Star radiates light. His glory and reign goes to eternity. Christ is the Light. Christ is Jehovah God the Light. Imagine how sweet the name of Jesus sound in a believer's ears. It is the Light that blinded Saul on his way to Damascus. Christ is the name known to the Father and the Son." A stroke of the cane is sufficient for the wise. Those who have ears to hear let them hear. May God bless His Holy words, Amen.

## BCS SUMMARY: ( by Elder W.B. Smith )

Brotherhood of the Cross and Star is the New Kingdom of God on earth. It is the fulfillment of our Lord's prayer as recorded in St Matthew 6 v 9 - 13: - "Our Father which art in heaven, hallowed be thy name thy kingdom come. Thy will be done in earth as it is in heaven.............." Brotherhood of the Cross and Star is the Kingdom that our Lord Jesus Christ has promised; for the will of God must be done on earth as it is done in heaven. The Garden of Eden was heaven on earth; a Paradise where everything was perfect. Man has lost that Paradise because of sin. Brotherhood of the Cross and Star is that Paradise regained. Brotherhood of the Cross and Star is not a church, prayer house, secret society or religious sect. It is universal, and includes all the nations of the world, regardless of race, colour, creed and status. Brotherhood of the Cross and Star is also the fulfillment of the words of God as recorded in Isaiah chapter 2 v 2 - 3. It is now fully manifested to unite the whole world into "One" in fulfillment of Ephesians 4 v 4 - 6.

**Brotherhood** is the Almighty God and all His creations put together. **The Cross** is bearing one another's burden without complaining. **The Star** is the reward at the end; no cross, no crown. From Genesis to Revelation, from the begining of the world until this day, no human beings or church denominations has ever succeeded in changing a sinner, and make him refrain completely from committing sins and vices. Not even our Lord Jesus Christ succeeded in changing a sinner. But, at this end of the age, come into the Brotherhood of the Cross and Star with all your sins, vices and problems; and through the power of the Holy Spirit, ( Read St John 15 v 26, and chapter 16 v 7 - 13 ), **you will be completely reformed, and brought up to the standard required by God to obtain salvation. It does not matter where in the world you reside, the B.C.S. Crusaders will be sent to baptise you. TAKE NOTE: that even if you are already baptised in the Churches it does not matter; because one has to be baptised by the Brotherhood of the Cross and Star in order to receive the Holy Spirit to Protect, Change and Save you. Why Brotherhood Baptism? Because we have to Repent, Confess all our sins and be Immersed in water THREE TIMES. This is the only way that our sins will be Remitted and open the way for the Endowment of the Holy Spirit that will Change Sinners. You can receive Brotherhood of the Cross and Star's baptism and continue to worship in your Church because God is Changing and Uniting all Churches and Nations as " ONE " and you will become God's Tool to execute that Change in your Church and Community. TAKE NOTE: that Brotherhood of the Cross and Star is not here to "Overshadow and Destroy" the Churches, but to 'Unite and Save' as clearly illustrated on the next page. The choice is ours.**

# THE KINGDOMS OF THE WORLD

## *We Must Change Or Perish*

**Disagreement, Quarreling, Anger, Fighting, Envy, Pompousity, Pride, Arrogance, Exasperation, Threats, Intimidation, Revenge, Retaliation, Hatred, Fastidiousness, Selfishness, Eye for an Eye, Deceit, Forgery, Insurrection, Commotion, Bribery, Swearing, Vindictiveness, Flippancy, Heresy, Gossipping, Jealousy, Fraud, Bullying, Whispering, Backbiting, Fear, Deceit, Animousity, Conceitedness, Blasphemy, Witchcraft, Necromancing, Soothsaying, Lovers of Money and Pleasures more than God, Abortion, Murder, Stealing, Fornication, Adultery, Child Abuse, Drug Taking, etc.**

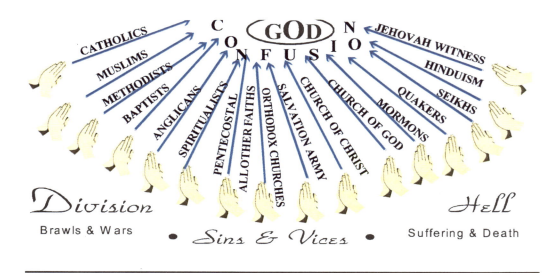

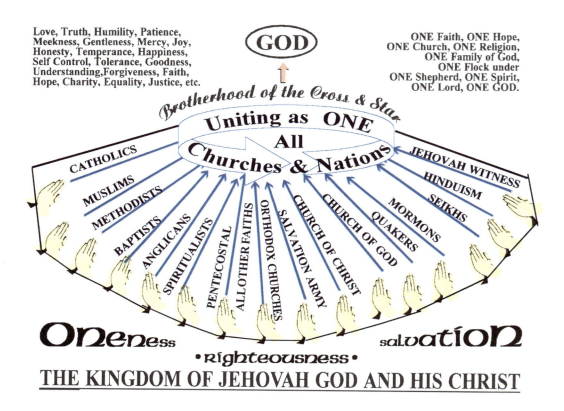

## THE KINGDOM OF JEHOVAH GOD AND HIS CHRIST

# CHAPTER 4

# CHRIST WAS NOT CRUCIFIED ON FRIDAY

Everlasting Gospel delivered by Leader Olumba Olumba Obu

Sole Spiritual Head of the Universe

**1st Lesson: Matthew 16: 21**

*"From that time forth began Jesus to shew unto his disciples how that he must go unto Jerusalem and suffer many things of the elders and chief priests and scribes and be killed; and be raised again the third day."*

**2nd Lesson: John 2: 19**

*"Jesus answered and said unto them "Destroy this temple, and in three days I will raise it up"*

**Golden Text: Matthew 12: 40**

*"For as Jonas was three days and three nights in the whale's belly; so shall the son of man be three days and three nights in the heart of the earth."*

It is said that by the Words of your mouth you are condemned or justified. Our Lord Jesus Christ said that He would go to Jerusalem where He would be tortured, condemned and finally killed. He said further, that He would rise on the third day. I want everybody to be in complete silence, so that the wax in your ears may be removed, and your bad eyesight, due to spiritual blindness, may be restored. As you read this gospel, all your encumbrances are taken away, and you are fully liberated.

It is pathetic to notice that the whole Christendom have lied to the world that Our Lord Jesus Christ was crucified on a Friday. But Our Lord Jesus Christ is the truth and His words are true. It is also absolutely false to construe that Our Lord Jesus Christ was nailed to the Cross on Friday. This claim has no substance and lacks the biblical foumdation and backing.

Many people have been to Bible colleges, or theological schools and seminaries, all in quest of studying religions and the Bible. Some have been to India, the United States of America, Russia and other places to study the Bible, for 20 to 30 years. If they still hold on to the argument that Friday was the first day and Saturday the second day, what about the third day? The orthodox churches keep on shouting Jesus, Jesus, Jesus, but they find it difficult to know when He was crucified. The knowledge, of when Our Lord Jesus Christ was crucified, has eluded the entire world. The significance of the Wednesday Watch and Pray, started during the time the feet of the disciples of Our Lord Jesus Christ were washed. The Thursday's weekly fasting and prayers symbolise the day He was condemned at 6 a.m, and at precisely 9 a.m. the same day He was crucified. I thank Matthew and John and a few other Apostles, who were able to document the teachings and the crucial events during the mission of Our Lord Jesus Christ. If these records were not kept, the enemies of Our Lord Jesus Christ could have succeeded in suppressing the truth, and of course the truth would not have been known. They would have permanently established their deceit and falsehood in the world for their own advantage.

## God's Words Are Sacrosanct

Our Lord Jesus the Christ had said that heaven and earth will pass away, but not an iota of the word of God shall pass away. The word of God is not deficient in power. That is why when the word of God is spoken; it will do mighty works, and can break mighty stones to manifest its purpose. From Genesis to Malachi, the words prophesied about Him had been consummated.

Our Lord Jesus Christ had said that as Jonas, the fifth of the minor prophets, was in the belly of the whale for three days and three nights, so shall the Son of God be in the heart of the earth for three days and three nights. He said; "I have many things to say unto you, but ye cannot bear them now. Howbeit when he, the Spirit of truth is come, He will guide you into all truth:"

Our Lord Jesus Christ was arrested and arraigned before the Elders, Pharisees, Scribes and the Chief Priests at 3 a.m. on Wednesday (Thursday morning). This was after the Last Supper He had arranged for that night. According to the Jews, from 6 a.m. to 6 p.m. was one day, and from 6 p.m. to 6 a.m. was calculated as one night. It stands to reason that from 6 a.m. on Thursday to 6 p.m. on the same Thursday was one day; and from 6 p.m. on Thursday to 6 a.m. on Friday, was calculated as one night. In the same vein, from 6 a.m. on Friday to 6 p.m. of that day, was two days. Similarly, from 6 p.m. on Friday to 6 a.m. on Saturday, made up two nights. From 6 a.m. on Saturday to 6 p.m. of the same day, completed the three days, and from 6 p.m. on Saturday to 6 a.m. on Sunday, concluded the three nights. This is the veritable truth, which had eluded the world. The spoken words of Our Lord Jesus Christ have materialized, and those who believe in all these truths are saved. And all those inexplicable teachings are wiped away.

## The significance of "Watch and Pray"

That is why we in the Brotherhood of the Cross and Star (BCS), do not joke with the Wednesday "Watch and Pray", and the love feast "which often follows the divine observance. This celebration reflects His acceptance and readiness to die, so that humanity might be salvaged with His stainless Blood. The Jews and the Scribes once asked why His disciples never fasted like the rest of the people. Our Lord Jesus Christ told them that it was not necessary for His disciples to do so, when the bridegroom was with them. That is why it is declared that those who believe fervently in Him are saved. I want you to observe these Wednesdays "Watch and Pray", from now till eternity. As many as will observe it, their problems, are wiped away. If you observe all these things, as spelt out of today's gospel, you are saved, and all your problems are taken away. I have other sheep which are not of this fold. They all must be brought in so that there might be one fold and one shepherd. Our Lord Jesus Christ had finished His works, and the ball is now in the court of the people of the world, to observe the three significant events in Brotherhood.

"Who are those that are clad in white garments? They are those who have come out from great tribulations and have been washed clean by the blood of the Lamb, who takes away the sins of the world." The three days (72 hours) dry fasting is a great cleansing exercise in this New Kingdom. The Watch and Pray is one of the events observed in respect of the death of Our Lord Jesus Christ. We who suffer with Him, and are tortured along with Him, are fully liberated from the bondage of evil. These observances reaffirm our belief in Him. This is also the enabling factor, which, by His grace, salvages us. We are also glorified with Him.

## Why BCS Hold Three Pentecostal Meetings in a Year

The April Pentecostal is significant, in that it symbolizes the period Our Lord Jesus Christ suffered untold hardship, torment and death, just for the atonement of the sins of mankind. It is a period to celebrate the three essences of His mission, torture, death and resurrection. In the same vein, the August Pentecostal Assembly comemorates the period when Our Lord Jesus Christ was baptized, and revealed to the entire world by John the Baptist. That is why the observance is so significant. It was then that He was exposed to the Jewish nation and the entire world, for acknowledgement and identification as the Lamb of God, who takes away the sins of mankind. Hitherto, He had been in the world for twenty-nine years, but they knew Him not, until He got baptized at the age of 30 years. That is why we usually rejoice greatly, in the commemoration of His revelation through water Baptism. We observe the December Pentecostal in remembrance of His Divine Birth. Had he not been born of a woman, He would not have been revealed as the Lamb of God, who takes away the sins of the world. If He had not been revealed He would not have died and shed His precious blood for the remission of the sins of humanity.

It is axiomatic therefore, that where there are those who investigate and ask questions, there must also be a person around to give answers to such questions. This can be likened to a lingering cough that would not leave its victim. The Zairians, the Liberians, the Americans, the Russians, the Europeans, the Germans and the rest of you, might have asked why the three Pentecostal Assembly Meetings are held.

Our Lord Jesus Christ must be glorified, as was written in the Bible. He must be glorified with activities featuring songs, dancing, testimonies and recitations, in sober reflections of the real essence of observance of these spectacular and historic events in the life of Our Lord and Saviour, Jesus Christ. While doing this, such worldly tendencies as beating of drums, burning of candles and incenses, and the pouring of perfumes should be avoided. His name can better be glorified and lauded without the use of all these things. The Spirit of truth has come to unfold all things for the salvation of mankind. Some people are saying that it does not matter. To assume such a position is wrong. This is a unique and important matter, which borders on the foundation of the Christian faith, life, and salvation of humanity. So it is wrong to treat the matter so lightly. The calculation from Friday will result in two days and two nights, during which time Our Lord Jesus Christ would still have been in the heart of the earth. This is wrong, and we cannot compromise or condone this satanic and misleading assumption.

I am opposed to any falsehood in the world, including the Jesus Christ's death saga. The calculation is misleading. The case of His birthday, which had been fixed for convenience could be tolerable, but for the death upon which the salvation of the generality of mankind depends, nobody should toy or falsify it on any account. I will not allow any false doctrine to be spread again in the world, and it is against this background that I am saying, that nothing should be added or subtracted at all in this case. It is said that if a tree does not fall, the axe shall not rest.

God is truth and all His actions are true and just. This should help us to realize that His words, sooner or later, must be fulfilled. Did Our Lord Jesus Christ not say that every plant, which my heavenly Father had not planted, shall be uprooted? That is why all false and misleading observance of His death and other issues must be crushed.

His death is the foundation, which must be celebrated with pomp and joy, His death has been the last covenanted arrangement, and that was why He said, "It is finshed", as He allowed His precious blood to be spilled for the atonement of the sins of men. This supreme sacrifice superseded other sacrifices of goats, sheep or rams, and has wiped away all sins To this end nobody has the right to impute sins to other people The sin of Adam had condenmed the entire hmnan race to death. But this unique and supreme sacrifice has come to redeem humanity from bondage and the clutches of evil; therefore if anyone says he suffers for anyone's sake, he is a blatant liar. It is Our Lord Jesus Christ who had really truly suffered for all mankind. It therefore becomes absolutely reasonable, <u>that Wednesdays and Thursdays should be regarded as Holy days. and must be set aside for the observances of these historic events.</u>

A stroke of a cane is sufficient for the wise. Those who have ears to hear let them hear. May God bless His Holy Words, Amen.

# CHAPTER 5

# VEGANISM

Everlasting Gospel delivered by Leader Olumba Olumba Obu

Sole Spiritual Head of the Universe

**1st Lesson: St Mark 1:6**

"And John was clothed with camel's hair,. and with a girdle of a skin about his loins; and he did eat locusts and wild honey."

**2nd Lesson: Romans 14:21**

"It is good neither to eat flesh, nor to drink wine, nor any thing whereby thy brother stumbleth, or is offended; or is made weak."

### Golden Text: I Corinthians 8: 13

"Therefore, if meat make my brother to offend; I will eat no flesh while the world standeth, lest I make my brother to offend".

## The Spirit of Truth

We do not speak out of our own authority, but we speak as we are empowered by Our Lord Jesus Christ. As John the Baptist had said, no man can have anything except it be given him from heaven. Our Lord Jesus Christ confirmed this when He said, "I have yet many things to say to you, but ye cannot bear them now. Howbeit, when He, the Spirit of Truth is come, He will guide you into all truth: for he shall not speak of Himself; but whatsoever ye shall hear, that shall he speak: and he will shew you things to come."

**Locust was not Insect but Beans**

The first correction that I have to make is the (Efik) translation which renders locust in our first lesson, as an insect of the grasshopper species. This is a blatant and misleading translation. It means locust beans and not locust as an insect of the grasshopper species. A sample of the bean is what I am holding up, which you should all look at. If you argue that it is locust (grasshopper), does that not mean that John fed on animal? Because locust the insect is an animal.

As God had said that the fruits and seeds of all herbs and trees shall be food for man; that was why John ate the locust beans. The misleading translation should be corrected with immediate effect. Since it was God who sent John to the world to practice the truth, that was why it was said beforehand that John would come neither eating meat nor drinking wine. This was in consonance with the commandment of God in the beginning, that the fruits and seeds of all trees and herbs should be man's food. It was for this reason that John the Baptist fed on locust bean and honey. Throughout his mission he was not sick but he was rather filled with power. That was a living example set for us. For this reason do not go back into your former ways of life.

**God Prescribed Food for Man**

You may begin to cogitate what manner of food you will eat. I am also going to tell you, what God had said in this regard. The type of food prescribed for man by God is found in Genesis 1: 29. From today that should be your food. Today is the day to sort things out.

" *And God said Behold I have given you every herb bearing seed; which is upon the face of all the eanh, and every tree, in the which is the fruit of a tree yielding seed; to you it shall be for meat:"* Genesis I: 29

Beans, melon, groundnut, orange, paw-paw and pineapple are food, and all kinds of fruits and seeds are food for man. The instruction is that the fruit and seed of every herb bearing seed and every tree yielding seed, shall be food for man. That is to say, all seeds and fruits of any herb or tree upon the surface of the earth, shall be food. You are true witnesses to the fact that beans, as foodstuff is rich in all nutritional requirements and sufficient as food. I know, as you know, the food nutrient in beans. You know too about countless number of fruits and seeds abounding everywhere upon the surface of the earth.

**The Essence of the Garden of Eden**

The Garden of Eden is not a folk tale. It is simply a reality. If fruit bearing herbs and trees are planted, they provide people with more than enough food. From the time the knowledge became elusive to the people of the world they departed from the path of God. The Spirit of God in man was dead, and the Spirit of God departed from man.

There was no time that God instructed man to kill and eat birds, animals, or locust insects, because these animals have their kingdoms. God's motto is "live and let live". The earthworm has its kingdom. Birds have their own kingdom. God does not tell you to have conflict with them but has spotlighted that all the fruits and seeds of herbs and trees shall be your food.

Have you fed on fruits and seeds, and not satisfied?

All the problems in the world which hinders man from knowing God and the imminent ruin of man results from eating meat and fish. By this act, the world has departed from the ways of God, to the path of perdition. Eating of meat brings about sickness, afflictions, gnashing of teeth and death to man. You can bear witness, that if God did not love man by sending John the Baptist in his fashion, the world would have perished. You will note that it was neither John's father, nor mother, or the priest who advised John not to eat meat, since they were killing and eating animals with bones and skin. As Our Lord Jesus Christ had said anyone who is filled with old wine will not need new wine, because he will always say the old is better for him. But in this case, what option do you have? I know many of you will not sleep. Your hearts are troubled about the seeming difficulty in practising the gospel. What is so difficult in practicing this gospel?

This is the first instruction given by God to man. Many people complain of what to do, and argue if they cannot eat things like egg or milk. Egg is a bird, Milk is taken from an animal and so it is part of an animal. Do not eat any of those things. The only food prescribed for man is either fruit or seed. If you love life, follow this prescription. Our Lord Jesus Christ at the end of every preaching would say those who have ears let them hear. The children of God, who are the children of this Kingdom, do not find it grievous to practice. It is rather pleasant to practice. It' you follow the prescription, you will no longer be sick, you will have no pains, and there will be no movements of objects in your body system, which you attribute to witches and lizards. The fish and meat you eat, causes these problems, because you have eaten of the forbidden fruit. I do not yet want to dwell on the repercussions of eating meat and fish. The penalties and disadvantages I do not treat. I am only dealing with the superficial aspect. At another time, I will speak on the disadvantages, repercussions, and the untold penalties to mankind. If I go on to expatiate on this issue, you will cry and shout to the top of your voice. If you eat a piece of meat, it is poisonous.

## Animals have Instinct but Lacks Thinking Faculty

Do you not know that animals are human? God your Creator also created goats, hens and all the animals. He first created them before creating you. Your brethren are the animals. Any animal is your brother, and you are a brother to the animals. If any cut is inflicted on you, blood will come out. Blood will also come out if a cut is inflicted on a goat or hen. If you compare the blood looks alike. You have instinct, and they too have instinct.

If there is a person in this building, an animal will know that there is a person, while humans are oblivious of such presence. When you speak, the animal hears. The animals equally speak. But since God has given you the power of superintendence over them, you should cater for their welfare. You are not told to kill them. Because of this role, God gave the reasoning faculty, which is the likeness of God in man. That is the only aspect that man surpasses animals. Otherwise the animals could manufacture guns and shoot you, as you manufacture to shoot them. Animals smell, see, hear, speak, walk. The only sense that eludes them is the reasoning faculty. God did this intentionally so that man can use it as the instrument of governing the animals.

## Animals and Trees Kingdom

I tell you that they enjoy themselves in their own kingdom more than you to the extent that they do not even imagine there are other kingdoms. When you see them gathering you may feel they are playing, not knowing that they are deliberating on a very important business. They have various institutions as we have. They have chiefs, police force, the army and every other institution. All animals created have both male and female. The trees have their own kingdom. They attend meetings, have their chiefs, converse and do their own thing, their own way. Their kingdom is equally very enjoyable. If I say that you are a member of either the plant or animal kingdom, you will wonder how. Do not bother about that aspect but believe that you are also a tree, or a fish, or an ant or bird. Therefore, you are a brother or sister to them all, and they are your brothers or sisters.

## The Use of Animals

In the northern part of the Country (Nigeria) and around the desert regions, animals are used as means of transportation. These animals carry loads, listen to instructions and do many other things. The horse is an example of such animals. If we were to know ourselves, we would train them all. They are the ones for man to govern. They can go on errands, carry loads, keep watch over the house, while a man goes about his normal business. When you try to exercise such control and power over a human being, you will be opposed. The power of superintendence of man over animals is the first grace man lost. If you were to cater for and feed the snakes, goats, dogs and other animals, they would watch the house, go on errands, sweep the floor and do other domestic chores. Brethren, the effort we waste in training men, if we were to concentrate our attention in training the animals, they would have given similar responses. We would use them for our errands and sit back to enjoy our glory. What obtains now? You are antagonistic towards <u>animals.</u> While you kill them, they also attempt to hurt you. With such a situation, can you exercise any control and authority over them?

### The Grace that Eludes Man

You can see how the whites train dogs, and other animals. If you keep a dog to watch over premises and it barks, it scares people off. There are various things animals can do if they are trained. If you train a parrot, for instance, it can call somebody's name and report situations. In your absence the parrot can keep record of all those who called at the house, and report when you return. That is one grace man has missed.

It is on this basis that we are told to love them. If we were to love them, re-direct our attention to training them, they would pick up. A human baby is born with the same characteristic features as animals, and into similar circmnstances. If the animal be given the same care, attention, and treatment, as its human being counterpart at birth, massaging and stretching the necessary parts of the body, cutting hair and clothing, the animal would respond as human beings. You are not more beautiful or handsome than animals. They hear when they are spoken to, and can move when they are told to do so. Some animals can convey you, as well as loads, from one place to the other. That is one grace man has missed because of stupidity.

### Animals are also human

More so, you do not know that when you kill an animal, you have killed a hmnan being. When, for instance a native doctor demands a cock and hen from you, he is in effect asking for a man and a woman. He does not know this and you do not know too. But the moment the cock is killed, a man is dead somewhere. When you kill a cock you have become a murderer and will stand betore the judgement seat of God to answer for it, and you will also be killed.

Can you realise why you are told not to kill any fish or bird or any other animal? It is because they are all human beings. Abel did not know that all the sheep he was tending were all humans. When God demanded that Cain and Abel should offer sacrifices unto Him, Abel chose the fattest of his lambs, and offered it to be burnt as a sacrifice. He thought that he was presenting a ram not knowing that he was offering himself. He gave his own life. It was not Cain that killed him; it was self-inflicted. Can you realise the wisdom I have brought to you? It is the recondite wisdom. If he did not offer that ram, he would not have given his life and nothing would have happened to him. You pray to God to take away death. Where do you intend Him to take death? You are still killing fishes, hens, cocks and other animals. Are those not human beings you are killing? People die as a result of what they do. Because of eating of fish and meat, man is overshadowed with darkness, and he dies. Sickness, anger, animosity are all found in you.

### Ist Lesson: St. Mark 1: 6

" *And John was clothed with camel's hair and with a girdle of a skin about his loins; and he did eat locusts and wild honey.*"

If you begin to eat fruits from today, brethren, you will no longer grow old. You will not be sick and you will not have any pains. You will ever be young. You will no longer know what it means to be angry, your eyes will be open and you will see God face to face, as you enjoy this Kingdom. You will have much blood, power, and vitality. When you refrain from meat, death, sickness and lack will be afraid of you. When you refrain from meat and fish, you will no longer know anger and troubled heart. You will experience real bliss and peace in your innermost heart. You will always be happy, because the Father dwells in you and you in Him. You will see His glory everyday.

It is because of disobedience that you kill animals for your meat, and as a result you suffer. When it is reported that somebody is fat, why is he fat? Is it not the result of stealing, prostitution and surfeiting? Is obesity a good thing? Come to think of the effect of meat on man. God created fishes, hens and goats and put them into very lowly and dishonourable places. When you eat their meat, where do you frnd yourselves? Can you not realise how you are liviing as beasts? Even animals are now wiser than you. If you no longer eat meat, mourning houses will cease to be kept, necromancers and juju doctors will fold up. All the secret societies in the world will cease to exist. Consequently, you will no longer have any problems. You will feel sound and happy, Brethren, I want you to come in and enjoy this Kingdom. People will no longer die, because the animals you kill are hunan, and when you stop killing them, they will no longer die, and human beings will consequently not die as a result. People will no longer be sick. Goats will not be missing. Animals will no longer be killed, but will be allowed to carry on their businesses while human beings go on with theirs. In that way, life will be worth living for both men and animals.

### What Makes up Civilization

Brethren, open-eyed blindness is a grievous sickness. When you claim that you are civilised and your eyes are open, what evidence of civilisation do you have? Do you think civilisation subsumes speaking and reading in languages? Engineering is not a product of any language. Language is not used in manufacturing or inventing anything. It is the product of God's knowledge. Do you think that the person who invented airplane was learned? It does not require being learned; God is the one who teaches man to do everything, without the direct application of any language.

It is said, when the Comforter comes, He will guide you into all truth. If we are able to maintain our purity and sanctity, and practice this injunction of God, we will be conversing and rejoicing with God. You will no longer argue that God is in the sky, but you will see Him face to face. He will use you to wrought mighty works. In all things you shall be free. When people talk of going to the mountains or to Jerusalem, what actually do you go to do there. Here is God before you, conversing with you, but your sight has been blurred and your ears blocked by the meat and fish, which God has directed you not to eat. God is not far from any person, but we ruin ourselves, most especially by eating meat and fish. This way, you defile the temple of God and it attracts perdition and sickness into our system. When you eat goat meat, the goat will seek a place of abode in you and begin to move around in you. These animals that you eat, move in you and you complain that you are poisoned or charmed. There is no one poisoning you, but you have introduced foreign bodies into your system. Whatever tastes delicious in the mouth of a sick man, that will he eat and die, says a local adage.

**Lesson Imparted Free**

Whoever continues to eat meat has been billed for perdition. The reason is that I cannot see why your life can be adversely affected if you do not eat meat. It rather helps you to live a better and more pleasant life. If you go to many parts of the world, like Jerusalem, they neither know nor have a lot of foodstuffs as we have here, but rather, they live on fruits. You claim the whites are powerful and civilised, that is due to the fact that more of them practice veganism. As I am teaching you now, it is not pleasing to those who have pre-knowledge of this truth, since they feel they had spent a lot of money to acquire the knowledge.

This lesson is not acquired free. It is a very significant and efficacious lesson but I have given to you free of charge. You complain that your dreams are confusing, or that you cannot remember your dreams as you used to do when you were young. Your dreams should be confused because of the meat and fish you introduce into your body, which defile the body. Experiment from today, now that you have heard this gospel. As the Scripture says, today, when you hear His voice, harden not your hearts. If you keep to the prescription of God and eat only what you are told to eat, you will witness a remarkable change, your eyes will be opened, your ears will be opened, and your understanding will be broadened. You will hear and witness the glory of God, as well as find peace for your soul and long life for yourself. The second lesson will now be read.

## 2nd Lesson: Romans 14: 21

*"It is good neither to eat flesh nor to drink wine, nor any thing whereby thy brother stumbleth, or is offended, or is made weak."*

I know that those who sell meat products will be angry, but their anger cannot affect me.

## The World seeks for Life where there is None

God kept time for everything. The time of foolishness has passed. This is the time for the Holy Spirit to lead you to the knowledge of truth. As has been rendered in a song by one of the choirs: "the world is looking for life where life cannot be found." Do not eat meat anymore. Do not drink wine. Do not kill and eat hens, goats or any animal, for they do us no good. Eating of meat does not admit you into the Kingdom of God. Refraining from meat does not remove you from the Kingdom of God, what therefore is the use of eating meat?

There are many people who will kill and eat human flesh in the absence of hens and goats. About 99 percent of the inhabitants of Africa are cannibals. If we no longer eat fish or meat, there will be no more killings and we will not only have peace, but we will see God, be alive, rich, and devoid of all problems. Complaints of meat poisoning, fish poisoning and so forth will be a thing of the past since you eat neither fish nor meat. Anger, troubled heart and repression will no longer be experienced. At all times you will feel please. At all times the Holy Spirit will dwell in you, and you will have the feelings of satisfaction, peace, good health and power.

**Meat Defiles the Temple of God**

When you eat meat or fish and pass effluvium, the obnoxious smell will cause every person around to run from you. The reason is that your system is dirty, and the air reflects your inner self. What do you think your body looks like in this light? God is not there with you, because the temple is defiled. You are the temple of the Most High God. It is said that whoever defiles the temple of the Most High, him shall God destroy. You destroy the temple of God by eating meat and fish. There is nothing that I can safely point to, as the benefit one derives from eating meat. I have not seen its usefulness to man. The only thing I see in meat consumption is itself punishment, death, lack, sickness, tribulations to man, and the departure of God from His own house. People always cry that God should help them refrain from fornication, but why is it that you cannot defeat the younger son, and you go to challenge the elder son to a fight? If you do not refrain from eating meat and fish, how can you refrain from fornication? If you do not refrain from eating meat and fish, how can you refrain from anger? If you do not refrain from eating meat and fish, how will the Holy Spirit dwell in your heart?

### Abstinence from Meat is Inborn in Me

I thank God immensley, because at first, I wondered what kind of life I was living without eating meat or fish, but I know that the Father was doing His work. You cannot have anything except God gives it to you. I tried as a man to eat meat or fish but could not. It is not that it is lawful to Me to eat meat or fish, but I neither need nor appreciate them. I have never tasted them since I was born. I have no business with such things. When one complains that he has the urge to eat meat, I wonder what stimulates such urges in man. I have no business with meat or fish. Since I know myself. I did not know that the Father wanted to do a significant thing for the people of the world. Were it not so, how will I preach this gospel?

When you argue that you want to be like the Father, what do you imply in your argument? But you have neither refrained from meat nor fish. Can you realise the cause of the downfall of many in BCS? Can you also realise the power in Brotherhood? You complain that the Leader has not shown you the source of power here in Brotherhood. Have I not revealed this power to you today? Those who eat meat are now very sorrowful, and do not knock their heads on the ground. God loves this generation immensely. As He had sent John to live that sort of life and to leave an example for mankind, so does He teach us purity and sanctity. You know that maize by itself is food. Banana, plantain, oranges, and other fruits are more than sufficient. I do not know what has become of the inhabitants of the world. The lesson taught to you now is not an extract from any book; neither is reference made to any authority . I was born with this understanding.

### The Gospel is a bombshell to the World

Brethren, it is high time that you are crowned. Do you see the gentle progression from simple to complex? We started with telling you to refrain from sin, removing all its vestiges from you. The gospel delivered today is a giant leap. I know that many people find it difficult even to say hallelujah, especially when they begin to weigh the possibilities of refraining from meat. Today , the urge to eat meat is taken from you. The inhabitants of the world will shout, when they listen to today's gospel, Leader Obu has 'killed' them, that He has instructed that people should no longer eat meat or fish. They will ask what does He want them to do? I have prescribed what is required of man to eat. People who sell animal/meat products and restaurant owners, some, who are even present in this hall, are almost petrified. They are thinking of what to do with the animal/meat they have in stock and pleading that I should give them a little more time.

Did you know all this while you were killing people and yourself, also defiling the temple of God? It is for this reason that your sensitivity to minor threats is high. When a little thing happens, you will die, you age out within a few years. If you begin today to refrain from meat and fish, you will ever remain young, healthy, and beautiful. All the body requirements will remain intact.

### If all refrain from eating Meat, Animals would not be killed

You may argue that you have not slaughtered any animals, you only buy and eat. If you stop eating, that person killing animals for sale will not find market for his trade. When you say that somebody is very troublesome, it takes two persons, and not one to cause confusion. It is good neither to eat flesh, nor to drink wine, nor to do anything whereby thy brother stumbles, or is offended, or is made weak. Meat and fish issue brings offence and confusion to the inhabitants of the world. Many of the calamities in the world come as a result of eating meat and fish.

Let all the inhabitants of the world thank God, because the Holy Spirit has come at this end of time to lead man to the knowledge of truth. If this type of gospel were delivered in days of old, that people should not eat meat, the preacher would not only be the object of ridicule but would stand the chance of losing his head. But now I am preaching this gospel with boldness because millions of people in the world have already become vegans today. Millions are also looking for the way to becoming one. That is why the Father throws the way wide open for the entire world to enter in and receive eternal life. When you light candles, burn incense, and accompany your worship with orchestra music in your church, I say stop drumming, go and practice this gospel. If you want power from on high, stop eating meat and fish, stop drinking, fornication and connnitting other vices. By that you will have power and will see the glory of God. Your eyes will be opened and you will see God face to face. I do not say you will only hear His voice, but that you will see Him physically. You will also swim in the ocean of good health and enjoy enormous wealth, you will express with surprise whether God had been around you all along.

### Golden Text: I Corinthians 8: 13

"Wherefore, if meat make my brother to offend; I will eat no flesh while the world standeth, lest I make my brother to offend."

### Acquire Land for Cultivation of Fruit Trees

In your community,whether it is mainland, or upland part of the country, donate land for the cultivation of fruits. Whether it is in Cross River, Nigeria or in Europe, acquire land to plant fruit trees. You will see the set up of the Garden of Eden with your naked eyes. The Garden of Eden means the cultivation of different species of various kinds of fruits extensively. When they eventually yield their fruits, you can pluck and eat without any problems. You will realise that by that time we will have no problem. As we begin to live on the prescription of God, you will witness the gradual unfolding of the glory of God, and a comparatively different atmosphere governing our living. All what you will witness and feel - power, happiness and joy, will not give room for you to be confronted with any difficulty. You have been hearing when we say, that we are staging a go-back to the Garden of Eden. In BCS, about ninety nine percent are now vegans. They no longer have anything to do with flesh. What remains of them is only one hundreth. These are the ones who will complain that what is left for them to do is to stop eating fish. It remains a little step for you to cross unto the other side and have eternal life.

It is a very lucky day for all the inhabitants of the world. This is so because I have been treating this subject on the surface. But today, it is elucidative and elaborately declared from the highest heaven; since God does not wish that we should perish, but that we should have eternal life, that is why He has sent the Holy Spirit to us at this end of time. Many people complain that they are bewitched and seek for powerful oracles to consult. Do not consult any oracle again. It is eating meat and fish, which is killing you. The reason you are recalcitrant with God is that you continue to eat fish and meat. What has darkened your eyes and blocked your ears, is that you are eating meat and fish. From this hour, as you have accepted Him, you have peace. You have seen and heard, and the stones are removed from the walls of your heart. You have witnessed the illumination of God.

## Resolve to be Eating Fruits Only

All the inhabitants of the world have a testimony from today. All those who are in prison, the sick, the barren, and people with various problems, from today, the Father has taken their problems away. Most of your calamities and encumbrances result from eating meat and fish. God has turned His merciful eyes on humanity. He has seen that we are all blind and stupid; and for this reason, sends the Holy Spirit to lead us, especially those who are in the universities. You fry here, roast there, bake and boil your food. Fry no more because that means death to you. If you want to pass your examinations, eat fruits. Wisdom, wealth, power, peace, beauty, good health and long life will be bestowed on you. You have heard that in the past, people lived up to eight or nine hundred years. Why was it possible? It was because they were vegans. Today, young people look older than their ages. Some are obese. Obesity is a disease resulting from eating of fish and meat.

Brotherhood of the Cross and Star (BCS) is neither a prayer house, nor service centre, nor healing home, nor church denomination. It is the Kingdom of God. Since we are back to the Garden of Eden, our food is as was first recommended by God <u>All fruits and seeds from trees and herbs are our food in this Kingdom.</u> If you eat something else, put yourself in prayer. Since we are in the Garden, that is why we have to be prepared, by planting trees - bearing fruits and herbs.

## Reward For Fruitarians

Many of those who are partially blind, or do not see their way, if they now begin to practice this gospel by eating fruits alone, their eyes will be opened. Those who are suffering from hypertension will have their blood normalized if they practice this gospel. Many who are certified anaemic, by practicing this gospel they will be filled with blood. The blood content of one person can be more than enough to donate to a hundred other people. Those who are left with ten days to one year or so to depart this world to the world beyond because of their disobedience; by beginning to practice this gospel, thousands of days are added to their days. All those whose faces are wrinkled, legs crooked and are old looking; by beginning to practice this gospel, they will be rejuvenated and will become handsome young men and beautiful women.

Because of eating fish and meat, we are disconnected from God. Our link to the fountain of living water is cut short from us, thereby rendering us ineffective. From this instant, the pipe is reconnected to that fountain. You can feel the pulse inside you. You will be surprised to see yourself look very young and smart. The swollen cheeks and protruding belly will be no more. When people look at you, they will see you as a beautiful young person.

You will be called beauty, and people will wonder how you come about such good health and beauty. More so, all forms of indiscriminate desires will be taken away from you. All the troubled hearts, exasperation and fighting, which have formed part of you, will be found no more. You will experience relative bliss and concord. This in effect is the Kingdom we were looking for. The knot that had loosened, which had caused the world to question what has brought about problems, and leading to some blaming it on women, money or other things, has today been righted. None of these or other imaginable things brought problems. We have been told not to kill and eat animals but to superintend over them.

I will not be tedious unto you. A stroke of a cane is sufficient unto the wise. Those who have ears let them hear. May God bless His Holy Words. Amen.

## Elder W. Smith's Recipe From Above
### For Replacing Meat, Fish, Animal Products, Alcohol and Nicotine ( and even Cooked Foods ).

All the above eating, drinking and smoking habits are responsible for about 99% of all sicknesses and diseases. The following recipes are 100% effective, bearing in mind also, that <u>fire is a destroyer and renders cooked food ineffective.</u> These recipes are healthy and quickly leads to the ultimate **'Recipe of Perfection'** which is the '**eating of Fruits only**' as prescribed by God our Creator and Father.

**BREAKFAST** - 7 A.M. to 8 A.M.

OPTIONS: 1. Fresh Orange or Grapefruit (eaten or liquidise) 2. Tea - Fresh Mint or 1 slice of Lemon and 1 slice of Ginger steeped in cup for 15 minutes and sweetened with honey if required. 3. Fresh ripe Bananas.
4. Cereals: 1 cup fresh Mix Nuts, 1 cup fresh Oats, 1 tablespoon Linseed, 1 tablespoon Pumpkin seeds, 1 teaspoon Sesame seeds, 1 teaspoon Sunflower seeds, 1 teaspoon Mix Spice, 2 - 3 tablespoons Honey, 1 cup boiling water, 1 cup cold water and 4 tablespoons Plamil Soya or Coconut Milk. Blend all in Blender or pulverise and mix all the ingredients. Number of servings depends on size of cups.
BREAD: Home baked - 1 lb Organic Flour, 250 mls water, 2 tablespoons Honey or Fruit sugar, 1 teaspoon Mix Spice, 1 tablespoon Extra Virgin Olive oil, 1 teaspoon Dried Yeast and Salt (if required). Bake as required and serve with Honey not Butter.

**LUNCH** - 11.30 A.M. to 12.30 A.M.

Assorted fresh Fruits and fresh Mix Nuts only. Recommended Options: Paw Paw, Pine Apple, Kiwi Fruit, Melon, Mangoes, Oranges, Soursap, Bananas, Peach, Pears, Strawberries; Cashew nuts, Brazil nuts, Peanuts, Pecan nuts, Walnuts, Almonds, Hazlenuts, Pine kernels, e.t.c.

**DINNER:** - 3 P.M. to 4 P.M.

OPTIONS:- 1. Broccoli, Cauliflower, Asparagus, Sweet Corn, Dwarf Corn, Mangetout Beans, Okra, Brussel Sprouts or Cabbage. Pour boiling water on prepared selection and allow to stand for 3 minutes. Pour off water, add salt, pour on more boiling water and allow to stand for 8 - 12 minutes. Pour off water and serve; or, add fresh herbs and spices, then blend and serve as Vegetable Soup. 2. Sprouted Mung Beans : Soak beans for 24 hours, pour off water, cover beans with kitchen towel, cover entire container for 24 - 36 hours. Mix Sprouted Beans with diced Red Pepper, Onion, Garlic and grated Carrots and serve. 3. Fresh Salad: Lettuce, Tomato, Cucumber, Radish, Celery, Onion, Green Sweet Pepper and Raw Mushroom with no dressings. 4. Avocado and Bread. 5. Pureed Ripe Plantain with topping of fresh mixed chopped Nuts. JUICE OPTIONS:- 1. Spring Water. 2. Jelly Coconut Water (eat the soft kernel). 3. Liquidised ripe Plantain and Coconut water with a dash of Nutmeg. 4. Carrot or Beet Root Juice. 5. Grape Juice. 6. Celery or Cucumber or Tomato Juice. 7. Soursap Juice. 8. Sugar Cane Juice. 9. Melon Juice.

**SUPPER**:- 6 P.M. to 7 P.M. Fresh assorted Fruits eaten or pureed + glass of water.

**NIGHT CAP**:- 1 cup of pure Camomile Tea with or without Honey.

These Recipes are effective, healthy and satisfying; the crave for Meat products, Alcohol and Nicotine will be eliminated within weeks. Always substitute the crave for Alcohol and Nicotine with a glass of <u>Spring Water.</u>

**FINALLY:** Take daily/regularly - 1 to 2 teaspoons of Fresh Aloe Vera ( remove skin first, then liquidise ). The Breakfast and Lunch Recipes are crucial and should be adhered to. **<u>Always Repeat These Words:</u>** "Thank You Father for solving my Eating\Drinking\Smoking or Dug problems, in the name of our Lord Jesus Christ, Amen."

# CHAPTER 6

# CELIBACY: ITS RELIGIOUS SUPPORT

Everlasting Gospel delivered by Leader Olumba Olumba Obu

Sole Spiritual Head of the Universe

**1st Lesson: Luke 20: 35**

"But they which shall be acccounted worthy to obtain that world, and the resurrection from the dead, neither marry, nor are given in marriage."

**2nd Lesson: 1 Corinthians 7:29**

"But this I say, brethren, the time is short: it remaineth, that both they that have wives be as though they have none."

**Golden Text: Revelation 14:14**

"These are they which were not defiled with women; for they are virgins. These are they which follow the Lamb whithersoever he goeth. These were redeemed from among men, being the firstfruits unto God and to the Lamb."

Here is a factual revelation of what has been, from time immemorial, to be confirmed as true, through the passage of time. Though some people may be angry while others may argue or quarrel over this word. It is not meant to disturb you beyond considering whether you are one of those to follow Christ.

### They made sacrifices for the Love of the Kingdom of God

The anxiety-ridden and frustrated world is making a last resort to following Christ. There is no other way to make mankind to be saved. Moreover, the position as a saint, apostle, or disciple of Christ holds out a charm for many aspiring Christians. Many people are called out of the world to serve God in order to have a share in the Kingdom of God. Among them are those who have made themselves eunuchs for the love of the Kingdom of God.

### Holiness a Sure Way to God

Whoever desires to be a child of God should be Holy. A fornicator or adulterer is defiled, and cannot inherit the Kingdom of God. Celibacy has proved a very reliable precautionary measure against defiling oneself with men or women. Though it is obvious that not all people can accept this truth, for those who want to follow Christ and forsake the whole world, the qualification is Holiness. Such a situation is not at all embarrassing if only it is understood to be simply the same as being faced with a choice between marriage and Christ: much as it is between the world and the Kingdom of God, or between life and death. You may then be going to church everyday, pass sleepless nights in long prayers, place your parcels of prayer request for a good and beautiful housewife at the sanctuary of God, marry or give in marriage, but without the full knowledge that choosing Christ is a different thing.

### Christ the Spotless Lamb

Christ is the lamb without blemish, a spotless Bridegroom whose virgin attendants are undefiled. Nuptial arrangement, in which virgins usually follow the bridegroom in this world though natural, is symbolic of the spiritual marriage feast of Christ to which those undefiled by men or women, are the only acceptable attendants: remember the five foolish virgins.

We do not want you to be like them. Where all are wishing to follow Christ, all are supposed virgins, but the number of those to meet and actually walk with Him are limited as illustrated by the unpreparedness of the five foolish virgins. Whether the story is of virgins without oil in their lamps, or of people without the wedding dress, or those who refuse to attend the wedding feast, one thing is meant to be illustrated; that any person who is defiled with women or men is unprepared and cannot walk with Christ.

### The Wages of Sin is Death

The wages of sin is death, and whosoever defiles his body with women is liable to suffer death. Today's world is filled with hatred, illness and sorrows caused by sin. Whoever is not pure is likened unto salt that has lost its savour - good for nothing, but to be thrown away and trampled under feet. Anyone in this condition is already dead.

### Follow the Examples of His Disciples

The holy life of the undefiled with women is not only to be envisaged, but practised as done by saints both living and of blessed memory. When Saul became Paul, he counted for nothing everything including marriage. Wishing that his examples be followed, he wrote:

*"But, what things were gain to me, those I counted loss for Christ. Yea doubtless, and I count all things but loss for the excellency of the knowledge of Christ Jesus my Lord: for whom I have suffered the loss of all things, and do count them but dung, that I may win Christ."* (Phil 3: 7-8).

Peter and the other disciples left everything and followed Christ. They remained for Christ, pure and undefiled in marriage.

### Prophetess Anna, an Undefiled Widow for 84 Years

Prophetess Anna married for seven years, then her husband died and she remained and died a widow, undefiled for eighty-four years. Why then should some women say that they could not do without lovers? God is love, health, joy and life. It is therefore foolish to condemn as harmful or inconvenient any condition that fashions our bodies for the indwelling of the Holy Spirit, Christ and God.

## Truth Is Bitter

Some prelates and laymen who have understood this gospel have successfully taken to celibacy for the same reason as Paul, Peter and Anna. Truth is bitter, but we are not to hide any truth, which has been highly acceptable to those who are anxious to gain the Kingdom of God. Christ is walking about here on earth, but you cannot see Him because you profane your bodies with (sex) men and women.

### Let Everybody Search Him/Herself

My dear Brethren let everybody, big or small search within themselves whether they have a share in eternal life. All those who are married look distressed at this word. This is not time for weeping or writing petition to the Author of the word. All those who are destined to live, and the resurrection from the dead are preserved by God. That is why those who are unfortunate in marriage should rejoice instead of lamenting over their ill luck. To them eternal life with Christ means more than compensation. It is a prize of triumphant life. It is the fulfilment of the highest Christian idea of living for Christ and for Christ alone.

### Following Christ has no Age Limit

Following Christ does not respect age or sex. We are simply asked to remain undefiled by men or women. You may have heard some people argue that the Kingdom of God is not for women or youths. This may stem from the observation that women and youths are most carnally inclined than elderly people. But God is no respecter of persons. Mary was a young virgin, Paul a youthful man. In Acts 21: 8-9, it is recorded that Philip the Evangelist in Caesarea had four daughters, virgins, who did prophesy.

### The Way Out

There is a way out for all those who are married already. A lot of what we regard as pleasurable are death. In order that our work as Christians may not be a waste, let us hear what the scripture says. Whenever you practice the word, even in a hundred years, only then will you see Christ. There is no wife, husband, church or government that can help; only individual determination can.

### Golden Text: Revelation 14: 4

*"These are they which were not defiled with women, for they are virgins, these are they which follow the Lamb withersoever he goeth. These were redeemed from among men being the firstfruits unto God and to the Lamb."*

### Defilement, a Stumbling Block to many Christian

The 144,000 who will follow Christ wherever He goes are those who have cut the time short to remain undefiled with women or men.

Let nobody deceive you, that there is any other condition. If Adam and Eve did not defile themselves, they would not die and there would be no want. You will be duly rewarded for whatever good work you do: Payiing of tithes, feeding the poor, visiting the sick and so on; but if you want to follow Christ, you must be undefiled by women or men. Following Christ is no joke. But what is impossible with man is possible with God.

Pray that God will help you to remain undefiled by women or men. Know that Christ is here with us. If we open the door for Him, He will come in and dwell with us and we in Him so that we may be heirs together for eternal life.

A stroke of a cane is sufficient unto the wise. Let those who has ears hear what the Holy Spirit has imparted to the entire world. May God bless His Holy Words, Amen.

# CHAPTER 7

# A WOMAN MUST NOT RULE OVER A MAN

Everlasting Gospel delivered by Leader Olumba Olumba Obu
Sole Spiritual Head of the Universe

**TEXT:** 1 Timothy 2 : 12 "But I suffer not a woman to teach nor to usurp authority over the man, but to be in silence."

Brethren, that is the revelation of this evening. It is a mortal sin for a woman to teach a man or have authority over him. The women folk all over the world suffer diverse afflictions, tribulations, anguish and death because they want to usurp the authority of men, which is strictly against the plan and will of the Almighty God. Any woman, who violates this law, does not disobey the law of man but the ordinance of God. Many women do not want to marry because they want to lord it over men. But for the entire world, churches, governments, communities and families to be in perfect peace, women must be in total subjection to men as was ordained by the Almighty God. And for this reason, a woman must obey a man with fear and trembling.

Many women are desirous to serve God, but since they aspire to usurp the places of men, they cannot serve God faithfully. And women who want to serve God must be ready to be subjected to her husband and other men. Your children are wild and rude because wives do not submit to their husbands, Sarah regarded Abraham as her father, master and king. To this end, she called Abraham "My Lord". That was why she had peace in the family and received God's blessings. Her son also was obedient to the father even to the point of death. For any woman to receive any blessing from God or who wants to see the glory of God manifesting in her, she must be in submission to the husband and other men. No woman under any circumstances should teach a man or rule over a man or for a man to be subjugated to a woman. God does not take it kindly. The reason all the matrimonial homes have no peace, stability and the sweetness of marital life is because women lord over their husbands. Any husband, who submits to the wife, causes the entire family to collapse. Death, sickness, poverty, division, stubbornness of children and all the vices beset such a family. The husbands must obey the word of God in the Holy Scriptures that a woman should not teach nor usurp authority of the man. The words of God will not pass away till all is fulfilled.

No matter your academic attainments, worldly position, even if a woman is a head of state or millionaire, she must not rule a man or give directives to a man even if the man is a slave. A woman should not use her beauty to enslave or give orders to any man. It is said that all are equal before God, but God created man to exercise power and dominion over a woman. Adam was the father and Eve was the daughter of Adam. The husband or man is the father to any woman; therefore, it is a sin for a child to be the head for his father. Any woman who wants the blessings of God must obey the husband in all ways. Brethren, let us hear the golden text so that you all will realise that you have overstepped the boundaries of old.

## GOLDEN TEXT: I TIMOTHY 2: 12

"But I suffer not a woman to teach nor to usurp authority over the man, but to be in silence."

## A Woman Must Not Rule Over A Man

Brethren, have you all heard the revelation of our lesson? Spread this gospel to all men who subject themselves to the rule of women or accept advice from the women. Any family, village, town, nation, or continent that a woman is at the head is under great punishment from God. Though a woman is a high court judge, lawyer, medical doctor or millionaire, never you make a mistake to subject yourself to her rulership. The decree of God is that a man should have authority over her. Any woman, who has the fear of God in her, must not usurp the authority of the man in order to escape the punishment of God. All the garments and bodily decoration of a woman are useless as far as rulership is concerned. A lot of men are living in fear and despair because their wives have authority over them. Some men spend most of their time in coupon houses after working hours because their wives do not allow them to have peace of mind in the house. Some of them are living miserable lives due to the maltreatment by their wives. If a man wanders and dies because a woman has authority over him, God will demand his blood from the hands of such a woman. God kept women as mothers to men. <u>It is out of ignorance, that some people say, the Leader does not travel outside 34 Ambo Street and 26 Mbupka Road. I am omnipresent and in your different houses, I have seen how women lord over their husbands.</u>

Now I want to ask the women fold this question; did God first create a woman before a man, or did the word of God first come from a woman to man or from man to woman? Did the serpent in the Garden of Eden first deceive a man or woman? The downfall of the whole world lies in the fact that Adam took advice from Eve his wife. Brethren, in order to have perfect peace in your family and to live long, women must be submissive to men and remain in perfect silence before them. Women will receive the blessings of God if they accept advice from the men in humility and meekness. Any house or nation divided against itself cannot stand. So what type of religion do you practice that before you go to the church, you quarrel and fight with your wife or husband? Ninety nine per cent of your families is governed by your wives and that is why there is no peace in the whole world. Since God gave Adam authority to teach and rule over a woman, any woman who makes any attempt to usurp the authority of a man is a rebel. The reason why all the churches, governments, corporations and other undertakings fail is because they accept advice from women like Adam.

All the advice, teachings and leadership roles played by a woman are useless because power was handed over to a man to teach and lead a woman. A woman must submit to his rule and authority in order to receive blessings from God. The whole world suffers, from heads of states; presidents, millionaires, governors, commissioners, judges, doctors and all categories of men do not have peace of mind because their women rule over them. Today the women are stubborn, self-willed and disobedient to their husbands. They behave exactly like Pharaoh in the land of Egypt. Therefore, take this message to the entire world that two cocks cannot crow on one roof. The women should return to their original position of submission to men, then peace, harmony, prosperity and other blessings of God will be their reward. If they fail to abide by this ordinance of God, they will receive their due punishment for disobedience to God's instructions.

The scripture says, *"Even as Sarah obeyed Abraham, calling him lord, whose daughters ye are, as long as ye do well, and are not afraid and with any amazement."*

Our great mother Sarah subjected herself to Abraham and called him, lord. All the pieces of advice, teachings and leadership role played by women power was handed over to a man to teach and lead a woman. Brethren, whether your husband is wicked, poor or whatever miserable position he may be, a woman must submit to his rule and authority in order to receive blessings from God. It is a shame for a woman to teach or have authority over the man but as long as women will obey and submit themselves to their husbands they will find the blessings of God surrounding them. No matter how beautiful a woman might be or the number of children she may have or any position she is placed in this earthly plane, a disobedient woman will never fail to receive punishment. Let those who have ears hear. May God bless His Holy Words, Amen.

# CHAPTER 8

# WHEN A MAN FIGHTS AGAINST GOD

Everlasting Gospel delivered by Leader Olumba Olumba Obu
Sole Spiritual Head of the Universe

**GOLDEN TEXT: ACTS 5: 39 -** *"But if it be of God ye cannot overthrow it; lest if haply* **ye** *be found even to fight against God."*

Beloved, this gospel intends to reveal to you that quite often, we fight against God in an attempt to correct one another. If we look round, most of the things we do in the world today amount to fighting against God. But, we think that we are mending. Today, a child is fighting against the mother, father against child and so on; all in a wrong attempt to correct one another.

The party that fails in the process accuses the other of using means. How true is this accusation? This other person who succeeds does not use "means"; he is simply directed by God, while the one who was fighting against him was fighting against God.

## WE SUFFER BECAUSE WE DISOBEY GOD

Very often, God asks us to give something to somebody. Perhaps, the person hates us, and whereas, God wants us to love Him; instead, we refuse, and as a result, what a loss and defeat we suffer! Very often too, our own spirit is speaking to us, but we turn to listen to the flesh instead, thus fighting against God. Lest you be found willingly, fighting against God, leave everybody to his own way, and take everything as you see it. Good or bad allow any event to come off naturally.

## NONE CAN OBSTRUCT GOD

If you are told that thieves are coming to burgle your house this night, do not try to prevent them by going to a necromancer for protection, or go packing, your things to somebody else's house. If you are told that you will be ill, do not buy medicines to prevent it. Thus, by not allowing anything to worry your mind, you will have peace. As long as we cannot prevent death, we cannot prevent anything from happening, for everything, including death is God's work. None can obstruct God in His work. None has ever done it since creation. God does everything in the way He thinks best. While man is ignorant of what is good or bad for him, God knows and does what is best for man.

Our only obligation should be for us to surrender completely to God's will. Man's continuous attempt to choose what is good for himself has often plunged man into regrettable mistakes and endless troubles.

## GOD MAKES NO MISTAKES

God Himself does not make mistakes, has no trouble or difficulty whatsoever. If He promises to give you money, you will have it. If He wishes to take all your wealth from you, He can do so very easily. Nobody can prevent Him. This being true, we should always say, "May God's will be done". Else, we shall be found, like our forefathers, unwillingly fighting against the Holy Spirit.

## ILLUSTRATION

A certain young king asked and obtained from God a dog that could foretell the future. One good year, the dog said to his master: "Thieves will burgle your palace tonight Sir". The King was very much disturbed. Without asking the dog what should be done, he set about gathering heavy bodyguards, soldiers and watchmen around himself. When the thieves came, they were chased back and the king was happy.

Two years later, the dog said again "Master, fire will consume all your things tomorrow". And again, without asking what should be done or what future such an incident was destined to bring, the king packed around himself a salvage party of fire brigades. He placed fire extinguishers in every home throughout his kingdom and asked all his subjects to stand by for any emergency. In time the fire burst out and was immediately put out through the mobilised operation by his subjects. No damage was done to life or property, again, the king was happy.

But after another two years an announcement that put the king at his wits end came "Master will die tomorrow!" announced the Future telling dog, looking sorry, yet announcing it clearly with his usual convincing tone. "What" the master asked "What shall I do, dear dog? "Nothing" replied the dog. And adding that, "You would be wise to have asked what you should have done in the case of the thieves and fire. And you would have been advised to let your riches go, for only by that means did God plan to take away your present riches so that your life might be spared to hoard and enjoy more riches afterwards. But you did not allow it. See whether you can save your life now."

## THE PREDICTION THAT CAME TRUE

The king could not save his life. He died the next day as predicted. My dear brethren, if that young king had known that the thieves and fire were God-sent prevention against his death, he would not have looked for soldiers, fire brigades and guards to protect his wealth. He would have allowed thieves to steal and fire to burn his property. But the fact that he prevented them caused him a lot of uneasiness, left him no peace and finally earned him his death. Read the lesson:

**GOLDEN TEXT: ACTS 5: 39 -** *"But if it be of God ye cannot overthrow it; lest if haply ye be found even to fight against God."*

The above text and the illustration are for us to see how disastrous it is to fight against God by trying to obstruct whatever He sends us daily as our own lot in life. It may be our lot to be involved in a court case, imprisonment, or suffer losses by thieves or fire, or ill treatment by a fellow creature. Whatever the case, we should not complain or find fault with anybody. Leave your wife, husband, and child to his/her own way, and do not be worried about how to prevent anything happening to you, else you would be found fighting against God. May God bless His Holy Words. Amen.

# CHAPTER 9

# THE STEPS TO GOD AND HIS KINGDOM

Several Everlasting Gospels of Leader Olumba Olumba Obu

Summarized by Elder W.B. Smith

**ST MATTHEW 5 V 20**

"For I say unto you, that except your righteousness shall exceed the righteousness of the Scribes and Pharisees, ye shall in no case enter into the kingdom of heaven."

It is not that easy for anyone to enter into the Kingdom of God. If it was that easy for anyone to qualify for entry into the Kingdom of God, why is it that only eight persons were saved in the world of Noah, and only three persons in the two cities of Sodom and Gomorrah? The world of Noah is the same world today. The people were eating, drinking, quarrelling, fighting, fornicating, stealing, backbiting, hating, murdering, and indulging in all kinds of sins and vices, until the great floods came and destroyed them. So also, was the behaviour of the people of Sodom and Gomorrah. In the case of the Scribes and Pharisees, they were deep in sins and vices but claim that they did not associate with Publicans and sinners; they observed the Mosaic laws, attend church and fast regularly, and they claim that they knew the scriptures very well. At this end of the age, after our Lord Jesus Christ had shed His precious blood, and made everything perfect, the inhabitants of the world are behaving worse than the Scribes and Pharisees, and the people of old.

Many people believe that since our Lord Jesus Christ came and shed His precious blood for the sins of the world, all their sins are taken away and they are free to continue committing sins, because our Lord Jesus Christ is a friend of sinners. There are those who continue to hate, fight, backbite, curse, fornicate, commit adultry, smoke, snuff, drink and indulge in other sins and vices; but claim to be christians because they attend church regularly. There are those who claim to be baptised in the church denominations and partake in Holy Communion, but cannot forsake sins. There are those who claim to be christians and preachers, but continue to get angry and drink alcohol; claiming that even our Lord Jesus Christ got angry and turned water into wine for people to drink. There are others who make sure that they own a big Bible; they read the scriptures regularly, concentrating on the Old Testament; they copy the actions of certain Biblical characters like Moses, Abraham, David, Solomon, etc., claiming that they also can commit murder, have many wives and girlfriends, have many enemies, take an eye for an eye and tooth for a tooth; then they conclude that they are going to heaven because God sent His Son to die for their sins, change them and give them new bodies to go to heaven. Others are members of Secret Societies and other Cults, but they claim that they are serving God. The Muslims claim to be very religious, but they conclude that anyone who speak against their religion should be put to death, eventhough God commanded that we should love one another and we should not kill anyone.

During the year 1990, Iraq a muslim country, invaded and captured Kuwait, a neighbouring muslim country. When many countries were united against Iraq for this act of aggression, the President of Iraq called upon all muslims to wage a holy war against his opponents, and declared that Allah (God) would deliver his country from the infidels. Is there such thing as a "holy war" when God commanded that we should not kill? See how pitiful and hypocritical human beings are in the sight of God? Our Lord Jesus Christ said, "Except our righteousness exceed the righteousness of the Scribes and Pharisees, we shall in no case enter into the Kingdom of Heaven." This statement of our Lord Jesus Christ, forms the basis of measurement of the righteousness of human beings. Today, the world is filled with Scribes and

Pharisees. At this end of the age, the Holy Spirit of Truth and Supernatural Teacher declared that to be qualified to enter God's Kingdom, one must be of the Brotherhood of the Cross and Star, where Oneness prevails; One Spirit, One Love, One Baptism, One Faith, One Hope, One Lord and One God.

## LOVE IS THE KEY

**1. St John 13 v 34**
"A new commandment I give unto you that ye love one another, as I love you, that ye also love one another."

**2. St John 14 v 21**
"He who hath my commandments and keepeth them, he it is who loveth Me; and he who loveth Me shall be loved of My Father, and I will love him and manifest myself in him."

**3. St Matthew 5 v 44**
"But I say unto you, love your enemies, bless them that curse you, do good to them that hate you, and pray for them which despitefully use you and persecute you."

These three passages from the Bible are only a few of the numerous statements made by our Lord Jesus Christ concerning Love; and at this end of the age, the Holy Spirit of Truth personified in our midst preaches Love from 1st January to 31st December every year. Love is God and God is Love. The Father is Love and our Lord Jesus Christ is Love. The Holy Spirit is Love and Brotherhood is also Love. Our Lord Jesus Christ gave us one commandment which is, that we should Love one another as he has Loved us. **Love is the Pivot around which all the other commandments revolves, and Love is the key to the Kingdom of God.** If we Love God we must Love one another. If we do not Love one another, it means that we do not Love God, because God and man are One entity. All human beings are equal; all human beings are brothers and sisters, therefore we must Love one another and regard other human beings as being equal to ourselves. God Loves all human beings regardless of whether they are good or bad. The thieves, liars, murderers, fornicators, adulterers, idolators, drunkards, homosexuals, blasphemers, those who murmur against God and even those who say that God does not exists, are all God's children. God Loves them all, eventhough the are wanted persons.

It is because of Love why God created human beings. It is because of Love why He saved human beings on the face of the earth till today, and did not destroy human beings completely during the Great Flood. It is because of His Love for human beings why our Lord Jesus Christ came to earth, and shed His precious blood to save mankind. Then why is it that human beings do not Love one another. It is the lack of Love that causes all the problems in the world today. Sickness, death, war, hunger, hatred, anger, deceit, lying, adultry, backbiting, confusion, division, lawlessness, drunkeness, racial discrimination, etc., are the result of lack of Love. Whatever is one's status in life, we must regard another human being as ourselves; the wealthy, the educated, the king, pope, president, archbishop, the white man, the black man, the coloured, the poor, the beggar; all are equal and must be regarded as equal. Failure to Love one another means that you do not want to enter into the Kingdom of God, because Love is the key to God's Kingdom. Our Lord Jesus Christ said that when we feed the hungry, visit the sick, clothe the naked and visit those in prison, we would have done all these things to God. All those who hate and discriminate cannot see God. If we Love one another, our Lord Jesus Christ will manifest Himself in us and dwell in us. What is the benefit of loving only those that Love you? Dont the demons do the same?

In order to inherit the Kingdom of God, human beings must return to that first Love; when man, animal, birds and all of God's creations lived together in Love, because God regard all His creations as one and the same. That is why our Lord Jesus Christ said that we should Love our enemies, bless them that curse you, do good to them that hate you, and pray for them that despitefully use you and persecute you. If you build a church for God, give all your possessions to the poor, or call the name of Jesus or Olumba one hundred times an hour, and you have no love, these are of no benefit to you because God would not recognise you. God does not require any other thing from human beings except Love. Love Jehovah God and His Christ and all human beings. It is the only way to the Kingdom of God. Love is the first and foremost thimg; every other thing comes after. Many people believe that to Love someone means to be intimate with one another, and exchange gifts with one another. Sexual intimacy is not Love, but rather lust of the flesh, and this leads to such sins as adultry, fornications, abortion, rape, homosexuality, wife swapping, child abuse, incest, and other sexual perverions and rituals. Love means to regard every human being as equal to yourself, regardless of race, colour, creed, nationality or status in life. The scripture said to, "Honour all men. Love the Brotherhood, fear God. Honour the King." We have to Love all types of men; rich men, poor men, black men, white men, old men, all women, all babies and living things. Love the Brotherhood. Who is the Brotherhood? It is God, Christ, Angels, human beings and all the creations of God. Brotherhood of the Cross and Star is Love. It is the gateway, the narrow path to the Kingdom of God. Our Lord Jesus Christ is the only Example Setter, and He is the only way to the Kingdom of God. Therefore to follow the examples of Abraham, Moses, David, Solomon, etc., means that you do not want to enter into the Kingdom of God, because these great men are saved only through our Lord Jesus Christ, the Redeemer.

## HOW TO WORSHIP GOD

**1. St Matthew 6 v 10**
"..............Thy will be done in earth as it is in heaven."
**2. St Matthew 26 v 39**
" And He went a little further and fell on His face and prayed saying, " Oh my Father, if it be possible let this cup pass from Me, nevertheless not as I will but as thou wilt."
**3. Revelation 11 v 16**
" And the four and twenty elders, which sat before God on their seats, fell upon their faces and worshipped God."
**4. Revelation 7 v 11**
" And all the angels stood round about the throne, and about the elders and the four beasts, and fell before the throne on their faces and worshipped God."

Many people worship God by the burning of incense and lighting of candles. Others sacrifice the blood of chickens, goats, sheep or cows. There are those who, even at this end of time are worshipping Heads of Countries as gods; also inanimate things such as statues, charms, talisman, crosses, paintings, photographs, etc. Others believe that to worship God means to attend church regularly. There are those who go on pilgrimage to Lourdes, Mecca and Jerusalem to worship God. Others build altars in their homes for God. There are those who believe that to worship God means to build a magnificent church for Him. There are others who claim to be worshipping God by being members of secret societies, and by the study of certain books. Others claim to worship God by possessing a big Bible, and reading the scriptures regularly, particularly the Old Testament; and being able to recite passages from the Bible. The Catholics worship God by conducting what they call "high mass," and by wearing the cross around their necks, and by reciting the Rosary. The Salvation Army and other church denominations worship God by the playing of musical instruments such as, drums, trumpets, clarenets, guitars, organs, cymbals, etc, and the clapping of hands. There are others who play what they call "gospel music," and they use the Words of God to compose gospel songs and worldly songs. Some people pray to God, standing up, others sitting down, others kneeling down, and others even lay flat on their backs. There are those who pray to God by looking at the sky with their hands stretched out, and shouting at the top of their voices.

The inhabitants of the world are in a great state of pity, confusion and division. Because of the lack of Love, human beings continue to suffer from divers tribulations and afflictions such as, sickness, death, poverty, fighting, wars and rumours of wars, hunger, wretchedness, lawlessness, etc; and no matter how they pray their problems are not solved. It is the quest for solution of these problems why their are so many church denominations, secret societies, occultism, mermaid, witchcraft, black magic, etc. Not even the people of the Old Testament era knew how to worship God. Our Lord Jesus Christ came and taught human beings the ways of God. His ministry work was a short one, because He came mainly to shed His precious blood. Due to the fact that His ministry was short, and because He realised how human beings were ignorant of the ways of God, He promised to send the Comforter, the Holy Spirit of Truth.

His mission would be to guide all nations into the accurate wisdom of truth, reveal the things to come and to remind the world of all the teachings of our Lord Jesus Christ. At this end of time, the Supernatural Teacher in our midst, is teaching the inhabitants of the world the ways of God; what God requires of human beings and how human beings should conduct themselves before their Creator. Our Lord Jesus Christ taught us to pray saying, "Our Father which art in heaven, hallowed be thy name thy Kingdom come. Thy will be done in earth as it is in heaven................" What is done in heaven must also be done on earth. We are told that the twenty four elders in heaven, fell on their faces and worshipped God. Our Lord Jesus Christ Himself, demonstrated to human beings that this method of worshipping God should also be done on earth, when He fell on His face and prayed to the Father in the Garden of Gethsemane. God does not want our money, church buildings, sacrifices of goat or chicken or any other thing. The one and only thing that God requires from human beings is that we should cover our faces on the ground, knock our heads on the ground three times; one to the Father, one to the Son and one to the Holy Spirit; and worship our Creator with our faces down, as demonstrated by our Lord Jesus Christ; so that as the Angels do in heaven, human beings must do likewise on earth. Is this too much to do to the Almighty God Who created you?

Man was not made for woman, neither was woman made for man, but God made both of them for Himself. All Human beings are the property of God, and He require all human beings to honour, praise, thank, fear and worship Him in this manner. From time to time, no matter where you are, no matter how well dressed you are, God require that man should kneel down and knock his head on the ground three times, to thank Him for what He has done for us and for the things which He has given to us. In addition, human beings must worship God barefooted as a mark of respect and humility before God. Remember what God said to Moses? He said, "Take off thy shoes from off thy feet, for the place whereon thou standeth is Holy ground." Only human beings resent and refuse to worship God in this manner. See how human beings are stupid and pitiful? The Angels in heaven do it, our Lord Jesus Christ who is the Son of man, Son of God and God Himself do it, but, human beings regard this method of worshipping God as demonic.

If human beings had known that God is dwelling inside us, no one would refuse to knock his head on the ground to his Creator, and worship Him with his face covered on the ground, and with no shoes on his feet. If God is in all human beings, and if all human beings are the property of God, whose head are you knocking, is it not God's? God is very pleased with human beings when they worship Him in this manner. There is no other method of worship which is acceptable to God. Of all the church denominations, the Muslims are the only people who pray with their faces on the ground, although some may do it ignorantly; unaware that God wants man to worship Him this way. In the Brotherhood of the

Cross and Star, which is the New Kingdom of God on earth, when one knocks his head on the ground, he does not knock his head to man; he knocks his head to the Almighty God who dwells inside him. The members of the Brotherhood of the Cross and Star are accused of knocking their heads to the Leader who is a Man; but Leader Olumba Olumba Obu knocks His head on the ground more times than any member. He may knock His head on the ground more than one hundred times in a day. To Whom is He knocking His head? He is knocking His head to the Creator of the Universe Who dwells inside Him. This is the era of the Holy Spirit. The Comforter who is the Holy Spirit of Truth, has arrived with tne New Teachings of Reformation and Reconstruction, to lead His children into the New Kingdom of God where the word of God is practiced, and where only righteousness dwells.

## EXAMPLE OF NEW PRAYERS TAUGHT BY THE HOLY SPIRIT OF TRUTH

*" Let thanks, praises, honour, dominion and power be given to the Father, in the Name of Our Lord Jesus Christ. Let thanks, praises, honour, dominion and power supremacy be given to the Father, in the Blood of Our Lord Jesus Christ. Let thanks, praises, homour, dominion and adoration be given to our Father, now and forever more, Amen. Holy, Holy, Holy, Lord God Almighty who reigns and rules in heaven above and on earth below, we your poor children have come before your throne as woeful sinners. We fall at your feet as the prodigal son, as Mary Magdalene and as the felon on the Cross. We have sinned against you in heaven and on earth. We have sinned against you through unholy utterances, untoward movements and unseeming behaviour. To this end, we are not worthy to be called your children. But because of the Cross on which divine Emmanuel your Son was nailed, and His precious Blood was spilled for the redemption of humanity; you have on account of this turned your back against our wrong doings. You have forgiven and blotted out all our sins, in the Name of Our Lord Jesus Christ, Amen.*

*We thank you, because you have forgiven and wholly blotted out all our sins, not minding how numerous our sins are before you. Daily, you continue to teach us to have love for one another; and to love you with our whole hearts, soul, mind; to love our neighbours as you love us. Let thanks and praises be given to you in the Name of Our Lord Jesus Christ, Amen. We thank you because you have washed us clean in our flesh, soul and spirit. You have endowed us with good and sound health and peace in Spirit and flesh. You have bestowed your love, peace, joy, happiness, hope, meekness, understanding, truth, faith, goodness, gentleness, patience, humility and temperance on all your children, and teach us to be truthful and honest in our lives. Let thanks be given to you Father, in the Name of Our Lord Jesus Christ, now and forevermore, Amen.*

*Let thanks, praises, honour, dominion and power be given to the Father, in the Name of Our Lord Jesus Christ. Let thanks, praises, honour, dominion and power supremacy be given to the Father, in the Blood of Our Lord Jesus Christ. Let thanks, praises, homour, dominion and adoration be given to our Father, now and forever more, Amen"*

This prayer is followed by Psalm 23 or 121; then the Lord's Prayer and ending with the Benediction (May the Grace of our Lord Jesus Christ........etc.). Finally you knock your head on the ground three times, and say Thank You Father. You must not pray to your CREATOR with your shoes on, and you must knock your head on the ground three times before you commence praying.

There you have it, we must take it or leave it, but the will of God must be done on earth as it is done in heaven. When you compare this prayer with the prayers of the Church denominations, **you must now realise that the Holy Spirit of Truth is now personified here on earth, and that what people are doing in the Churches and Secret Societies as their method of worshipping their CREATOR, is very pitiful, comical and hypocritical indeed. It is a fact that human beings are proud, arrogant, pompous and prejudice. It is also a fact, that the things which human beings regard as foolish, degrading and demonic, are the things accepted by God.** There is more benefit in repeating the Lord's Prayer and knocking your head to the Almighty God, than attending Church service for three hours. The way to the Kingdom of God is like a Ladder. The Father has come down to earth from His throne above to teach, reform and prepare His children to climb the Ladder step by step to His Kingdom. There are FOUR STEPS to GOD:-

# THE FIRST STEP TO GOD

**1. St Matthew 3 v 13**
"Then cometh Jesus from Galillee to Jordan, unto John to be baptised of him."
**2. St John 3 v 3**
"Jesus answered and said unto him, except a man be born again, he cannot see the Kingdom of God."
**3. St Mark 16 v 16**
"He that believeth and is baptised shall be saved, but he that believeth not shall be damned."
**4. Acts 2 v 38**
"Then Peter said unto them, repent and be baptised everyone of you, in the name of Jesus Christ, for the remmission of sins, and you will receive the gift of the Holy Ghost."

Of all the Biblical characters from Genesis to Revelation, **the one and only person whose example all human beings must follow is our Lord Jesus Christ.** He was the Almighty God in Human Form, and He demonstrated and taught human beings what we should do and what we should not do. Today, the Holy Spirit of Truth personified here on earth, is reminding us of the things spoken by our Lord Jesus Christ; teaching us the ways of God, and bring us to the accurate wisdom of Truth. Our Lord Jesus Christ demonstrated how human beings should worship God. Before commencing His ministry work, He got baptised by John the Baptist, thus demonstrating to human beings that we must first be baptised. He told Nicodemus that one has to be born again of the water and of the Spirit, in order to enter into the Kingdom of God. Therefore the First Step to God is, that **we must repent and confess all our sins; be baptised by immersion in water three times, in the name of the Father, Son and Holy Spirit; and refrain from all sins and vices.** This form of baptism is known as the **Baptism of our Lord Jesus Christ, and it is administered only in the Brotherhood of the Cross and Star.** The church denominations have several types of baptism which they administer according to their worldly wisdom. In the church denominations you are only ask if you believe in Jesus Christ and accept Him as your personal Saviour, when you reply in the affirmitive, you are baptised by one emersion in water and then told to attend church regularly and pay your dues. Such baptism does not work, because you did not repent and confess all your sins, and so you do not receive the Holy Spirit.

With this form of baptism your old sins are not remmitted, and you cannot therefore refrain from sins. That is why anyone baptised in the church deniminations continue to fight, hate, quarrell, backbite, fornicate, commit adultry, steal, tell lies, smoke, drink and indulge in all kinds of sins and vices. John the Baptist practiced the baptism of repentance. Some of the church denominations practice the baptism of repentance. Of all the various types of baptisms practiced in the church denominations, the baptism of John the Baptist is the best, but it is not the end because the baptism of John does not give you the Holy Spirit, and without the Holy Spirit you cannot forsake sins. Only the disciples of our Lord Jesus Christ were given the Holy Spirit. John the Baptist himself declared that, "He baptised with water for repertance, but He who come after him baptise with the Holy Gost and with fire." This is the baptism of our Lord Jesus Christ.

One must repent, confess all his sins, believe that our Lord Jesus Christ is the Son of man, Son of God and God Himself; and then be immersed in water three times in the name of the Father, the Son and the Holy Spirit. After this, he will receive the Holy Spirit and he will be able to refrain from sins and vices. It is only the Holy Spirit that gives one the ability to forsake sins and vices. If after baptism you continue to sin, it means that you did not receive the Holy Spirit and He has not given you the ability to refrain from committing sins. It is only the Brotherhood of the Cross and Star that practice the baptism of our Lord Jesus Christ. After baptising in the Brotherhood of the Cross and Star, so long as you repent and confess all your sins, it means that all the sins that you have committed from Adam till now will be forgiven; you will receive the Holy Spirit and you will be able to refrain from sins and vices. This does not happen after you are baptised in the church denominations. That is why, even if one is already baptised in the Churches, he has to be baptised again if God reveals Brotherhood of the Cross and Star to him.

Many church goers claim that they would not be baptised again. This is nonsense because one can be baptised several times. Our Lord Jesus Christ has said, that after baptism by repentance and confession of sins, He would reveal Himself to you and manifest Himself in you. To complete the First Step to God, one must repent, confess all his sins, be baptised and refrain from all sins and vices such as:- anger, witchcraft, charms, talisman, drinking of wine and other alcohol, smoking, lying, stealing, backbiting, fornication, adultry, quarrelling, fighting, murder, hating, maliciousness, lawlessness, suing people to court, homosexuality, abortion, child abuse, being members of Secret Societies or Lodge, consulting of Oracles and Delawrence, weeping, mourning at funerals, murmuring against God, etc.

After these are done, one will be pure in heart and will be able to see our Lord Jesus Christ. Brotherhood of the Cross and Star is not a Church, Group or Society where you pay fees or dues to become a member. It is the New Kingdom of God on earth. It is only God Who reveals Brotherhood of the Cross and Srar to you, and call you into Brotherhood. If you are not convinced, or if you do not understand or accept what you are now reading about the New Teachings of the Holy Spirit of Truth now personified in our midst; and about the Brotherhood of the Cross and Star, it means that God has not revealed Himself to you nor called you.

## THE SECOND STEP TO GOD

**1. 1 Corinthians 5 v 11**
"But now I have written unto you not to keep company. If any man that is called a brother be a fornicator; a covetious or an idolator, or a railer, or a drunkard, or an extortioner, with such an one do not eat."
**2. John 1 v 10**
"If there come any unto you, and bring not this doctrine, receive him not into your house, neither bid him God speed."
**3. 2 Corinthians 6 v 17**
"Wherefore come out from among them, and be ye separate said the Lord, and touch not the unclean things and I will receive you."
**4. Luke 14 v 26**
"If any man come unto Me and hate not his father, and mother, and wife, and children, and brethren, and sister, and his own life also, he cannot be My disciple."
**5. St Matthew 10 v 37**
"He that loveth father or mother more than Me is not worthy of Me, and he that loveth son or daughter more than Me is not worthy of Me."
**6. St Matthew 12 v 49 - 50**
"And He stretched forth His hand towards His disciples and said, behold my mother and my brethren, for whosoever shall do the will of my Father which is in heaven, the same is my brother and my sister and mother."

The First Step to God tells us to repent, confess our sins, be baptised and refrain from committing all manner of sins and vices. The Second Step to God is, that we must separate ourselves from sinners.

If you refrain from committing sins you should not keep company with sinners, nor get entangled with the worldly things. If God gives you the ability to refrain from sins and vices, then you should not keep company nor associate with evildoers; fornicators, adulterers, extortioners, drunkards, backbiters, thieves, liars, dance and party goers, gamblers, indulgers in witchcraft, occultism, secret societies, and other ungodly practices. **Our Lord Jesus Christ is no longer known as a friend of sinners after He has shed His precious blood. He has nothing to do with sinners now, and God does not hear the prayer of sinners who do not repent, confess and refrain from committing sins and vices.** Once God has called you out of the world, you must abandon the worldly things such as wealth, money, men, women, children, fathers, mothers, sisters, brothers, relations, worldly music, jewellry and all other abominable things.

To keep company with sinners and partake in their worldly activities and vices, is a sin against God, and He does not answer the prayers of such persons. Some people takes pleasure in listening to those who speak evil words against God, but are annoyed when evil words are spoken against their carnal father. Who is the Father of all human beings, is it not God? The child of God works for his Father. The Psalm says, "Blessed is the man that walketh not in the counsel of the ungodly, nor standeth in the way of sinners, nor sitteth in the seat of the scornful." Our Lord Jesus Christ said that, to be true followers of God, we have to hate fathers, mothers, wives, husbands, children, brothers, sisters and our own lives. If you refrain from sins and decide to follow our Lord Jesus Christ, you must be prepared to forsake your families for the word of God. You dont hate them, but their bad ways. Our Lord Jesus Christ does not make any mistakes in making such statements. Did Adam and Eve obeyed God's voice? It is because of them why we are suffering today. If your parents are pagans, how can they teach you the ways of God? Who killed Abel, was it not his brother Cain from the same womb? About 99% of the problems in the world today are caused by our relations from the same womb. Who sold Joseph into bondage in Egypt, were they not his brethren? David's children suffered because of his sins. Who hated Jacob, was it not his brother Esau? Who got Esau's birthright by fraud, was it not his brother Jacob from the same womb? Who stole Esau's blessing by deception, was it not his brother Jacob? Was it not their mother Rebekah who engineered the whole fraud in favour of Jacob? Was she really a real mother to Esau? The father Isaac loved Esau more than Jacob, while the mother loved Jacob more than Esau, were they real parents? Parents and families cannot do anything to save you.

The brethren of our Lord Jesus Christ did not believe in His teachings, and so were the inhabitants of His native city. He was killed by His town's people. Who told Job to curse God and deny Him, was it not his wife? Who betrayed Samson, was it not his beloved wife Delilah? Our Lord Jesus Christ when on earth rejected His father, mother, and brethren for the service of God. When He was told that His mother and father sought for Him, He replied by declaring that whosoever hear His teachings and practice them, are His mother, father and brethren. God advised Adam and Eve not to eat of the tree of good and evil, but they disobeyed God, thereby bringing into the world the issues of good and evil. There is no court to judge them, but the flesh and the Holy Spirit always remain at war.

If you are the only man of God in your family or village, all other members being worldly will continue to oppose you. The world today is divided into two classes, namely, good and bad. God knows that our sickness, sufferings and death comes from wicked parents, etc., so why should we not forsake parents and families for the work of God? To forsake your parents and families and continue to indulge in adultry, fornication, stealing, lying, hating, cursing, fighting, drunkeness, smoking, etc., is of no benefit to you. If you are going to hate families for the work of God, you must refrain from all sins and vices, and disassociate yourself from sinners and worldly things. The people of the world love worldly things more than God. People claim to be christians but continue to drink alcohol, smoke, backbite, hate, fornicate, steal, quarrel, tell lies and indulge in abortion, divorce, homosexuality, child abuse, etc; does it mean that God does all these things and advise you to do all these abominable things? Can you claim to be a christian when you do all these things?

Do not love your parents and families because they are your relations, but rather love them because they love God and do the work of God. It is impossible for one to have two fathers. God is the only Father, and our Lord Jesus Christ the only Brother. Anyone who is baptised into the Brotherhood of the Cross and Star becomes a child of God, and there is no class distinction. Anyone who practicalise the words of God is your brother and your sister; no matter where he or she comes from; whether he or she is black, white or coloured; all are One in God.

## THE THIRD STEP TO GOD

**1. St Luke 12 v 48**
"But he that knew not and commit things worthy of stripes, shall be beaten with few stripes. For unto whomsoever much is given, of him shall much be required; and to whom men have committed much, of him they will ask the more."

**2. 2 Corinthians 8 v 14**
"But by an equality, that now at this time, your abundance may be a supply for their wants, that their abundance also may be a supply for your want, that there may be equality."

**3. St Luke 3 v 11**
"In reply He said unto them, let the man that has two garments, share with the man that has none, and let him that has things to eat do the same."

The Third Step to God is that we should share all that we have with those who are less fortunate than ourselves. Heaven and earth and the fullness thereof belongs to God, therefore all the things that are made by God are meant to be shared equally amongst the children of God, so that no one is lacking and so that equality prevails. It is because of the lack of this wisdom of truth, why man accummulates everything for himself in one place, so that these wealth which he accummulated get rotten; some wasting away; others destroyed by rodents and wild animals; but the children of men are dying from hunger. If you have two coats you have to give one to the person who has none; as God has blessed you, you have to share all your resources equally with those who are less fortunate than yourself. Our own salvation, and that of the whole world hangs on this teaching. Having been bestowed with the manifold blessings of God, you are now being called upon to share all that you have with those who are less fortunate than yourself. You should not wait until someone ask you. It is intended to be a voluntary or humanitarian service.

God created all things first before He created man, so that man may use all things to maintain himself, so that all human beings may live happily and in peace. The rich will never enter the Kingdom of God, so long as they continue to accummulate wealth and do not distribute their resources to the poor and needy. That is why our Lord Jesus Christ said that it is easier for a camel to go through the eye of a needle, than for a rich man to enter into the Kingdom of God. He also said, "What does it profit a man if he gains the whole world and lose his own soul; and what can a man give in exchange for his life?" Wealth is an instrument to human beings, and human beings are instruments to God. We have to employ these resources in the services of God, that there may be satisfactory service in the Father's Vineyard. All money and food throughout the world, should be distributed to the poor and hungry. Failure to do this is the cause of confusion, division, rebellion, death, sickness, tribulations and afflictions affecting the whole world.

It is said that a hungry man is an angry person. The souls of all those who are dying of starvation will haunt the rich. A great many people argue erroneously that food is nothing, but food is a very important thing. People commit murder and cause physical injury because of food. A hungry person will steal and commit other offences in order to obtain food. Of all the things created by God, food occupies the first position. Abraham used food to entertain Angels and received manifold blessings. It was food that God finally used to free the Israelites from bondage in Egypt. God instructed Moses to conduct a feast, using the male from each group of animals, roasted and eaten in great jubilation by the congregation; after which Pharoah would release the Israelites. It was food that Jacob used to usurp the birthright of his brother Esau. It was food that Isaac requested from Esau in order to bless him. You did not come with anything into the world, nor will you carry anything when you leave the world.

Our Lord Jesus Christ taught us to pray to the Father saying, "Give us this day our daily bread." God provide things for all His creations. Whatever is left over after your daily bread does not belong to you, you should therefore share whatever is left over with those who have none, because God will continue to give bread day by day. It is because of selfishness, greed and lack of love, why all the things created by God are not distributed equally amongst His children. Regardless of race, colour or creed, God's instruction is that if you have much, you must distribute to others who have nothing. We should not accummulate or reserve anything for ourselves, but all resources should be distributed to the poor and needy, the orphans, the wounded, the sick and the maimed. It is the promise of God, that every person born into the world is being provided for by Him; not only human beings, but also animals, birds, fishes and creeping things, plants, etc; even the sand on the ground is being catered for by God.

Failure to distribute your wealth brings suffering. Not only wealth or food, but if God bless you with children, good health, education, etc, you must use these to help others who have none. Whatever you are blessed with does not belong to you; whether it be money, food, land, children and all other things. Everything belongs to God; you are only a steward or caretaker of these things. Poverty is the worst sickness in the whole world. We should regard ourselves as borrowing all the parts of our bodies. God only loan His eyes, ears, hands, brain, etc to us, as well as other things. In Brotherhood of the Cross and Star, all are equal, and the Father is uniting the entire world so that all will be One. Prayers cannot take poverty away, therefore we must always help all those who are less fortunate than ourselves.

## THE FOURTH STEP TO GOD

**1. St Matthew 12 v 50**
"For whosoever shall do the will of my Father, which is in heaven, the same is my brother and sister and mother."

**2. Acts 4 32 - 33**
"And the multitude of them that believed were of one heart and of one soul, neither said any of them that ought of the things which he possessed was his own, but they had all things common, and with great power gave the apostles witness of the resurrection of the Lord Jesus Christ, and grace was upon them all."

**3. Luke 20 v 35**
"But they which shall be accounted worthy to obtain that world and the resurrection of the dead, neither marry nor are given in marriage."

**4. 1 Corinthians 7 v 29**
"But this I say brethren the time is short; it remaineth that both they that have wives be as though they had none."

Whosoever does what God likes is a child of God, regardless of his race, tribe, creed and nationality. **The Fourth Step to God is to practice the Words of God as taught by our Lord Jesus**

**Christ, and recorded in the New Testament, particularly St Matthew chapters 5, 6, and 7 and St Luke chapter 6: and the New Teachings of the Holy Spirit of Truth now personified in our midst.** We are told to have love, peace, mercy, kindness, temperance, self control, endurance, meekness, humility, tolerance and forgiveness. These Godly Virtues will unite us in Oneness, and give us the right to enter into the Kingdom of God. The Children of the New Kingdom are the Children of Promise, and are those who do the will of God. The right to enter into the Kingdom of God is obtained by hearing and reading the words of God which are delivered daily by the Supernatural Teacher and Holy Spirit of Truth, at the Everlasting Gospel Centre of the Brotherhood of the Cross and Star, Calabar, Nigeria, Africa: and putting all these teachings into practice.

Our Lord Jesus Christ is the Way, the Truth and the Life. In the begining human beings and all of God's creations lived together as One. Today there are divisions among families, communities, villages, towns, countries and nationalities. This situation has brought hardships, tribulations, afflictions, poverty and death into the world. There can be no peace in the world except we practice the Words of God. That is why our Lord Jesus Christ said, "I am the Way, the Truth and the Life, no one cometh to the Father except by Me." All blessings, glory and peace hangs on the Fourth Step to God. Our Lord Jesus Christ died and resurrected for those who hear and practice His teachings, and they are like buildings set on a rock. The Words of God unifies all races of people. Abraham became a friend of God, because he did what God likes. Only those who practice the Words of God are brethren. Our Lord Jesus Christ said, "If you do what I tell you I will not call you servants but friends."

We should not call a brother a thief, if you do you are also a thief. The term brother or sister means maintaining a state of equality with those who do not commit sins. The scripture says that, the eyes of the Lord are upon the righteous, and His ears are open to their prayers, but His back is turned on the evil doers. If one or two people practice the Words of God they are better than fifty thousand people who do not practice the Words of God. By practicing the Words of God, your eyes will be opened and you will be united with God.

## CHASTITY AND CELIBACY

God prefer those who do not marry, and those who do not indulge in sexual intimacy. Marriage is an enemy of God, and it is marriage that set the whole world ablaze. Fornication is sexual intimacy between man and woman. It is because of the fornication committed by Adam and Eve why there are so many problems in the world today. God did not create woman for man, nor man for woman, but He created both of them for Himself. We have to purify ourselves since God is the Bridegroom. We should keep our bodies undefiled. Fighting and quarrelling between men and women emanates from sexual intimacy. Christ dwells in those who are not intimate with one another. It is erroneous to say that if men and women are not intimate with one another, they cannot be fruitful and multiply. Did Adam and Eve had parents? No they did not. It is the Word that God used to bring everything into existence. Our Lord Jesus Christ came into the world through Mary who had not been intimate with anyone. It is by this same manner that people would come into the world. All those who indulge in sexual intimacy cannot declare that they and the Father are One. Fornication destroys the body and affects the Spirit. Our Lord Jesus Christ said, that not everyone that say "Lord, Lord" will enter into the Kingdom of God, but only those who do the will of His Father Who is in heaven.

Knowing what God has now revealed to us, we should now pray to God to remove the sexual urge from us. All those who indulge in sexual intimacy are still in the world and drinking the old wine. To be carnally minded means death. Human beings are the temple of God, and so when we commit fornication and adultry we have done great harm to God, and this is an hedious sin against God. God requires that we should abstain completely from sexual intimacy, because it is imperative that God must dwell in human beings. The Tabernacle of God is now with man. Chastity and celebacy is the way to salvation. Those who are not married are warned not to marry or be intimate with one another. Those who are already married should now live as brothers and sisters, refraining from sexual intimacy with one another since the time is short, for the Owner of the Vineyard has come. His dwelling place with men is the Brotherhood of the Cross and Star.

Our Lord Jesus Christ now rules over our mortal bodies. He reigns in the Spirit of the flesh, therefore we must now surrender ourselves to God. The number of people that God want is 144,000 virgins, therefore we should no longer indulge in fornication and adultry. God does not say that it is evil for you to marry since you did not know, but since the time is short you should surrender yourselves to God, and refrain totally from sexual intimacy.

## THE NEW COMMANDMENTS, INJUNCTIONS AND INSTRUCTIONS OF GOD.

The Holy Spirit of TRUTH and Supernatural Teacher in our midst at this end of time, has delivered the following **warning to all the inhabitants of the world.** Read between the lines and surrender yourselves to the CREATOR of heaven and earth and the fullness thereof, because **the Owner of the Vineyard has arrived for vengeance:-**

*" LOVE YE ONE ANOTHER. I am shouting and pleading with you, that all those who indulge in the following will not enter the Kingdom of God:-*
*Fornication, adultry, stealing, lying, deceit, envying, cunningness, anger, quarrelling, fighting, gossipping, smoking, snuffing, heresy, lasciviousness, sedition, unrighteousness, jealousy, cowardice, vindictiveness, pomposity, division, laziness, coveteousness, argument, flippancy, pride, fraud, bullying, murder, insult, rancour, vain thinking, aggravation, whispering, cursing, herbalism, traditional plays, worldly dance, worldly songs, swearing by blood, oath, inordinate, lust and evil concupiscence, both native and english treatments, occult science, burning of incense, ogboni society, playing of bands and drums, weeping, frowning of face, sighing, bribery, being bribed, selfishness, beating of children, wife or servants; disobedience, lamenting, wearing of gold, pearl earings, necklace, finger rings; piercing of ears, drinking, offering drinks to people, keeping company with fornicators, mourning, keeping a mourning house, secret societies such as Lodge, Rosicrucian, Abu, Ekpe, Ekpo and others; court actions, backbiting, sacrifice, eating of meat from strangled beast or meat from animals which die by themselves, and such ungodly manners."*

The Church denominations do not have the Holy Spirit to forgive sins. That is why a person who is baptised in the Church denominations find that his troubles and afflictions still remain with him, because his sins have not yet been remmitted. This is the reason why people jump from one Church to another seeking salvation, all to no avail. Baptism in the Brotherhood of the Cross and Star gives you salvation, because all your sins from Adam up to today will be forgiven; and all sicknesses, afflictions and sufferings will be solved immediately. Our Lord Jesus Christ said that, "God is a Spirit and they that worship Him, must worship Him in Spirit and in TRUTH." What is TRUTH? TRUTH is that God is Man and Man is God. TRUTH is that our Lord Jesus Christ is the Son of Man, Son of God and God Himself. TRUTH is that our Lord Jesus Christ is Man, and The Holy Spirit is Man. TRUTH is that God and Man are One Entity. TRUTH is that God is now dwelling on earth with men. If you accept these TRUTHS then "Love ye one another and worship God in Spirit and in TRUTH." Amen.

# CHAPTER 10

# THOSE WHO WILL GO TO HEAVEN

Everlasting Gospel Delivered by:
Leader Olumba Olumba Obu, Sole Spiritual Head
of the Universe

## PART ONE

| | |
|---|---|
| **FIRST LESSON:** | Revelation 14 v 4 |
| **SECOND LESSON:** | St Luke 20 v 35 |
| **GOLDEN TEXT:** | St Matthew 19 v 12 |

"These are they that were not defiled with women for they are virgins. These are they which follow the Lamb wheresoever He goeth. These were redeemed from among men, being the first fruits unto God and to the Lamb."

Brethren I want to divide this gospel into three parts. I will give the first part today, and the other two parts on the following sundays. We are going to illustrate those who will be taken to heaven. If any of the signs is seen in you, then you are one of them. This gospel is not going to be long because it is self explanatory. I am not giving this gospel to set a division between husband and wife. I do not also want wagging tongues. This gospel does not belong to any particular member. It is just a revelation of the eternal truth as God has it. I am giving this gospel because I had already promised you that I will reveal to you, those who will be going to heaven.

### Heaven is for Heavenly People:

You cannot ascend up to heaven because you are wealthy, or because of your wisdom, or because of any righteousness or goodness in you. You may be the cleverest person; you can make up your mind not to get married and stay unmarried; you may use your money to prepare yourself for heaven, but if you were not meant for it you cannot go there. Even if you were put in heaven, you cannot stand the condition of things there. People have different gifts from God. God give people advice to marry only one wife and after union to fast. St Paul, from the day Christ called him, had nothing to do with woman. At the end of His sermon while here on earth Christ would say, those who have ears to hear let them hear. The gospel given out is like a big net thrown out into the sea. It takes with it various kinds of fishes, so when the gospel is given, you must pick out whatever portion that belongs to you.

When our Lord Jesus Christ preached to His disciples that if they divorced and married another, they have committed adultry for the rest of their life, the disciples became very sad. Because they were annoyed, He made it clear to them that the sermon belonged only to those who were destined to hear it, those who could digest it. Do you remember an instance when the disciples of John the Baptist saw the disciples of our Lord Jesus Christ baptising, how they were annoyed and went and told John the Baptist what the disciples of our Lord Jesus Christ had done? John said that he had told them that nobody could do anything along these lines except the power is given to him. Therefore the capacity to marry one wife and be satisfied with just that one comes from above. Also the capacity to marry two or more wives must come from above. There are some men who if they put two or more wives in the house, become almost dead. There are those who cannot stand women at all. That is just how they are made because they are meant for the Kingdom. This revelation of God is plain. When you see others marry you start to immitate them, some even marry more than one wife; has God given you the capacity? Many women say, our companions have husbands and still keep as many boyfriends as they like outside, let us immitate them; have you ask God whether you can do so?

### The Signs that Follow Them:

On the other hand you may find some women marrying one husband and keep to him alone. They do not want to know the number of women that their husbands has made contact with outside. There are others who may marry one husband but have many boyfriends outside. I tell you that in each case, they are not responsible for this behaviour. They were created like that, so do not try to immitate them. If you do you may become wretched. There are people who were not meant for marriage, but because of the circumstances of this life, they marry. You will find that they would carry on for some time, then finally separate because they always fight and quarrel in the family. There will be no settled life in their midst, because they are not meant for this world, but for heaven. Some of these women become sickly in their husband's homes because of sex. But as soon as they stay away from their husbands they become well.

Some men or women will be lovely to look at but they remain single; this makes you wonder why such lovely persons should not have wives or husbands. They have been approached for marriage but they refused because of their position in heaven. The world is blind. When a thing like this happens, people begin to talk and gossip and start to consult juju doctors to prepare them lucky charms to make them find wives or husbands. There are some women who are born exactly like men, and some men who are born exactly like women. The Bible says, that there are some who are born eunuchs; but when this happens to a man the individual becomes perpetually grieved, and is ridiculed by men and women. As a result, he starts worrying and looking for treatment. This is how human beings fight with God. There are others who because of the Kingdom, separate themselves from husbands or wives, and wait for the coming of the Kingdom. They are not responsible for this action.

### FIRST LESSON: Revelation 14 v 4

" These are they that were not defiled with women, for they
are virgins. These are they which follow the Lamb withersoever
He goeth. These were redeemed from among men, being
the first fruits unto God and to the Lamb."

Brethren, have you heard the word of God read as a witness? People say Oh! where can God get such people these days? People who dont want to marry or people who haven't defiled themselves with women? I tell you that there are lots of men and women who have never defiled themselves. They are not responsible for the level in life which they have attained. It is God that has given them that power of resistence. Some of these people may be highly educated; some may only attained a basic standard of education; some may not be educated, before the trumpet setting everything in order, sounds. There are other people who have been in preparation against this time. Among them are the Reverend Mothers and Fathers who have kept themselves from fornication, etc.

Dont make the mistake that Elijah made when he saw all other Prophets killed, and asked God to protect him for the people have decided to kill him, as he was the only one left. What was God's reply? God told him that He had sent down seven thousand men to him, to protect him. Some very young ones are coming. When the number is completed the trumpet will surely sound. Some of them, as soon as they are born into the world show no interest for man or woman, because they dont know the difference. You can find a girl undressing in front of a man or sleeping in the same bed with him; but with our carnal minds, if we see such a thing we would conclude that they have known each other sexually, because it is believed that a man and a woman cannot sleep in the same bed without having sex.

**God's Way Is Mysterious**

These children of God so born, do not even know that they were created like that for the Kingdom of Heaven. God passes in a mysterious way to do His work. That is why in Brotherhood of the Cross and Star, we do not struggle for anything. Stay where God keeps you. Philllip had four beautiful daughters, and none of them was given in marriage. They remained without husbands all their lives and waited for the fulfillment of God's wish. Prophetess Hannah married, but when her husband died she stayed, worked and served God without a man. There are many Hannahs among you today. Do not feel that you are lost when you hear this gospel. God knows what He is doing. Do not make any choice because the Father has already made it.

I told you of those heavenly ones that will follow the Lamb wheresoever He goeth. In the same sense there are children of perdition. Dont you see clearly, that this does not depend on anybody who looks for it or runs away from it. There are Prophets who will go to heaven, and there are Prophets who will inherit the earth, and there are those who will go to hell. Today I tell you that those who will be selected to go to heaven, are those that never marry nor defile themselves. Everybody is saved by grace, but we should not, because of this, become people with questionable characters. Those who are destined to go to heaven will be separated from their husbands or wives to get themselves prepared before the trumpets sound. You may count a miserable prostitute who goes from man to man as lost, but I tell you if his or her name was destined for heaven on that day he or she will refrain from all this and will surely go to heaven. Can you say why women are prostitutes? It is because they do not see the truth.

You may see a husband and wife and recommend them to be good partners. You may be wrong in your recommendation, because you may not know their internal problems. The husband may not be truthful to the wife. The woman, because of this may retaliate in like manner. They come back to the house and no one questions the other. You will also find a woman who is married to a man who goes from woman to woman, the wife will not be satisfied because she wants a loyal husband. The woman eventually leaves the husband to look for another man. She is not a prostitute, but she is looking for loyalty. This thing also happens to men, and when they make up their minds they decide never to marry again. The whole town will take them to be prostitutes. A woman who becomes a prostitute does so because of some unavoidable circumstances. They want loyalty that is why they go from door to door. The same thing happens to men.

Brethren, why is there so much dissatisfaction in marriage? It is because God does not create some people for marriage. They just marry for the purpose of security, and when their husbands demand sex, they refuse because they have no interest. The same thing happens to men, some have no interest in marriage, they just marry to be free from women's molestation. When their wives demand sex, they refuse and they will be called eunuchs. There are also some men who are impotent, they become miserable and dispirited and may even commit suicide when they know that they can't play the part of a man. They dont know that God created them for Himself. They can pay large sums of money in ignorance to juju doctors, to make them virile. God in fact loves the world very much. If He should follow our evil ways, He would not keep us alive till today.

## SECOND LESSON: St Luke 20 v 35

*"But they which shall be accounted worthy to obtain that world and the resurrection from the dead, neither marry nor are given in marriage."*

### They Are Not Married

Those that are counted worthy are not married nor given in marriage. You may say, "I will be carried up to heaven," which heaven? If you still think of material things, you will not be carried up to heaven as you think. You may look around and say, my friends are all married and have grown up children. Those who are married think of how to please their husbands or wives, but those who are not married think of how they will be pure in body and mind so as to please God. Those who are for heaven do not have marriage in mind. If you talk to them about marriage they will refer you to heavenly things, and depart from you. But they are only happy if you take them as brothers. Brethren, do not be deceived that those who will go to heaven are given in marriage. The choice of who goes to heaven is left to God alone. If it falls on a woman she will remain without sex. If it falls on a man, he also will remain without sex. God wants to use us all, so stay where you are placed and do not be annoyed.

Our Lord Jesus Christ said, that it is better to go to heaven with one hand, than go to hell with two hands. There are some people who were not born eunuchs but later they changed and became eunuchs. There are some, from the day of their conversion they resigned from all forms of sexual intercourse. Yes, it was stated by God that within the twinkle of an eye they will be changed. Many of you are still fornicating eventhough you are meant for heaven, you do this because you do not know where you stand. There are those who are kept for the fulfillment of the scripture, and those who will be changed within the twinkle of an eye. If you are among those for the heavenly home, dont worry you will be changed before you go to heaven.

### Christ Is Preparing You

Some grumble, that ever since they came to Brotherhood no woman or man has shown interest in them anymore. Whether they have become too ugly they wonder. No, I say you have even become more beautiful. You are being prepared for heaven by driving the desire out of you. So do not be surprised if you no more have the desire for sex, eventhough you are not old. When God puts up a sign like this you worry and abuse Him, not knowing that He is preparing you for heaven. You will find that since you came to Brotherhood you have no more peace at home; you face a threat of divorce every now and then from your husband. Yes, Christ wants to prepare you for that day. Some men, when their wives divorce them, they become worried and marry another woman, not knowing that this will not give them peace of mind. Christ does not want you to marry and perish, hence the divorce. Why then do you worry when you are given the knowledge that you are being prepared for the Kingdom? You all have seen these signs in you and have ignored them in ignorance. Now that God has come to save you please heed the advice.

## GOLDEN TEXT: St Matthew 19 v 12

*"For there are some eunuchs which were so born from their mother's womb, and there are some eunuchs which were made eunuchs of men, and there be eunuchs which have made themselves eunuchs for the Kingdom of heaven's sake. He*

that is able to receive it, let him receive it."

**The Power of Resistance Is Not Yours**
We hope you understand our lesson. That is why Christ said that it is simpler for a harlot to go to heaven than a rich man. There are people born eunuchs and remain so till they die. Yes, that is their share. They were not born eunuchs because of their sins or the sins of their parents. Another class of eunuchs is made of men. God has given another person power to make you eunuch so that you may go to heaven. The third set are those who decide within themselves to remain eunuchs for the sake of the heavenly home. They are perfectly sound in health, but because of the Kingdom of heaven they decide to stay without sex. Are you now aware that this decision cannot be made by man? Now you will find a compatatively young man surrounded by lovely girls, but he does not want union. Dont you see that the power to resist sex is not yours but the power of God? When He gives you this power He has given you a place in heaven.

Those who are born eunuchs are made by God. You cannot ask Him the reason. He made them for a purpose. .The self made eunuchs often revert back to fornication and other bad life, because they cannot resist the temptations of life. Do you remember when God wanted the children of Israel to suffer tribulation from the hands of the Egyptians; how they later came to realise the power of God? Without suffering you cannot know the power of God. When you meet a very wicked husband or wife who punishes you, you will decide to stay alone. God wants it so, so that you may know yourself. In every court today, you see divorce cases. These things do not happen for nothing.

**No Marriage In Heaven**
The scripture says that when the Lord Jesus Christ shall come, His angels shall be sent to remove whatever will be obstacles in the ways of the children of God. One of these stumbling blocks is marriage. You will remember the statement which says that two people will sleep together and one will be taken away. The one that is taken goes up to heaven and the other will be left behind. If something that you love very much is not taken from you, you will be chained to it, and you are lost. If you are meant for heaven, God will take away from you whatever job you are doing, if He sees that it will be a stumbling block to you.

You are not told here that a man and a woman will not stay together. They are to remain as brother and sister. The capacity to do this does not come from man. Be thankful to God when you can perceive these things Spiritually. Even if it remains one day, God will cut off your relationship with the world so that you will be fit for heaven. There is no marriage in heaven. It is inhabited by Angels. You will be told of those who will remain on earth. You have been told that you can stick to your one or two wives, but there is no place for you in heaven. Those who will go with Christ are not to marry. This is the first sign. There are two more signs. So dont rejoice and say that you have no husband or wife so you are for heaven. Wait for the three signs which signify the supreme Godhead. You may decide not to have sex but in Spirit you are doing it. It means that you were forcing yourself. If you force yourself to stay without sex, you may become mad. Some say, "I am not going to marry, I want to devote myself to the service of God, for the rest of my life;" but as soon as you set yourself for this purpose, your desire for sex becomes worse. Those that God has destined for these things have no difficulties and no regrets.

People tell women that if they stay without sex they will have no blood in them. It is false because God does not reason this way. This can happen to those who force themselves to stay without sex. Therefore brethren, let everyone stay where God has kept him or her. You who will not marry, do not tell another woman to leave her husband, etc. If she leaves her husband and comes to you, will you be of help to her? As God gives grace to those that are married and have children, so does He gives grace to those who are unmarried. Their wealth is in heaven. On that day there will be much lamentation. Those who have ears to hear let them hear. May the Lord bless His Holy Words, Amen.

# PART TWO

**FIRST LESSON:** St Luke 18 v 22
**SECOND LESSON:** St Luke 14 v 33
**GOLDEN TEXT:** St Luke 12 v 33

**"Now when Jesus heard these things, He said unto him, yet lackest thou one thing: sell all thou hast, and distribute to the poor, and thou shalt have treasure in heaven, and come, follow Me."**

Last week we told you certain signs that those who will go to heaven shall bear. That was the first part and today we give you the second part. You can now see why our Lord Jesus Christ said that it is difficult for a rich man to enter into the Kingdom of God. To them, the god of this world is nothing else but money. They believe that without money you are lost. If you tell them that one who loves the wealth of this world will not go to heaven, they laugh you to scorn and tell you that heaven means comfortable living which money provides. They have eyes but they cannot see; they have ears but cannot hear; they have brains but they cannot reason, because they have been led astray by the author of confusion, the Satan. How then can people who put their hearts in the riches of this world go to heaven? Did I not tell you that there are those who will be taken alive to heaven, and those who will inherit the earth and those who will go to hell?

You may find some people with bags of money today, but before they know where they are the money has all been spent. People take this to be misfortune and attribute it to the power of evil spirit. Yes, the money finnishes because he gives it away freely at anytime. He is not responsible for this action. It is because his kingdom is not of this earth, and he is laying up treasures in heaven. As I said before, the will and the power to do this does not come from anybody, it comes from above. If you are this type of person, you will go to heaven. The children of God does not regard money as anything in this life. In spite of this, they don't lack money, rather money finds them. But one thing is certain, they are never in peace if they do not distribute it.

### This Is All False
People say that if you do the work of God you will be perpetually poor. This is all false. The children of God are banks themselves, and their work is to give out money left and right to others. If you examine the different tribulations that confronts you, you will see that it is due to your actions. People will always advice you wrongly, and will tell you that, if you give alms to others freely you have no gain, you will only become poor in the end. You take their wrong advice and you stop giving alms, this works against you, you will be in want. The children of God should therefore be contented with any position that God has placed them in life. If you say that you are tired of doing good and stop doing it, you can't enter into the Kingdom. What helped the Gentiles to have a share in this Kingdom? It was through Cornelius the commander of an Italian army, who was giving alms to people. The people of the world laugh at a man who gives alms freely, because they say that he is bound to be poor and wretched in the end. Brethren, you have been told that what God loves is what the world hates and vice versa. If you keep all other laws such as honour your father and mother, etc., yet you do not give alms, you have no

share in the Kingdom of heaven. Suppose you pray for someone who is hungry and penniless; and after the prayer and the Word of God you send him away saying, "God be with you," which God? What helped Abraham? It was generousity; by giving freely Lot also was saved. When the two angels were sent to destroy Sodom and Gomorrah, they called at the house of Abraham. They were Angels in the form of human beings and neither Abraham nor Sarah knew this, but as soon as Sarah saw them she prepared food for them. This showed that Abraham and Sarah were children of God. As they were eating the Angels told them about their mission to Sodom and Gommorrah. Then Abraham mentioned Lot his nephew to them, and begged them to save him and his house; the Angels agreed to save them and went on their way.

When they reached Sodom and Gommorrah, Lot treated them with the same generousity as Sarah did. The Angels told them that they came to destroy the cities but that they will be saved. Lot and his house were warned not to turn back while going out of the city. Lot's wife met her doom because she turned back when she started to think of her box of trinkets and became a pillar of salt. You can now see clearly, our Lord's lessons on how hard it is for a rich man to go to heaven. A man who loves money cannot love God.

### Money Is Nothing

We think money is important, has it hands and feet? It is unwise to bury our minds in money; after all Nigerian coins are different from those in Ghana, Gambia, etc. Even in Nigeria, how many times the currency note has been changed? Dont think of money as God. Anybody who does not put his heart in money is the person that money goes to. This indicates that he is the child of God, and that his duty is to give freely to the poor. Some people complain of having a lot of money in their dreams, yet in real life they are poor. Yes, because their minds are on money, so each time they close their eyes they dream of money. I told you that the children of God are very rich; money means nothing to them. Job declared that he came into the world naked, and naked will he return. We came with nothing into this world. We shall go with nothing.

### Blessed Are The Poor In Spirit

That is the reason why we have the teachings from our Lord Jesus Christ; He said, "Blessed are the poor in Spirit for theirs is the Kingdom of heaven." They that come from heaven do not regard money as anything. The children of the heavenly Kingdom have no money in their pockets, but when they want something their Father send them cheques. The heavenly children are the top root of the family of many children, everybody else feeds from them without caring to know where the money comes from. In short, they take them as their bank; strangers are always coming to the house, and the Lord gives them the ability to care for them. The heavenly children don't draw money from this earthly bank, but from the heavenly bank. When they are in difficulty they find that nobody helps them but God and His Angels. Whenever you give alms you are placing your wealth in heaven. When you see a person who is fond of giving alms freely, know that such a person is from heaven, and will be taken alive to heaven. He can never be at rest if he doesn't give his neighbour what he lacks.

If he has but one cup of garri, he shares it with everybody, and he can never be alone in a place. If you give him a small room to sleep, he will call everyone in. The power to do this comes from above. People who comes from heaven do not attach any importance to agreement papers when transacting business with ohers. They know that God Himself is their agreement. These people never claim anything as their own. If they work for the government they use the money to help others who complain of being in difficulty. Should they give a loan to someone, the person will not care to return it, instead they abused the giver. People always like to borrow money from them, because they will never ask for it again. The children of God are always cheated by others and because of this they are always blessed by God.

## FIRST LESSON: St Luke 18 v 22

"Now when Jesus heard these things, He said unto him, yet lackest thou one thing, sell all that thou hast and distribute to the poor, and thou shall have treasures in heaven and come and follow Me."

Brethren do you see the truth? Tell Me then how many rich people will go to heaven? People seem to think that when a man is rich he is in heaven. They say that if you have no money you cannot enter into heaven.

### A Rich Man Becomes A Murderer

What are you doing with money in heaven? A man is wealthy because he does not use his money in giving alms and feeding the poor. A rich man finds it difficult to give out even five shillings to a person who is in need. He complains of lack of money. Now if the person in need dies through lack of help from the rich man, the rich man becomes a murderer because he refused to render help. A person who can save up to 40 Naira, hates man and God. All those who are created for destruction always have the interest of money in their hearts, and they cannot do anything free of charge. If they are asked to sing or dance, they first want to know whether they will be paid for it. Now these same people will turn round and say that when they die, they will go to heaven. Who will take them there? The first lesson says that you must sell all that you have and give the money to others. All those who are meant for heaven use their money, voice, strength and health for the service of others.

Those who can read and write must teach those who cannot. If you are well, use your health to make others well. If a person has no faith, go and give him faith. A man who has no clothes, give him from your trunk which is full of clothes. Why not give them out? Let us obey these instructions so that we may go to heaven. We are but storekeepers of our Father's treasure house, and we are to give out anything as required by others. If it is faith, if it is intelligence or if it is gospel that is wanted, we must give them out freely. Regard all things as belonging to the poor and must be distributed. Our Lord Jesus Christ knew that the world had nothing to offer Him so He stored His wealth in heaven. Go and distribute what you have and follow Christ.

## SECOND LESSON: St Luke 14 v 33

"So likewise, whosoever of you that forsaketh not all that he hath, he cannot be My disciple."

You say that you want to go to heaven, you cannot go there with the thought of worldly wealth. Christ says that we must surrender all the things of the world before we can follow Him. Many of you must have met beggars on the way as you were coming to the church; you did not give them anything. Your coming to church means nothing, because you do not know they are Christ's, Who is the Head of the church you are hurrying to attend. Do you remember the incident in which Christ said to the people on his right hand, "go to eternal joy prepared for you because I was hungry and homeless and you cared for Me?" He also said to the people on His left hand, "go to eternal destruction, because when I was hungry and homeless you did not care for Me." In as much as you did it for the hopeless ones, you did it to Me. If you have a house and you meet someone without one, house him. Name the person who has surrendered all that he has and followed Christ. I tell you, there is none. All the twelve disciples of Christ surrendered all that they had. They left their wives, mothers; some left their canoes, nets, etc. They sold all their belongings and the money was given to the poor. Matthew was a rich Tax Collector as well as Levi. They all put their belongings into the common purse.

### This Is A Revelation, Not A Gospel

St Paul said, "Things that would have been gain to me I count them but lost for the sake of the Kingdom." What will be your gain if on the eventful day we are left behind? Do you want to be left behind? People witnessed Enoch and Elijah taken up alive. Our Lord Jesus Christ after blessing His disciples was taken up in front of them. Those from heaven come down here to work and return to heaven afterwards. It is just like an expatriate who comes over to Africa to work, and returns to his country at the end of his contract. Many of us now sitting in this room comes from different places. We may stay at these places to do different businesses and have children. But one day we may decide to return to our different places of birth. It is exactly so with the heavenly children. One day they will go back to heaven where they belong. Those that will go back to heaven are not many. If you do not give freely to the poor you can't climb up even as far as this roof. The power to do these things doesn't come from us, but from above. People begin to ask whether there are such people in the world today. Yes, God has prepared them from the beginning of the world.

Brethren, this is not a good gospel, but a revelation of the truth about those who intend going to heaven. If you have the noble qualities given here, continue with them for you are among those who will go to heaven. If you do not have these qualities, don't struggle to do them because your name is not among those who are going to heaven. I tell you these things because I have already promised that I will explain the three categories to you. You see, members of other churches say that they will go to heaven, when heaven wants only 144,000. Those who will go up to heaven are those who come from heaven. Some said that, "if their parents had lived till this generation they would have gone to heaven," but I tell you, if they were not meant for heaven they won't go.

### GOLDEN TEXT:    St Luke 12 v 33

"Sell that ye have and give alms; provide yourselves
bags which wax not old, a treasure in the heavens
that faileth not, where no thief approacheth neither
moth corrupteth."

If we have Europeans in our midst today, they will surely send home anything they have, that they attach importance to, at least for security purpose.

### They Are Strangers Here

It should be the same with you. Every good thing that Christ did was stored for Him in heaven. All those who are heavenly give all that they have to the poor knowing that they are but strangers here on earth and will go back to heaven. Don't deliver this gospel to the rich person for he will lock you up. Don't give this gospel to the people of the world for they will laugh at you. I am not even asking you to practice this gospel because you can't practice it. Look at the young Lawyer who asked our Lord Jesus Christ what he should do to inherit the Kingdom of God; when he was told to sell all and give to the poor, he was greatly disturbed and went away sorrowfully. Those of the earth only think on how to get rich.

The heavenly ones think of heavenly glories and how to please God. If you were not meant for the Kingdom, but after hearing this gospel you decide to sell all you have and give the money to the poor, you will find that in a short time you will go back to your former life. There are people here in Brotherhood who sold all they had but are now looking for those things again. Dont worry yourself if, as a rich man you find yourself penniless because of alms giving, you are storing in the heavenly bank. Our Lord Jesus Christ did all His good work without counting the cost, because He knew what He was doing.

Now that this gospel reveals to you where you stand, continue doing good so that when that great day comes you will go up to meet your wealth where no moth or rust doth destroy. Thieves or moths may break into the earthly bank. There is no other bank for the heavenly children than helping the needy. You dont do them to the poor, but to God Who will reward you. Of what use is your preaching if you do not give water to the thirsty and food to the hungry one? Heavenly children have no other assignment but this. The good Samaritan had his hope in heaven. He was not a rich man. Whereas the other two well to do people who passed by the wounded man and offered no help have no hope for heaven. The good Samaritan is a good man of God. In Brotherhood our hope is in heaven, that is why we are instructed to give alms, because it might happen like a cinema and it is done for ever. People from your family often tell you that the money you would have used for the family, is used for your brethren in your church. The power to do this does not come from you but from above. Brethren we shall not take you further.

Those who have ears to hear, let them hear. May the Lord bless His Holy Words. A-men.

# PART THREE

**FIRST LESSON:** St Luke 14 v 26
**SECOND LESSON:** St Mark 8 v 34
**GOLDEN TEXT:** St Matthew 10 v 37

"If any man come to Me and hate not his father and mother and wife and children and brethren and sisters, yea and his own life also, he cannot be My disciple."

Brethren, this is the third and last instalment of those who will go to heaven. On the first day when the gospel was given, people feel that because they have left fornication, they are free, but that is not all. The second instalment was about distributing your wealth to the poor. What about that of today? Many people call themselves christians and say that they wait for Jesus Christ. Can it be done without faith? The gospel of today proves to you, those who are in readiness to go to heaven. Christ spoke these words clearly not in parable. He told His disciples that if they did not do these words, they can never be where He is and they can never reign with Him. He said, I am going to prepare a place for you. So that where I am, there you may be also. Brethren, if you cant follow Him on earth how can you follow Him in heaven? Christ said, that after the days of John the Baptist the Kingdom is gained by struggling for it.

Now show Me a single individual who is a follower of Christ, with the members of his family and his friends? Did Christ do His Father's work with His mother and father? Don't you remember an occasion when His mother and brethren sought for Him, and His disciples told Him that His mother and brethren were looking for Him, how He stretched His hands over His disciples and said, "Those who hear what I say and do what I teach are My mothers and brethren?" When Christ was taken by the Spirit into the desert to pray, did He go there with His mother and father? He forsook His mother, father and brethren and He never stayed in Nazareth. Up till today, people wonder whether Christ had sisters and brothers. He forsook personal enjoyment to do the work of His Father.

Brethren, I put this question to you, what is your preparation to meet Christ? Don't you know it was written that there will be anti-Christs? When the people of the world talk about false Prophets they mention Brotherhood. If all these churches say that they are followers of Christ, yet they dont practice His teachings, are they not false prophets? Peter asked our Lord Jesus Christ, "as we have left all things and followed you what will be our gain?" Christ replied, that all those who left their father, mother, children, wife and relations, and all the pleasures of this life and for their own lives; when all things are perfect and He will be in the Kingdom of His Father; they will sit on the twelve thrones to judge the twelve tribes of Israel; and they will receive a hundred fold of what they left, plus eternal life. In the wide world today which person has forsaken father, mother, children, sisters, brothers, wife, to follow Christ? Who has surrendered his life to Christ? Now, since you haven't done this, what is in your mind? He says, . "I am a jealous God." If you love mother or father, then you dont love Christ.

**Paul surrendered Everything To Follow Christ**

People carry their Bibles every day and proclaim themselves followers of Christ, which Christ? When you go home, read the scriptures again for they are the real Words of God. Christ became poor for His Father's sake. You who say you have God, have you surrendered your wealth so that you may have Christ? St Paul said, what would have been gain to me I count as loss so that I may have Christ. Paul forsook his profession, wife, children, relations, etc, and suffered many indignities for the sake of the gospel, so that he may possess Christ. Peter and other disciples did the same, so that they may have even a small place in heaven. The Apostles, Levi and Matthew did the same. Now brethren you have faith that on that day you will be taken up. On what do you base your faith? Don't you know that Christ has come back; not to have anything to do with the world, nor go from street to street preaching; but He has come to take those who forsake all and even their lives, and carry them to heaven? Dont you see that today it is your mother, father, brother, sister, wife, husband, children and the enjoyment of life that has hindered you from following Christ?

It is written, that all those who love their parents or children and the pleasures of the world have no share in heaven or in the New Earth. Those who are ashamed to confess My name to people on earth, I will be ashamed to confess theirs before My Father. I will forsake those who forsake Me. You find people saying, Christ the good friend of all. If He is your friend do you keep His commandments? How many people believe His words and do them? God has come down with His only Son to strengthen all things, so that they may take to heaven those that belong to heaven and leave the earthly ones on earth. The Holy Angels are telling us what we should do and what we should not do. Who are those people prepared to go up, who are those prepared to remain on earth?

Remember the barren fig tree? Christ cursed it because there was no fruits on it and the next morning it withered. To whom does the parable refer? To the churches, you and Me. Who in the churches are prepared to do His work and His words? Who in this house where we are now is prepared to own Christ and make up his mind to follow Him? You cant follow Him by words of mouth, you have to follow Him with your whole heart and mind. Let each person ask himself today whether he loves Christ. Christ says that he who loves Me will keep My commandments, and My Father will love him and we will make our abode in him. Therefore if we love Christ we will keep His commandments today.

**FIRST LESSON:     St Luke 14 v 26**

" If any man come unto Me and hate not his father
and mother and wife and children and brethren
and sisters, and yea his own life also, he cannot
be my disciple."

Of all that is counted in this text, which is the one that concerns money? I dont ask you to do this gospel. I am only revealing the gospel of truth to only those who will be going to heaven. I told you before that there are three marks that indicate those who will go to heaven. I am merely revealing these marks to you, to get you prepared for anywhere you may be taken to. I am not asking you to leave your parents or brethren. I tell you these things so that you may work with hope and gladness, so that you may not feel disappointed when those with these marks will be carried up to heaven. At that time, you will not turn round to say that the Leader has deceived you. To be forewarned is to be forearmed, so do not be satisfied with saying "I am Brotherhood." Yes everything else is Brotherhood; the trees, the water; Lucifer himself is Brotherhood. But the scriptures clearly states, that only those who possess these heavenly qualities will be taken up to heaven to be with Him. Let us ask ourselves whether we have these signs. Because heaven and earth will pass away, but not the Words of God.

Do not interpret the word of God to suit yourself. Some people say that it does not mean that one should hate his mother. I tell you that it means so. Now, is it not your wife, parents, child, etc, that made you to be in enmity with God? Dont you remember the young man who was called by Christ to follow Him? He gave Christ the excuse that he wanted to go and bury his father first. Christ said to him, "Let the dead bury the dead." Now your complaint is that your children or husbands have stopped you from knowing God and going on ministry work. Are they not stumbling blocks? You keep on saying, "who will look after my children; what will they eat?" Supposing a charriot was brought down here now for you to enter and go to heaven. How many of you here will be ready to jump into the charriot leaving all the children, parents and relatives behind? I tell you that you wont be able. You will think about the children and relatives; that they should come as well.

Our Lord Jesus Christ said, don't keep your treasures on earth, because where your treasure is there will your heart be. How can you go up to heaven when your heart is still on your relations? When your child is sick you querry God, asking why the child should be sick. Do you see your setback? If you dont follow Christ these are the things that hinder you, so whatever happens to you as a result of this, Christ is not responsible. Christ has said openly that if you don't hate your relations, you can't be His disciple. This is not a law or commandment, it is just the simple gospel of truth. It is now left to you to make up your mind whether you will follow Him or not. Those who Christ has given the power to do this gospel will do it because the power to do it comes from above.

Dont you remember when Christ said, "blessed are the barren and the wombs that never bear and the paps which never gave suck." Don't you see how children worry you? A pregnant woman is not sure of what will happen to her till the day she delivers the child. She continues to live in fear till that day. When a pregnant woman goes to church, it isn't for the love of God, but for God's protection against that day of uncertainty.

**Abraham And The Sacrificial Lamb**

Now we place before you Christ, children, wife, mother, etc., choose one. Christ says that if you choose Me you must forsake every other thing. He also said that one who looks for his life shall loose it, but one who forsakes his life for His sake, will save it. Don't you remember Abraham's faith? He walked three days and three nights to the place where he was to offer sacrifice to God. He got everything ready for the sacrifice but there was no lamb. Isaac his only son question him about the lamb and he replied that the Lord will provide; and the Lord did provide a lamb just as he lifted up his hand to cut off Isaac's head for the sacrifice. Did Abraham not hate his only son? Did he refuse to offer him for sacrifice? The same Abraham was going with his wife to buy corn, and he was instructed in a dream that when they go to the place, he should say that Sarah was not his wife. Now when the king of that country saw Sarah he loved her and sent someone to go and find out whether she was Abraham's wife. The reply was no; he therefore asked that Sarah be brought to him. Abraham raised no argument. But here today, you cant stand someone else conversing with your wife, even if they say he is Christ. At night God sent an Angel to rebuke the king for his action, and he explained that he did not know that Sarah was Abraham's wife.

Today you may say that you are a good Brotherhood member, yet you dont allow your wife to go on missionary work for fear of her being loved by someone. If your husband go on missionary work you fear that he will love another woman. If your wife sends a present to a brother you misinterpret her action, and then confusion comes between you. If a brother bought a soutane for a sister the wife will get annoyed. Now ask yourself whether it is not your wife or husband who prevents you from serving Christ. If you quarrel with people you are a confusionist, you cannot be Christ's follower and you cannot go to Heaven. Christ said that He separates Himself from the joys of this world for our sake so that the truth may be ours. Don't you see that if you separate yourself for Christ, you will see the truth and the truth will help you to separate others for Christ? But today you find it difficult to separate yourself from your wife and children.

Well the question is, how can you go to heaven? The advice your wife or husband gives you will not save you. They say that because you attach yourself more to members of your church, you forget about your family. If you dont let go of the ways of your wife, husband, children, mother, father and relations and follow Christ you will be lost. You must follow Him because He is the Light, the Truth and the only Way to heaven.

**SECOND LESSON:     St Mark 8 v 34**

"And when He had called the people unto Him
with His disciples also, He said unto them,
whosoever will come after Me, let him deny
himself and take up his cross and follow Me."

**You Must Deny Yourself The Comfort Of Life**
He said that he who follows Him must be ready and willing to suffer, and to deny himself the comforts and pleasures of this life; and must leave pride and arrogance and humble himself by going from house to house preaching the gospel of our Lord's sufferings and death. As you spread the gospel along, you may meet with opposition; this may lead to abuses and beatings and other kinds of disgrace. This is how to carry the cross of Christ. The carrying of the cross will let you talk to people you would not have talked to.

It will also compel you to enter into houses you would never have entered. When rain nor sun does not stop you from spreading the gospel; when you accept humiliations because of Christ and complain not; when you are prepared to go naked because of Christ, you will surely go to heaven. You must be very accommodating by agreeing to see another person's point of view. You must be prepared to go on ministry work at any time the need arises. You must bear one another's burden. This is christianity pure and simple. He said, "if you want to be My disciple take up the cross and follow Me." He did not say take your wife, children, money, cars, relations, etc, and follow Me. By bearing one another's burden and taking up the cross, you are letting the light of Christ to shine everywhere. This is difficult to do but it is the only sure way to heaven. For it was the only narrow path that our Lord Jesus Christ took, and anybody who wants to go to heaven must surely follow His footprints. He must be very humble. He must teach his children this humility by doing the least job in the house, such as fetching water, etc.

You can see a well to do man going about without shoes or costly and expensive clothes. When they prepare him good food in the house, he cannot eat it because he is always fasting. He teaches people the importance of mortification of the flesh. This teaching takes one to the new Kingdom. It is said that he who does not keep these commandments and teaches others not to do so will have no place in the Kingdom; but he who receives it and teaches others the same is saved. We must be prepared to forego anything to gain the Kingdom. If anyone spits on you or slaps you, just say, may the peace of God be with you. If you dont behave in this way you are not for the Kingdom. Don't think of what to put on or what to eat. If you cannot go to spread the word of God in all the corners of the earth, how will people know Christ? Christ denied Himself of all pleasures and took up His cross to do His Father's work.

Show Me a follower of Christ who lies comfortably in his bed and sends others to do the work for him. Paul suffered a lot and was beaten many times. When you go on ministry work, you may return to find all your things stolen. When you come back, all you ought to say wholeheartedly is, may the peace of God be with the thieves. This is the life that the heavenly ones must live. How pleasant would it be for one to leave his car and go to do things for others, and to see him walk without his pair of shoes, even in his house. How nice would it look for one to see a Lawyer with all his knowledge, going about without his pair of shoes, serving his juniors.

People may say, of a truth God is on earth. That is not all. If you dont attach yourselves to the lower class of people you are not fit for heaven. Money is money, but you have special duty to do with your hands. You cant see God in your money, but people can see Christ in your lives. There is Christ in all the parts of your body. People will see Him in you and what He tells you to do. It was because of St Paul that certain great men were converted. Peter and some of his disciples were mere fishermen, and the higher class of people wouldn't have listened to them. Those great men were saved through Paul. By going out to serve others people will be drawn to God.

### GOLDEN TEXT:  St Matthew 10 v 37

"He that loveth father and mother more than Me
is not worthy of Me; and he that loveth son or
daughter more than Me is not worthy of Me."

Now have you seen the point? If your child is sick you won't attend service because you love the child more than Christ. Anybody who loves Christ have no time for the things of the world. Christ does not think about the things of this world. You cannot serve two masters. If you love Christ you must hate your parents, children, wives, husbands, etc. Those who hate Christ hate His gospels because they are the children of darkness. They have no share in the Kingdom of heaven. Those who will follow Him are those who love Him more than father, mother, child, etc. The behaviour of all those who are for Christ must be able to win the children of perdition for Christ.

All those who hate Christ love all those who hate Him. If their parents were juju makers and snuffers, their children will support them either financially or otherwise. You always take the advice of the people you love. The instructions you receive from your parents often lead you astray. You remember king Solomon. God advised him to leave the woman he was keeping or else he would go astray, he refused. Because he loved the woman, he did what she wanted by building a temple for her goddess. For this reason God departed from him, and Babylon fell to rise no more. You see where the love of children, parents and other people lead us to. Therefore if you follow them you are lost.

### Christ The Only Adviser

Christ alone is the only One who can advise properly. I do not say that you must hate your people, this gospel is not for flesh and blood, but for the Spiritual ears. Your wives or children dont take you to heaven, no matter how strong and healthy they may be. Christ alone can take you there because He reigns over heaven and earth. If you love Christ, you can no longer love your relatives and the material things of the world. Those who will be taken up alive are those who love Christ only. What Christ love is what they love. Christ said, he who loves Me should keep My commandments. Therefore what Christ doesn't love, they dont love. You cling to your village, what do you get from there? Christ gives you blessings but you take them to the people of the world. Christ loves you so much that He gave His life for you. What have you done for Him? Instead you centre your thoughts on your children who disobey you, and are fornicating and doing all sorts of evil. Your father is snuffing and fornicating, yet you cling to him and you dont leave him. If they are ill you prefer to stay with them. For this reason you find it difficult to serve God. Brethren do you see your love? Is this your preparation for heaven?

Those who have ears to hear, let them hear. May the Lord bless His Holy Words. Amen.

# SUMMARY

**FIRST LESSON:** James 2 v 5
**SECOND LESSON:** 2 Corinthians 8 v 9
**GOLDEN TEXT:** St Matthew 19 v 28 - 29

People have wondered why you have been asked not to marry, even the young beautiful ones have decided not to marry. Today we are going to summarise the gospels of the past three weeks. Our first gospel revealed that those who will go up to heaven never marry. They are the ones who go with the Lamb whithersoever He goeth and they will reign with Him. The second gospel was that which asked us to sell all we have and give the money to the poor before we can follow Christ. We became sad when we heard this. The wise men of the world think that this is a parable. Those who will be rich in this New Kingdom of heaven are those who are selling their wealth in order to give the money to the poor. Our Lord Jesus Christ used to speak in parables, but when He decided not to do so, He spoke in His plain language. The same thing is happening today. Moreover the Holy Spirit, the Comforter has come as promised. Dont you see that the words spoken by Christ are true? How difficult it is for a rich man to enter this Kingdom of heaven.

### You Dont Enter By Force

When the scripture says that it is difficult for a rich man to enter the Kingdom, those who are poor rejoice and feel that the Kingdom then belongs to them. They don't struggle to improve their status, they are glad to be poor so that they may enter heaven. This is an entirely wrong idea. The rich here mean, that although they are rich their minds are not on the riches; they give freely to the poor for the sake of the Kingdom. That is why Christ compares the Kingdom to precious stones that one finds buried in his garden. He sells all that he has and buys this garden. If a rich man gives out his wealth, then he is storing wealth in heaven. There is nothing more pleasing in the sight of God and Angels than distributing to the poor. God has promised that those who will inherit the Kingdom and be His children forever, are those who are giving freely to the poor in material things. All their minds and beliefs is in heaven and as they do not want others to suffer, they give them freely. I will show you why they act in this way and what will be their gain. You cannot enter the Kingdom by force or through accummulated wealth.

### FIRST LESSON: James 2 v 5

"Hearken, my beloved brethren, hath not God
chosen the poor of this world, rich in faith and
heirs of the Kingdom which He hath promised
to them that love?"

Brethren hear what the scripture says; that those who are poor in the material things of this world, are rich in heaven and are heirs of the Kingdom. They do not bury their minds on houses, cars, clothes, etc. A child of heaven does not attach importance to any material thing. He gives out such things freely and his mind is not there. A person who is rich in faith is a person whose mind rest entirely with God and heaven. In all that they do they think of how to get to heaven. Their minds are not on children, clothes and wealth. God knows that everything in the world belongs to Him, therefore you being His children can never be poor. Any person who loves God is poor in Spirit, because he is prepared to give all he has to the poor.

### This Is Wrong

There are people who go about consoling themselves that they are poor, therefore they are meant for heaven. When they are poor physically it means that they are rich in Spirit, because all their minds are on how they could be rich, how they could have money, have cars, houses, children, clothes and food; to mention a few. When they sleep they always dream about these things because their minds are there. Do you think that anyone who loves God loves money? Anyone who loves God does't like to hear anyone complain about God, he is prepared to share things in common with others. His greatest desire is to do things for God and to please all those who are sad. He has no regard for money. He knows that God has everything, so he needs not strive for anything because everything that belongs to God belongs to him.

Does a person who heals free of charge loves money? Does a person who gives the Words of God free of charge also love money? If he doesn't love money, what does he love? Can a man serve two masters? People who love God are wealthy in the Kingdom. They are riches. Christ said to the young Lawyer, come follow Me and you shall have more than what you left behind plus eternal life. Therefore don't rejoice because you will go to heaven if you are poor physically. Heaven is for those who have one mind, one heart and one Spirit in Jehovah God and can give freely; this class of people surrenders everything to the service of God. This does not mean that if you go to their houses you will not see cupboards, chairs, motor cars, etc., but they know that these things belong to God. They built their houses to accommodate the poor. With their money they buy clothes for the poor. These are those that are poor in Spirit.

### SECOND LESSON: 2 Corinthians 8 v 9

"For ye know the grace of our Lord Jesus Christ,
that though He was rich, yet for your sake He
become poor that ye through His poverty might be rich."

Do you see what is meant by being poor in Spirit? Because of the Words of God, because of the love you have for God, you become poor in Spirit. Who is the richest person in the whole world? We are like God. The likeness of God in us is wealth, power and wisdom. Do you realise now who you are? The children of God are stewards and storekeepers. It is their duty to give out from their Father's storehouse, to those who haven't, knowing fully well that wealth belongs to God. Anybody who calls wealth his own, whether it be money, children, etc, has no faith in God. Did we come into the world with any children or wealth? Yet we claim that this is our child, this is my wife, this is my house. Empty handed you came and so you will return. Those who realise that these are those who will inherit the Kingdom; what is it now you have that you didn't receive? If you receive what you have why then do you puff up when it was all given to you?

You pray to God to give you appointment, He gives you; when another person comes to you in the office for help, you drive him away saying, "go away from my office." Are you really in your correct senses when you say this? He who is poor in Spirit knows that he cannot do anything by himself, but God can do everything. Christ Himself said that He cannot do anything by Himself for it is the Father that does everything. When sick people were brought to Jesus He knew that His Father would do the work and heal them. Now tell Me why your mind is always on money? You sleep and think of money and you see bags of money. If your thoughts and mind is on money, etc, how can God see a space in your mind? Do you think that if you fail to think about money, you wont have money? Some of you dont put your minds on money, yet you see people giving you money.

All those who will move with Christ believe that they dont possess anything; even others who come to borrow their things never return them. Christ our Lord, dressed like His disciples. He did everything in common with them so that He could not be distinguished from others when they came to arrest Him. The children of God, even if they have houses they sleep on the floor and give their beds to others, without caring. The text of the gospel says, leave your wife, children and relations and follow Christ.

**They Do Not Belong To You**
Yes, this makes up the other class of wealth. Leave your wife and children to serve God. Let them serve God so that they may have wealth in heaven. Your wife and children do not belong to you. Let them go, stay as if you have none. If you count upon the pleasure of wife and children, when will you serve God? If the love of children and wife fill your heart, how can you serve God? That is the reason why Christ said, that if you love children, wife, etc, more than Me, you have no place in the Kingdom. Eventhough our Lord had a father, mother, sisters and brothers, He left them so as to serve God. At what time did He ever say, " as the first born I must look after the others, or why did you not ask for My permission before doing anything in the family?"

Today we are going to tell you what you will have when you surrender all that you have to God. Any man who loves God is poor in Spirit. Any man who loves his children, etc, is rich in spirit. Those who are poor in Spirit, whose hearts and minds are with God will inherit the Kingdom of heaven. God does not say that you should not have mother or father, etc; because He had said "Go ye and multiply." Whether you have a father or not you must realise that you have them in Spirit. Now tell Me why a person should pray to God to give him a child, wife or husband? Do not put your trust in man, whether Paul or Appollus; sickness, poverty and wealth belong to us. We have Christ, and Christ have God. God owns all of us. Why then do we complain that we have nobody, momey, houses, cars, etc. We are the children of God. God owns everything in the world. Whatever God has belongs to His children, therefore we lack nothing. Aren't these persons owned by God? Don't love these things and put your heart in them, they belong to God, and you.

### GOLDEN TEXT: St Matthew 19 v 28 - 29

"And Jesus said unto them, verily I say unto you that ye which have followed Me, in the regeneration when the Son of man shall sit in the throne of His glory, ye also shall sit upon twelve thrones judging the twelve tribes of Israel. And everyone that hath forsaken houses or brethren or sisters or father or mother or wife or children or lands for My sake, shall receive an hundredfold and inherit everlasting life."

Brethren do you hear this statement? Haven't I told you that I will reveal those who will go to heaven? Those who have forsaken wives, mothers, children and even their own lives for My sake will inherit the Kingdom, and in the regeneration they will sit with Christ, and with Him rule the whole world. Now distribute your money, clothes, houses, stores and wealth to the helpless, so that you will have an hundredfold and eternal life. Those who leave all types of earthly things will go to heaven and rule with Christ and go wheresoever He goeth. Now see if your name is written among those for heaven after going through the first, second and third lessons of today. See if you are among those for marriage; those who surrender their goods to the poor; those who leave their fathers, mothers, children, wives, husbands, relations and their very lives for the Kingdom's sake; those who dont tell lies, those who love Christ and God and those whose hearts are with Him; those who don't regard themselves as anything; who go about preaching and teaching about the sufferings of our Lord; those who dont mind being cheated, and those who regard earthly glory as nothing.

See if you are among those who meet with shame and disgrace for the Kingdom's sake. See if you are one of those who go hungry because of the gospel. Those who work day and night enduring all conditions of life for the Kingdom, will have everlasting life and everlasting rest. See the small sacrifice you make and the glory it brings to you. If you have these signs then you have this glory awaiting you. Because you don't defile yourself with women, because you give out freely, you will have an hundredfold plus eternal life and you will reign with Christ. Everything will be changed but the words and promise of God stands forever.

God speaks these words, not an Angel, not St Paul, not St Peter. Whenever Christ made a statement He would say, "These words are not from Me but from God." Think brethren, what is greater than eternal life? If we were to see the glory awaiting us, we would readily surrender everything for this glory in heaven. Earthly glory soon passes away but heavenly glory lasts forever. Life itself is but a shadow. The glory of this world is transitory. You may be king today and tommorrow you are dethroned. Christ Himself didn't want the glory of the world. Those who are from heaven want everything directly from God. Those things are everlasting. Those who do this gospel are those who will reign with Christ the King of Kings and Lord of Lords. They will judge Angels, Trees, Moon, etc. Their wealth will have no begining nor end, and they live everlastingly in joy and glory. Those who have ears to hear, let them hear. May the Lord bless His Holy Words, A-men.

# CHAPTER 11

# THOSE WHO WILL GO TO HELL

**Everlasting Gospel delivered by:**
**Leader Olumba Olumba Obu, Sole Spiritual Head**
**of the Universe.**

# PART ONE

**FIRST LESSON:** John 3 v 8
**SECOND LESSON:** Revelation 13 v 10
**GOLDEN TEXT:** St John 8 v 48

We have a publication for those who will go to heaven. I am releasing to you another gospel for **Those Who Will Go To Hell.** The names of those who will go to heaven are in the Lamb's Book of Life; while those who will go to hell are in the Devil's Book of Doom. The number of those who will go to hell are countless, but those who will go to heaven are numbered. Many of us may put on the white robes, calling ourselves Brotherhood when we are not victorious over sins. The white robes and girdles are for those who are victorious. Satan does not put on the white robe.

All those who dive deep in sin are those who will go to hell; know it, that it is satan with his hosts; including his false prophets, false evangelists, false apostles, false pastors, false popes, reverend fathers, mothers and sisters, etc; any person therefore, who continues in sin is of the devil, and his abode is in hell fire. This was why Jesus Christ, in His prayer stated categorically that He did not pray for the children of perdition, but for those whom the Father had given Him. Christ never said that all were saved. He knew that the disciples were clean; but even in this case, not all of them. He knew that there were twelve but one was a devil. He knew that there were children of perdition, so He always ended His sermon saying, "He that hath ears, let him hear," satan has no "hearing ears." His ears have been stopped from hearing the Word of God.

I have been teaching you from January to January, but the amazing thing is that nobody has repented by refraining from all manners of sin. Your persistence in sin would have been reasonable if satan had been mounting up to teach you, when I come down from the Altar. But in the consequence, satan has nothing to offer you, than a place in hell fire. The pity of it all is that people are competing in sin. You must not allow any angel or spirit to deceive you that a sinner will inherit the Kingdom of God. The Brotherhood of the Cross and Star is the Kingdom of God, and not that of satan. If you have been taught but you continue in sin, it means that you have been predestined for hell. It is clear that no matter how the two palms are clasp together (in pretended prayer) no sinner will inherit the Kingdom of God. **Satan and his hosts must go to hell.** Now you find people competing in sin. They sow the seed of discord and disunity and defile themselves. They hate their own bodies. The Son of God has been sent to destroy the works of satan. Therefore satan with death, the various elements, including the sea and the havoc done by these elements will all go to hell. Satan had been vanquished and his judgement is eternal destruction in the bottomless pit of hell. Satan in frustration has established all the cults, Lodges and Secret Societies. All the black magic powers and lying wonders are employed by satan to sustain his empire. **All the socalled Churches are the network of satan's telecommunication systems. They are ushered in by satan. Governmentally, God never established any court or prison. All these are introduced by satan.**

All the good virtues of God dwell in man. Any person who sins takes up the likeness of satan. You have been exhorted to refrain from telling lies and from living in falsehood. You have been warned not to lie to the Holy Spirit. Our Lord Jesus Christ came to reveal God and His Kingdom on earth. He came in Trinity as the Son of man, Son of God and God Himself. The likeness of God is man, the Son is man, God is Man and Man is God. God in Human Form has revealed His nature as mercy, forgiveness, humility, patience, love. These virtues of God are indwelling in man. Therefore if you deceive or tell lies to any human being, it means that you are telling lies to God. You have seen God, the way He lives and you must also live as He lives. The Son of God came to put an end to the shackles of satan, so that satan might not deceive you to be revengeful, or tell lies, fornicate, lack mercy and patience or to be arrogant. Death is not serving God; satan is not serving God, but himself, by seeking his own glory. This gospel is therefore given to differentiate between God and satan, and where those who serve satan will end up.

Satan has impressed upon you that you are graciously saved. It is no grace to continue in sin. The grace that is given to mankind is our Lord Jesus Christ. That grace is grace, when you practice telling the truth, being pure, humble, kind, patient, merciful, forbearing, tolerant, etc. What does it cost any person to refrain from fornication, idolatry, anger, annoyance, quarrel, disputes, etc? Any person who knows that God is mercy, love, truth, kindness, gentleness, lowliness, humility, etc, must endeavour to resemble Him in these virtues. Why did God dismiss Adam from the garden of Eden? It was because of sin. What has been the root cause of sickness, poverty, anger, greed and starvation today? Why did God destroy the world of Noah? All troubles facing mankind is caused by sin. Satan is responsible for them. Some people may say that Satan is a spirit or a snake. No, **Satan is a man.** He might get some followers who are apostles, prophets, pastors, evangelists, reverend fathers, mothers, sisters, etc.

Do you not remember Christ saying that one of the disciples was Satan? That disciple was sitting close to his Master. Judas Iscarriot is the son of man; he was a man and was Satan. The trinity of the godhead is also manifested in Satan. Our Lord Jesus Christ likened the Kingdom of God to a sower who sowed good seeds on his farm during the daytime, but at night satan went and sowed bad seeds amongst the good seeds. The owner of the farm making a remark to the inquiring servants who saw a mixrure of good and bad seeds, said that it was the work of the enemy. Our Lord Jesus Christ making this analogy, was referring to satan as an enemy to all Godly virtues. The enemy is the person who blasphemes, kills, fornicates, backbites, gossips, steals, reckons sins on others, etc. These are the enemies of the glory of God. This is why Christ said that many are called but few are chosen. A great many people are putting on white garments, professing to be Brotherhood. They go about as wolves in sheep's clothing. They go about causing untold harm and havoc to people in high places. They may be married but will keep many girl friends. They will use their cars and riches to trap girls and misdirect them into careless living. Surely such persons will go straight to hell. A native doctor, a magician, an idolater or a society man may boast to you that his wife, who was barren has become fruitful, while you are still childless despite your claims of devoted life to God.

He may boast of getting his promotion from time to time when you have none. If you say that God loves a sinner and turn round to follow such a person, you are going to hell with him. Why was Lot saved and his wife perished? If you allow worldly surroundings to mislead you, your abode will be in hell fire. It was because of sinfulness why the great flood destroyed the world of Noah. Was it not satan who was responsible for the death of Peter, Stephen, John the Baptist and other prophets and Apostles? Was it not satan who was responsible for the death of God's messengers? Was it not satan who tempted, blasphemed and killed our Lord Jesus Christ? It was satan who asked our Lord Jesus Christ to jump from the pinnacle to demonstrate His sovereignity. It was satan who asked Christ to fall down and worship him. It was satan who passed death sentence on Christ. It was satan who killed Him.

Lack of steadfastness, patience, endurance, mercy, forbearance, etc, will take many people to hell. Our Lord Jesus Christ had set an example: when He was spat on, abused and cursed, He overcame satan and his agents. St Paul is another example; he was beaten, imprisoned, opposed here and there, but he suffered so that he might win Christ. Daniel was steadfast because he knew whom he trusted. In your own case, why do you fall to the suggestions, that when you continue to sin and continue to confess your sins, you should be pardoned? Do you not know that a son or daughter must resemble his or her father? So, those who came to receive instructions, and also to resemble My practical life but continue to sin, believing that they are saved by grace, have got their names written in black letters for hell. Satan's teachings always leads one to death. The churches founded on the code of life of Satan will resemble their father, the devil. Let the first Bible lesson be read.

### FIRST LESSON: St. John 3 v 8

"The wind bloweth where it listeth, and thou
heareth the sound thereof, but canst not tell
whence it cometh, and whither it goeth, so
is everyone that is born of the Spirit."

You always shout that Christ is a friend of sinners and that He is your Leader. Is He a sinner? Do you know that whosoever you trust, is your Master?
The person you serve, the person from whom you receive commands, to whom you listen and from whom you take instructions is your Master. The entire universe is an object of great pity. But yet they claim to know God and His ways. Who has ever deceived you that a sinner has any place in heaven? The population of the children of Israel who were above twenty years in the wilderness, totalled 600,000 but only two entered the promised land of Canaan. The report showed that their corpses were scattered on both sides of the road. 23,000 of them died in one day because of fornication, several others died because of idolatry; thousands of them died because of murmuring against God, etc. If all these people died because of one sin or the other; why do you console yourself with the fanciful suggestions of Satan? Can Satan continue to deceive you by asking, "if all liars will die, who will remain for God?" Or, "if all those who drink wine will die, who then will remain for God?" I tell you that if a single murderer or fornicator or a liar ever enter into the Kingdom of God, you will have to challenge God on His righteousness.

I assure you that the Great Day of the Lord has not yet come. But when that comes, it will be disastrous and tragic, and you will have to challenge God if anything unclean, any sinner, will enter into His Kingdom. God created all things in their respective places. He created man as an autonomous being and equipped him with all the thinking faculty. But man has surrendered his glory to the lower creatures. Man has made the trees, the dead wood, the stones, angels etc, to be his god by worshipping them. The lesson of today is to show you all those who will go to hell. God has given man freedom of choice and he can go anywhere he likes. If you decide to tell lies, you can continue with it; but be assured that no liar will enter into the Kingdom of God. If a man has a son, that son must resemble his father. God created Satan holy and undefiled in His own likeness. Just as a child will fail to resemble his father by getting into bad company, so does Satan left his first state of holiness, righteousness, truth, peace, etc, and became an opposition to God. This is the way satan started his life.

When a child start to do some good things, the mother or the father will praise him, but when he starts to exhibit evil practices, the parents will give him a name that is descriptive of his evil deeds. If the child is fond of going out with boys to fornicate, she may be called an "harlot." The parents will often say to her, "You, this harlot." If he is a boy and goes into the company of other boys to pilfer, he may be called "a rogue." The child is given a name to show his pattern of behaviour. When you were not an harlot nobody called you an harlot. Similarly, when you did not engage in highway robbery or in pilfering, nobody called you a thief. In the same way you gained the title of being an Amorc member when you joined the Amorc Cult. When you serve or render services to satan and his agents, your place is in hell fire.

You will find people the world over joining societies to do one kind of havoc or another. The Bible says that those who raise up the sword against others will die with the sword. Have you not heard that if you kill by the sword you will also be killed by the same instrument? Why do you pre-judge others by passing death sentences on people that God created by Himself? Why do you destroy what you cannot create? The power of taking away any life is solely and wholly in the hands of Jehovah God and His Christ. God authorises no government to take away any life.

Is there any government greater than that of Nebuchadnezzar or that of king Pharaoh, who along with his armies were drowned in the depths of the sea? Did God command that you should take the law into your hands and use human laws to pass death sentence on the highest creation of God? If you do this your place is in hell fire. Those judges who argue that it is the law, and not they who condemn; or the executuners who plead that they are doing their assignments by law, are gravely mistaken, because their abode is in the deep pit of hell. Didn't Pilate do the same thing? Did that save him? You always claim that you are saved by grace and you continue to sin. The world is faced with all kinds of troubles, sicknesses, tribulations, sufferings, deprivations, etc. What you see and hear are no judgements yet. These are merely preambles. **The real judgement of God will be very terrible and drastic.**

The scripture says that if you think evil of somebody, someone else will in turn think evil of you. If you point an accusing finger at someone, four fingers are pointing at you. This is why deceitfulness and falshood will continue to multiply. You will notice that when you take bribe before you do a favour for someone or discharge your lawful duty, someone will also demand bribe from you when you are in similar plight. As you deceive someone to get money, you will also be duped by another person. If you force out somebody's wife, your wife will also desert you. This is the reason why tthe entire world is in confusion. Tell Me, have you found peace anywhere in the world? A sinner has no peace. A sinner lives in hell fire. You are never in peace with your family. Every human institution is in hell.

## WHAT IS HELL?

**Hell is a condition of eternal torment, torture, lawlessness, all types of killing, cheating, a den of thieves and robbers, falsehood, hatred, anger, sickness, death; yes, the wicked has no peace said the True God.** Satan keeps on deceiving you that you are saved by grace. My question is, has that Salvation by grace come to you? If so, why do you live in torment, deceit, fear and danger? If you continue to live in sin, the obvious fact or bitter truth is that a sinner has no place in heaven. His abode is Hell, a condition that can give him no peace. Let the second Bible lesson be read.

## SECOND LESSON: Revelation 13 v 10

"He that leadeth into captivity shall go into captivity;
he that killeth with the sword must be killed with the
sword. Here is the patience and the faith of Saints."

I want to give you an example from the contemporary world. What is the relationship between Egypt and Israel today? Have you seen this grace that is brought? The Arabs and the Israelites have no peace because they continue to destroy themselves. To look for peace when you continue in wickedness is a day dream. You are obviously in hell and therefore cannot get peace. This is the day of vengeance by the Spirit of God. I remember proclaiming to the various governments of Nigeria to refrain from war, as it would be very destructive. The proclamation was ignored. The Nigerian conflict later took such a dimension, that you all were witnesses to the wanton destruction to human lives, either as an outright savagery or because of sickness and starvation.

No prayer can put away this fact, that when you killed with the sword you also will be killed with the sword. Christ had taught that you must love one another. Love does no harm to a neighbour. Whatever instruments you use in killing, the same instruments will be used in killing you also. Why is that grace by which you claim that you are saved, never let you know that Christ has shed His blood to give you peace? Why does the name of our Lord Jesus Christ reigns supreme in the whole Universe? It is because He did not kill. If He had not come, the world would have continued to destroy themselves. The names of Moses, Abraham, Melchezedek, Elijah, etc, are not entombed in the Kingdom History because they killed others. None of the people of old had any peace. Moses had no peace, neither in his home life nor in his official capacity as Leader of his people. In the same way Solomon had no peace because he killed. Any person who kills must be killed. In spite of all these examples, you stiffen your necks and continue to say, "but for Brotherhood I would do this or that."

Have you not heard that any person who kills, will be killed? Why was Moses prevented from entering the promised land? Do you not remember what Jacob told Levi and Simeon, that the instrument of cruelty would never depart from their habitation, because in their anger they killed a stranger who defiled their sister. They killed this stranger after the man had pleaded for an exchange of marriage, and Jacob accepted his plea. Simeon and Levi felt that it was an unpardonable crime. They went and lay waited the man and killed him in cold blood. Their father pronounced a curse to their anger, and from that time the sword had never departed from their household. Their offsprings have been suffering violence. Have you not seen that fornication and murder are twins? They brought untold sorrow to the houses of Simeon and Levi. This is the cruel effect of sin.

You claim that you are a beloved son of God when your name is in hell. Give this gospel to the various governments of the world. Give it to the so called churches of christendom. Give it to the other highly placed men in the society; give it to the soothsayers; give it to the labourers on the farms; give it to the traders in the markets, for them to re-assess themselves. Let the golden text be read again.

## GOLDEN TEXT: St John 8 v 48

"Then answered the Jews and said unto Him, say we
not well that thou art a Samaritan, and hast a devil?"

There is no small sin. Sin is sin. There is no magnitude of sin that is free from penalty. All evils emanate from Satan, and their end is hell. Any person who kills is Satan. Cain who killed his brother Abel was the son of Satan, the son of man and Satan himself. It is human beings that tell lies. They are the children of Satan. They are Satan incarnated in human flesh. It is man who commits fornication. He is the son of Satan and he is Satan. Who ever told you that a sinner is a son of God and is loved by God? The disciples sold all they had and put the money in the common purse. Annanias and Sapphira his wife, out of their own volition, went and sold theirs but kept back part of the money. Peter who was filled with the Holy Spirit said to Annanias, "Why hath Satan filled thine heart to lie to the Holy Spirit, and to keep back part of the price of the land?" He died because of telling lies. His wife who was a party to the deceit also died. People regard telling lies as a trivial sin. You may say that you are only telling small lies. You are sinning against God and your place is in hell fire. Satan is the chief and author of every sin. Satan entered the heart of Judas Iscarriot. He betrayed his Master. Satan is so mobile and free to enter into any victim, and to leave him when he finnishes his work. The same thing happened to Judas Iscarriot. When Satan left him, it was then that he knew himself to have smeared the blood of an innocent person in the palms of his hands. He threw his thirty pieces of silver at the elders, but this was too late. Satan had already accomplished his work in him. He did not enjoy the money, and finally killed himself.

### WHERE IS HEAVEN?

**Heaven is here on earth. It is righteousness, goodness, humility, love, long-suffering, patience, lowliness of mind, peace, kindness, joy, mildness, self control, etc. A condition of faithfulness in harmony with God; the habitation of God.** On the other hand, when you have none of these Godly virtues, you are in hell. When evil thoughts surround you, fear grips you under worried atmosphere, sleeplessness and restlessness. Man, you are in deep hell. Take a look at Adam and Eve. They were quite happy in the Garden of God. They suffered no tribulation, no hardship and they were served by the lower creatures. They had dominion over the lower creatures. They enjoyed good fellowship with their Creator God. They were in heaven. They were commanded to eat of every fruit found in the garden, except that of the forbidden three in the middle of the garden, which was the tree of knowledge of good and evil.

### DRAWING AWAY FROM GOD

When you are tempted, do not say that you are tempted by God. Do not say that it is God who causes you to sin. It is your driving passion and lust which drags you into sinfulness. When you look for your personal glory, fame and profit, you are drawing away from God. In the same manner that Eve was convinced by her passion, greed and lust, you also succumb to temptations. Both Adam and Eve decided to break the law of God, by yielding to their own lust; lack of self control. They were free moral agents, having free minds and free thinking faculties. Eve took her idea to Adam, who, in his endeavour to please his wife, accepted her suggestion. God's nature was shelved and man's lust enthroned. The tree in the middle of the garden that they ate was nothing else than fornication. The proginitors of the garden of Eden, in frustration, waved off all the restrictions of God.

It was not God who drove them away from the garden. Both of them ran away and hid themselves. Adam argued that it was Eve who induced him to eat of the forbidden fruit. Eve on her part said that it was the serpent. The serpent was the lust and driving passion to which both of them yielded. From that time, God closed His mercy door against man, and pronounced sentence on both of them. To the woman, God said, that she would scratch the ground, in deep pangs and pains at childbirth. Adam was similarly cursed, to win his bread through the sweat of his face. Human troubles had their start from here. Have you not seen that you have no peace? What other hell do you think of than where you are now?

### THE NEED FOR A REDEEMER

Our Lord Jesus Christ saw that the punishment of man was too great, so He came to return man back to the garden of Eden, by giving a simple law that we must love one another. But you continue to hate and devour each other. What do you want God to do after He had provided a Redeemer? Adam was the house of God, the dwelling place of God. He was the Christ of God, but he polluted the dwelling place of God by sinning. God did not like what he did. So, from that time onward tribulation, hardship and sorrow dogged the footsteps of man. You have been told to refrain from fornication, but some of you say that you will do it bit by bit. You will certainly end up in hell as you continue in it. The names of all those who continue in these sins are boldly written in Hell. You always hear people saying that the Leader is good, no matter how you sin, and even if your sins are in the worst category, He will always welcome and embrace you. The Bible says, that not all those who call Me Lord, Lord, will enter into the Kingdom of God. When you steal do not say that it is God who induced you to steal. It is your greed, passion and lust dragging you to sin. All sinners who violate the laws of God will end up down in everlasting Hell fire that burns with sulphur.

# PART TWO

**FIRST LESSON:** 1 Corinthians 6 v 9 - 10
**SECOND LESSON:** Galatians 5 v 20 - 21
**GOLDEN TEXT:** Revelation 21 v 8

Satan is deceiving the whole world today that if you steal, fornicate and commit all forms of abomination, but call on Jesus as your personal Saviour, you are saved; that since Jesus Christ came and shed His blood for the redemption of sinners, you can go ahead drinking wine, committing adultery, murdering and coveting and be licentious. This is an outright deception. All those who are led by those precepts are going headlong into hell and they are in hell right now. This is no time for false claim or a time for showing false front. It is no time for saying that somebody is God, Christ or an angel, but it is the time for everyone to repent and refrain from sin, and to abide with God's righteous principles. I want to point out to you, those who are the children of perdition. Have you noticed what the golden text has in context? Those who practice those things are in hell right now. You are not forced or bound to do what is right, but you must know that any sin that you commit leads you into hell. Let it become known to you that from time immemorial, all sinners have their abode in hell till now.

Is there any person in the world that can point to any portion of the Bible that says, if a person fornicates, steals, commits adultery and indulges in lawlessness, that such a person will inherit God's Kingdom? Let such a person come out and prove his case. How can you have hope of entering into God's Kingdom and at the same time remain lawless? This shows that you have no hope at all. Some people having seen that they are lawless, have decided not to attend any church, for they conclude that they are good for nothing and are in hell; in this they are correct. There are others also who are aware that they are chronic immoral persons, yet they are the best church goers. What is the sense in going to church when you are lawless? Are you not the same as the one who does not attend any church at all? However, the sheep must be separated from the goats right now.

## SEPARATING THE SHEEP FROM THE GOATS

This is the time to separate the sheep from the goats. Since you know that you are a goat why do you come in here? We do not keep goats here. You know that the thief only comes to steal. Since you are licencious, or a sex maniac, your intention is to come and corrupt the sheep that are kept chaste and undefiled by God. Your destination is in hell and the sheep only are for heaven. Today many people are rushing into the Brotherhood of the Cross and Star, with the intention of being healed of their sickness or to have an improved condition of life. But little do they think of refraining from sins. Christ said, "come to Me all of you who are loaded with heavy burden and I will give you rest." He further said, that it is the sick that looks for the physician, and not the physician that looks for the sick; that He did not come for the righteous but for the sick sinners to repent and get saved.

With this text in mind, many have been brought into Brotherhood with a heavy load of sin in order to get saved and get out of hell. But they must refrain from sin, they must repent whole heartedly now, for survival into eternal life in heaven. The Brotherhood of the Cross and Star is the Kingdom of God, it is for the righteous ones. No lawless fellow has any share in this Kingdom. Obedience is better than sacrifice. Instead of spending your money celebrating sumptious feasts, why do you not refrain from sin? Why do you not repent and get saved from this adulterous generation? Instead of suffering yourself in fasting for a number of days and nights, and going to unecessary ministerial tours, why not refrain from sins? Instead of becoming regular confessor of sins, why not heed God's instructions now and live? For it is written, for if they did not escape from him who begged and from him who was giving divine warning upon earth; how much more shall they not escape if they turn away from Him who speaks from heaven?

## YOU ARE OBLIGATED TO REFRAIN FROM SIN

God gives us life, protects and heals us, and bestows all good gifts on us. There is every reason then, why we should and must obey God. It is because of this fact why you are given this gospel. God has given you all that you need for your daily sustenance, why then do you choose to go to hell fire? If you were to abide by the gospel of Christ, you would not spend your time going about telling people that the Leader of Brotherhood is God, Christ or an angel. This is a wasteful exercise. All that you are required to do is to practice the Words of God and get saved. It is written that not all those who call Me Lord, Lord will enter into the Kingdom of God, but only those who practice the Words of God. The choice is before you now; either you abide by the instructions of God and enjoy life in God's Kingdom; or practice lawlessness and be condemned into hell. Why do you choose to go to hell? You do not come here to work for anybody, or for the interest of anyone. You are here to save your soul. God and His Christ are here to save you. Many people think that if they refrain from fornication, adultry, stealing or telling lies, they are doing another person any favour. Not at all; it is for your own good and welfare, it is for the salvation of your soul. Why? For under no circumstance, shall a sinner go unpunished.

The world is full of blind and crippled leaders. Satan invites you into his organisation with false promises. You are told that if you pay your church dues, partake in the so-called communion, and be baptised, that you are saved; and that when you die you are going straight to heaven. This is absolute falsehood. Others believe that to carry the Bible about, parading in front of every door and in every street, in pretence of preaching, that they are saved, eventhough they do not live up to what they preach. This is also another self deceit. Any person who commits those things mentioned in the first Bible lesson is in hell now. Read the first Bible lesson distinctly so that you may have discernment. All those who practise such things will not inherit God's kingdom.

## REAPING WHAT YOU SOWED

This gospel will save you just as it happened to that robber on the cross. For one of the evildoers on the cross began to say abusively to Christ, "you are the Christ, are you not? Save yourself and us." But the other robber rebuked him and said, "do you not fear God at all, now that you are in the same judgement? We indeed justly so, for we are receiving in full what we deserve for the things we did, but this man did nothing wrong." At this point he pleaded with Christ to remember him for good. It is your place now through this gospel to take stock of yourselves, and know that all that befalls you daily are due to the sins you commit. For example, I mentioned that marriage is hell in one of the gospels. That fact still stands true. If you are involved in this marriage contract, do not complain to anyone about the consequences of its torment. You know that Christ is the only Bridegroom. Why do you come to report to Christ when you have stolen a woman; yes, His wife from Him. You must suffer the penalty. There is no amount of fasting that can take away the sufferings of this hell. This is the judgement.

Your sufferings are no part of God's service, you are receiving in full what you deserve. Because the scripture says, that those who are counted worthy to partake in this new system of things, neither marry nor are given in marriage. If you turn a deaf ear to this instruction and marry, then you must be prepared to face the heat of fire from this hell. Do not call on God either, do not complain to anyone, you must reap what you sowed. You who take fornication for your hobby, why do you complain when you are struck with the fire of hell? You who commit adultry as you take breakfast, be prepared to face the consequence of it. Tell no one about it; do not complain; accept the blows; this is what you wanted. It is so also with the thieves. Continue to steal, but know that you are in hell. There is no turning of the shadow from here. You must drink your cup of evil. There is no sense for a thief to seek a defence. He is already in hell. Consider from your youth all the sufferings that you have received, because of the sins that you commit. Are these sufferings not enough? Listen to the first Bible lesson.

### FIRST LESSON: 1 Corinthians 6 v 9 - 10

> "What, do you not know that unrighteous persons
> will not inherit God's Kingdom? Do not be misled.
> Neither fornicators, nor idolaters, nor adulterers
> nor men kept for unnatural purposes, nor thieves,
> nor greedy persons, nor drunkards, nor revilers,
> nor extortioners will inherit God's Kingdom."

Just as I have already told you, hell is a condition of suffering, a state of perpetual punishment, afflictions, tribulations, gnashing of teeth, poverty, distress and torture of extra ordinary kind. It is a place of torment, where you will look for life but will not see it, and pray to die but death flee from you. It is a terrible condition ever thought of. Stealing, fighting, murdering, anger, lying, hatred, lawlessness; in short all manners of evil are found in hell. Ask the soothsayers, the sorcerers, fornicators and adulterers whether they have the required joy and happiness. Anyone who seduces another person's wife cannot have rest and peace of mind. He lives in fear, eats in fear, walks in fear, he is in hell. Or someone that defiles another person's daughter, he can never have peace of mind; he is in hell fire, poor soul. He lives in fear, moves about in fear and perhaps die in fear.

The world is on fire. In every home the fire is blazing high, but of course without visible flames. Nothing physical can extinguish this fire. The only capable extinguisher is for one to follow the instructions of God. The sins of mankind has now reached the climax. The fire is perfectly heated now for lawless fellows. You who want to get rich over-night and steal another person's money, have you actually enjoyed what you stole? You who indulge in dubious ways of getting money, either by immoral conduct or otherwise, have you enjoyed this hot money? There is no enjoyment in hell. You do not even get to hell with these things that you possess, the fire quickly consumes them.

Today thieves are shot because of the increase in highway robbery. The prisons are full of lawless men. The hospital beds are insufficient because of diseases due to immoral conduct; the doctors are on the run. The courts are filled with cases that are not able to be disposed of. Retirements, dismissals, terminations with immediate effect, are prevalent everywhere; yet you are warned to refrain from sin, but you refuse. Even as you are here in Brotherhood, if you are a fornicator or immoral person, know that you are in hell. What cause a person to steal, fornicate or drink wine? It is mere greed, lust, selfishness. Unless you refrain from these things, you will have no share in this ¬Kingdom of God. But someone may say, I want to help myself in one way or the other. Some want to enjoy themselves; there is no happiness or enjoyment in hell fire. It was because Christ preached to the people saying, "all those who are loaded with heavy burden should come to Him and He would give them rest," that made many people rush to Him. Fornicators, drunkards, adulterers and all types of persons rushed to Him. But no sooner had Christ given them this solid food- "that unless they ate the flesh of the Son of man and drink His blood they would not have life in themselves," that many started to grumble, murmur and leave Him. According to the report they said, "this speech is shocking, who can listen to it?" Yes, who can eat the flesh of someone and drink his blood? Impossible; they concluded and went away.

The gospel is the begining and the end. If you want to be saved, practise it. But if you have signed a bond with satan and you are bent on committing sins; if you do not come here to be saved but to corrupt those that are here; the best thing for you to do, since you have concluded like those people of old that what you are hearing from this gospel is impractical; you better stay out and face the penalty that is due to you. All I know; heaven and earth will pass away, but no particle of the Word of God shall pass away until all are fulfilled. God had sworn by His Name, that all those who practise these sinful things will not enter into His rest. God is the Word. His Word is the Truth and His pronouncements are irrevocable.

When you have time, examine these texts carefully. If you are suffering, sick or afflicted, know that your name is on the list of those who are in hell. If you are an angry fellow, a liar, know that your name is there in hell. You have yourself to blame for being disobedient to God's instructions. All evildoers should not ask God for any help. If you want to be free from all your sickness, refrain from anger, immorality and live with God your Creator. Christ came and preached this gospel, but people rejected it. Today no church denomination attaches importance to Bible principles. People claim to be christians; the people of God, but they do not know who Christ is, nor follow His instructions. You have yourself to blame. May we read the second Bible lesson.

### SECOND LESSON:   Galations 5 v 20 - 21

"Idolatry, the practice of spiritism, hatred, strife, jealousy, fits of anger, contentions, divisions, sects, envies, drunken bouts, revelries and things like those. As to these things I am forewarning you, the same way that I did forewarn you, that those who practice such things will not inherit God's Kingdom."

If you are hardened in mind and remain here in Brotherhood and commit sin despite this vital warning, know that you are in hell. Does it not surprise you to hear that someone is attacked by evil forces right in the altar or in the Bethel? On the other hand, that there is a person in the bush enjoying his sleep undisturbed by anyone? This shows that someone can be in the presence of God and yet be in hell. I do not say that you must come to Brotherhood, but what I am saying is; wherever you are, if you practice these things mentioned in the three texts of this gospel, you are in hell and the Kingdom of God is not for you. On the other hand, I can see that many of you that are here, are in heaven while others are in deep hell. Those who, though in Brotherhood are in hell, are those who do not care to receive and practice the instructions given them from God's Words. They brush them away by saying, "as the Father likes it." You must understand that hell is everywhere. If you practice what is good, wherever you are, you are in heaven. If you practice what is evil, no matter where you are you are in hell.

Go and tell the world, that all evildoers are now in hell. Why sympathise with the sick, or someone who has got into trouble? Rather advise him to repent, confess his sins, and refrain from sin, so that all will be well. For this reason, it is written; Is there anyone sick among you, let him call the elders of the church and let them pray over him, annointing him with oil in the name of the Lord, and the prayer of faith will make the indisposed one well, and the Lord will raise him up. Also if he has committed sins it will be forgiven him. This is no hospital business, it does not require any black magic priest. The black magic priests themselves do not have peace. There is no point in saying that you will refrain from sin gradually. You cannot continue in sin and the grace of God abound in you; for if a person like David did not escape the punishment for taking someone's wife, who are you to evade God's judicial judgement? All what God told David happened to him because of taking Uriah's wife. David did not escape from any of the punishments, so why then are you toying with sins? When you refrain from sins all your troubles will be over.

Do not be afraid of the angels, spirits or any person; but flee fornication, adultry, stealing, anger, telling lies, cheating; flee sin, because anything short of this leads to hell. But, if you would discern what yourselves are, you would not be judged. However, you are judged, you are disciplined by the Lord, that you may not be condemned with the world. For example, in the prison yard, there are those who are for one day imprisonment, such persons are not tortured at all. They are given all delicious dishes and cared for until that ONE DAY. Whereas, there are those who may be there for two or three weeks, but are punished and tortured and then freed after this period of discipline. The latter refers to the children of God, while the former refers to the children of the world. When the children of God commit sin, they are punished and restored, unlike those of the world who will continue to enjoy themselves though in sin, until the ONE DAY condemnation. These One Day prisoners may continue to mock you when they see that you are being disciplined. There are those whose sins are revealed immediately and they are punished, whereas there are others whose sins are concealed, and later will become manifest; too late to amend, too late to be corrected; Condemnation. Today there are people who are good but they are rejected of men. After their lifetime, their good works will become manifest and people will speak well of them. This happened in the case of Christ. He was killed as a lawbreaker and troublemaker. But, today He is being searched for; He is called the Good Friend of mankind. He is in heaven. And so it is with everyone who abides in His Words. Wherever you are, even if you put on the white robe all over your body, if you commit sin you are in hell. You should not be surprised therefore, if you see people committing all sorts of abominations even before the altar, or in the house of God. Such people are in hell. A fornicator, a thief, a drunkard has no respect for anyone. They are dangerous persons, when you see them, take care of yourselves.

You have heard that satan said he would not remain alone in the bottomless pit. Who are with Satan? Are they not the fornicators, thieves, adulterers, murderers and all lawless people? They campaign for people to join their company. Therefore, beware of these men. The drunkards will always give you the reason why they drink. No good person will take snuff and eat tobacco. It is stated, "Give wine to the one who is about to perish and drink to those who are bitter of soul, let them drink and forget their poverty, and let them remember no more." Of course, under the influence of alcohol they may forget their sorrows and poverty; but when they become normal, their problems will surely come back to their headache. So you can see that wines or drinks are not for good people, especially not for the children of God.

If you see men and women running around like sex maniacs, it is because they are in hell; and of course no one can help you in hell. The heat of the fire in hell is the cause of your high temperature, and such high fever that sometimes could cause a wet cloth to become dry when it is placed on your body. Do not even ask yourself where this heat comes from, without any flames in your body. Man you are in hell. Why do you not do something now to erase your name from the list of those in hell? It is because you were in hell while in the world, that you were requested to confess your sins and repent of your evil course and get baptised; removing you from hell into God's Kingdom. May we read the golden text.

### GOLDEN TEXT: Revelation 21 v 8

"But as for the cowards and those without faith
and those who are disgusting in their filth,
and murderers and fornicators and those practising
spiritism, and idolaters and all the liars; their portion
will be in the lake that burns with fire and
sulphur. This means the second death."

**Let no one deceive you, all those who practise these things have no share in heaven, their destination is in hell.** Show them those who will go to heaven, and those who will go to hell.

All those in Brotherhood who are still complaining of sickness, afflictions, tribulations etc, are not yet in Brotherhood. They are still in hell, although here in Brotherhood. Poor souls, if they can simply discern what hell and heaven are; if they could but abide with God's instructions, this would erase their names from hell, and be written here in the Kingdom of God. You who believe in the eating of communion as a guarantee of salvation; you who believe in baptism as a sacrament; do you know what is the actual communion as taught by Christ? This bread is the Word of God. You must eat the word of God. That blood is the suffering that comes through the practise of the Word of God. Yes, as for your contest against sin, you have not started until you have shed blood. This is the time for you to enrol your name in the book of life, so that it may go well with you.

Today in the world you may look at some people as wealthy people, blessed with children, but you do not know that there is a canker worm in them. Remove Jonah from the boat so that the boat may move. Yes, unless you take away those things that are meant for destruction, that are now in you, you cannot escape God's punishment. You Jonah class, repent now otherwise you will have no peace. Do not hope to repent in hell. Now is the acceptable time for salvation. Evildoers are head-strong and disobedient. Fornicators and thieves have no need for church services. They do not see any good in worshipping God. Someone will say, I have been a member in all the churches. Is that a good report for someone to say that he has been a member in all the churches? Or someone who say, I have toured the world in search for power. Why not refrain from lawless practises and have God's favour now? Or do you prefer to be burnt by this fire? How long will you choose to remain there? It is not the wish of My Father that any of you should perish, but that you should repent and get saved. This gospel is for that purpose, to help you out of hell. If you reject this gospel, there is no alternative. It means that you have been destined for hell.

Decide now or never. Be transformed by making up your minds to do God's will. If the people of old were to have this gospel, do you think that they would have chosen to be destroyed? But if you now, are determined to refuse the warning contained in this gospel, I am confident and convinced that millions who are now on their way into this Kingdom; who have already got themselves prepared for this glorious treasure in heaven, will enjoy these eternal blessings now and forevermore.

# PART THREE

**FIRST LESSON:** St Luke 3 v 11
**SECOND LESSON:** 1 John 3 v 17
**GOLDEN TEXT:** St Matthew 25 v 45 - 46

Brethren, when you read the first, second and third lessons, you will actually see what is now at stake.. The subject of our discussion must have become apparent to you. Many people have construed hell to be a literal place of torment, where fire is stored up and people descend there to be burnt alive. In this revelation, it is clearly shown that hell is a condition of perpetual punishment, a damned condition, a condition of wickedness, torture and death. Whereas, heaven is eternal joy, peace and happiness. There is everlasting life and everlasting punishment. Therefore in this world, there is eternal punishment and eternal life. The whole world is placed in a damned condition of eternal punishment from Adam till now. Mankind in general has been plunged into hell fire.

In times past, some of you had believed that your forefathers were taken to heaven at death; but may I ask, where were they when they were alive? Some of you talk of the rich man having a better place in heaven, this is impossible. For the scripture says, that the minding of the flesh means death; how then can a rich man have a place in heaven? Christ spoke vehemently that it will be difficult for a rich man to enter into the Kingdom of God. How can a rich man have peace of mind, when he is busy thinking how to increase his wealth and secure the ones he has acquired? Since he has rejected the Word of God, he is a saboteur; for the word of God says, if you have two garments, you must give one to the person who has none. But a rich man has more than two and he is keeping them to himself. He has much Naira with him, but on the wayside are the needy and the poor who do not have a Kobo, but he fails to share with them. There are others who build houses but refuse to give to those who are hanging around, but boldly write on the building, "house to let." To whom does he want to let out his house? He wants more money from the needy who cannot afford to pay the rent for a house. Such people are in hell.

The way to heaven is open and here it is; that, if you have two things you must give one to the person that has none, otherwise you are in hell fire. All those who refuse to practise the first lesson of this gospel are in hell right now. What is called the Kingdom of God is the Word of God, and the first Bible lesson has shown you what Brotherhood is. Therefore let it become known to all of you, that anyone who fails to practise the first lesson is deep in hell fire. Some people may say that they refrain from fornication, adultry, drinking of wine and taking of drugs or injections and telling lies; that may be true, but what about giving out those things that you have more than one, to another who has none? This is the greatest sin; it is the sin of selfishness, greed and coveteousness; it is a state of voraciousness which is punishable by eternal torment in hell fire. That is why, it would be highly impossible for a rich man to make a showing in the Kingdom of God.

The children of God are mocked for being generous, and for practising this lesson of giving one of the two things that they have to another who has none. They are regarded as foolish for their hospitality. But I tell you that it is an act of wisdom on your part, for yours is the Kingdom of God. Anyone who fails to practise this lesson, I repeat, has no place in the Kingdom of God.

Does this not identify to you, those who are in hell? Certainly it does. No rich person in the world, who fails to practise this scriptural text has peace, he is in hell fire. Inform your parents, relations and the entire world who reject this principle of the scriptures, that they are in hell. A way of salvation is now open to all; use this chance to get out of hell. If you realise that your name is in hell, due to the fact that you have not practised this gospel, do so now and use this chance to erase your name from hell, and have it written in the Kingdom of God for your eternal salvation.

Some fancied preachers and misguided individuals say that the statement of Christ was a parable when He said, "Go and sell all that you have and distribute to the poor, and come, be My follower and you will have a portion in the Kingdom of God." Our Lord Jesus Christ demonstrated this Biblical principle Himself. He distributed all that He had to the poor; His faith, His power, His love, His wisdom; He willingly shared and distributed equally to those in need. For your sake He, though being rich become poor, so that you may be rich. The scripture says, do not love the world or the things in the world; if anyone loves the world the love of the Father is not in him, because everything in the world; the desires of the flesh and the desires of the eyes, and the showy display of one's means of life, does not originate with the Father, but originates in the world. Think of it yourself, **your suitcases are full with different types of soutanes, costly ones and the less costly ones, old and new; among them also are other dresses which perhaps you may not want to use now or in the future, but here are your brothers and sisters without a soutane or something to put on, and you are shouting "Hallelujah," what is the meaning of your jubilation?**

The things of this world have blinded such people, just as the Word of God says, now that the gospel is unveiled among those who are perishing, yes, those in hell. But as for those who desire salvation, they have taken this chance to practise this gospel and get saved. During the time of the Apostles, the record shows that there was not one among them in need. Why? For all those who believed, and were possessors of houses or fields, would sell them and bring the values of the things sold, and deposit them at the feet of the Apostles. But, of course, a certain man name Ananias sold his possession and secretly held back a part of the money for himself and gave the Apostles the rest. Today we have the "Ananias" class, people who are selfish and greedy, who would not share their surplus with others. You may not be a fornicator, adulterer or a liar, etc, but bear in mind that today, you cannot be more fortunate than Ananias who was unable to get away with his devices, he was condemned to hell immediately.

The Angelic messengers told Lot and his household not to look behind, when they were getting out of Sodom and Gommorrah. To look back would mean that they have interest in the things that they left behind; it would be a sin. But alas, the wife looked back; she was condemned to hell instantly. You also remember Judas Iscarriot. His mind was bent on riches. This led him astray, headlong into everlasting punishment in hell. Do not be deceived, for all what you possess now are not yours. It was written, that in the later time a Prophet would be raised up, and whosoever would not listen to that Prophet would be cut off from among the people. Whatever you are, be you a doctor, a lawyer, and whatever position in life that you must attain, if you do not give out one of the two things that you have to the one that has none, you are now in hell fire. It is because you allow these worldly things to occupy your minds, that you cannot please God the way you should do. What did you come to this world with? And with what are you going away? Who makes you to differ from another? Indeed, what do you have that you did not receive? If now, you indeed receive it, why do you boast as though you did not receive it? God does not say that you should not be rich for He is the one who bestows all these things on you. You are the storekeepers, and things kept in your care are for you to distribute to the needy. It is out of selfishness, lust for these material things, that you are now kept under eternal torment in hell fire.

To possess cars and other material things of this world is not in itself satanic, but it is the love that you have for these things that makes them worldly. You must give out one of the two things that you have to the needy in order to gain salvation in God's Kingdom. God has given this instruction to the rich men of this world; that those who are rich in the present system of things should not be high-minded, not to rest their hope on uncertain riches but on God, who furnishes them with good works, to be liberal, ready to share; safely treasuring up for themselves a fine foundation for the future, in order that they may get a firm hold on the real life. This is your passport to heaven, otherwise you are in hell fire. Read the first Bible lesson again.

### FIRST LESSON:   St Luke 3 v 11

"In reply He said to them, let the man that has
two garments share with the man that has none
and let him that has things to eat do the same."

That is the beginning and the end of the gospel. Abraham was used to entertaining strangers, and he eventually entertained Angels. God gave him one child and later demanded that the child be offered as sacrifice unto Him. Abraham obeyed. If Abraham had disobeyed God, that would have led him to hell fire. Lot was also liberal and generous. That was why he willingly entertained those strangers without knowing that they were Angels. Liberality is required from all those who are longing for this Kingdom of God. **You must be liberal even with your beauty or handsomeness; you must mix freely with the unfortunate ugly people, be ready to share with them your beauty, thereby consoling them of their unfortunate condition.** By doing so you will not be criticised by the ugly ones since you accept them with open arms. God does not use two persons to save the world, but He uses only One. **If you are blessed with wisdom, children or with any wealth of this world, you must be liberal and ready to share with those in need; otherwise you are in hell fire.**

**For example, you may be blessed with many children, but only one is your child.** The one that listens to you and obeys you at all times, is the one that you love most. Although others may be with you, notwithstanding, only that one is your own. Therefore, be liberal, **you must distribute these children to those who do not have, so that you may be saved with those children. You may build so many houses, but it is only one house that you will live in. That house will have so many rooms, but it is only one room that will be your own. You may have many beds, and many pillows on these beds, but it is only on one bed that you will sleep, and only on one pillow that you will lay your head upon. Think of it right now, you have many dresses and soutanes, but it is only one soutane that you are using now; why not give the rest to those who have none? Can you use two spoons to eat at the same time? Look how many spoons you have in your box. You have so many tables and chairs, but it is only one table and one chair that you can use at a time. Why not secure your life by giving out those things which you do not use to those in need?**

**From these examples given, you can see that polygamists are rebels. You may marry so many wives, but only one is your legal wife. Why not give out the others to other men who have none? You can only put up with one wife in one night, while other concubines are kept without someone to care for them that same night. This is selfishness, it is theft, and is punishable by fire in hell.** Solomon committed this offence. You who boast of marrying so many wives, you will agree that you can only eat from a wife at a time. It may be said that there are other men, and so you women greedily get hold of them; sister, only one is your own. You must be liberal.

The Word of God is also applicable to the polygamists. Take only one wife and give out others to other people. **If you are selfish to accummulate concubines, you are in hell fire. You women and girls who are keeping thousands of boy friends at all corners, you must keep only one, and release other boys for those women and girls who are not yet successful in this contest. The same thing applies to those who are holding more than one job. You are a civil servant and at the same time, you are a private businessman, a contractor, etc. Why not be liberal and share the other jobs with those who are applicants?** In this light of Truth you must be ready to share with others. In the name of our Lord Jesus Christ.

In fact this is what is troubling the nations of mankind today. One man has a hundred jobs; one man has a hundred plots of land, while there are millions of people without a job and without allocation of a plot eventhough they qualify for it. It also applies to occupying positions. You can imagine a man who is a Chairman or President in five different meetings. Can you? Only one post is yours. You must give out the other four posts to those who has none. **If you are selfish and want to be Mr President everywhere, you must know that you are in hell fire.** If you are not liberal and generous, then, writing "Jesus" "Jesus" on your door post will not save you.

This is the time to practise the Word of God so that you may enjoy everlasting life in God's Kingdom. It is easy to deceive someone that you love God, but God cannot be mocked. How? While on your way, you come across the beggars by the wayside and the needy who beckon to you for help, but you say that you are running to meet Jesus. Do you all know Jesus? Today many say that they do not joke with money, children, their jobs, even their lives. What then are you to joke with? Abraham did not consider his child as too important. That was why he readily obeyed God when God asked him to sacrifice his child. Our Lord Jesus Christ did not even consider His life as something important to Him. In fact He gambled with life; He joked with His mother and father while here on ministerial activities. Therefore brethren, anyone that has this world's means of living and does not give out his extras to the needy ones, does not love God either. As long as you fail to share or to give out one of the two things that you have to the one that has none, or food to the one that is hungry, you are in hell fire.

Faith without work is dead. What is work? It is liberality. Being ready to share. Jesus asked Peter, "Do you love Me more than all these things?" Peter answered, "Lord you know that I have affection for you." Christ told him, Feed My little sheep." Who are these sheep? They are the needy, the poor, the afflicted, depressed widows and orphans. In the writings of Paul and James, they both wrote about the caring and honouring of the widows and orphans. For instance, when you go to preach to someone who is without food or clothing, and after your sermon you say, -"May God be with you." How? You must be practical, you must be liberal, you must be hospitable. They need the necessities for their bodies. This is where works come in to meet faith.

Whom do you think the false prophets are? They are those type of fancied preachers who are not interested in the physical needs of the needy. They are also the false apostles; those who are selfish, lustful and greedy with the things of this world. Such persons are the anti-christs. May we have the second Bible lesson read.

### SECOND LESSON:    1 John 3 v 17

"But whoever has this world's means for supporting life, and beholds his brother having need and yet shut the door of his tender compassions upon him, in what way does the love of God remain in him?"

Brethren, the context of this lesson is clear and practical. Anything short of this keeps one under eternal punishment. Take a look at the so many churches today with wealthy people. Do you see those huts built around the city and are labelled "the house of God?" Even the churches are debtors. Such wealthy people in their midst are in hell fire. For instance, in a function, there may be a levy of One Naira for every one. The rich will pay the One Naira and expect the poor to do the same. **Such a rich person is mocking God.** Any person that has this world's means of living and he is not liberal, has no love of God in him. It is written, that anyone to whom much is given, much will be demanded from him.

If it is money, wisdom or any wealth that you are blessed with, much more will be demanded from you. If you fail to comply with this demand, you are a rebel. Of what use is it for God to bless you with all things, but you fail to honour God with these things? You are the Storehouse kept in the stewardship of God. Therefore you must not shut the door of compassion to the needy. You must do this indiscriminately. God has kept you in this position as intermediaries to distribute to the poor and needy people that you come across. If God gives you truth, love, self control, faith and hope, you must be liberal with these qualities given to you by God, to those who do not have; otherwise you are in hell fire.

There are others who would not go to people's homes, or eat the food of other people, or touch things belonging to others, in order to avoid trouble. Such people who are self centered are likened to the unfaithful stewards, who buried their talents and were kept under torment for doing so. Paul was a lawyer, but because of this gospel he decided to share his knowledge with the needy, and because of this action he converted many people to Christ. You may be a driver, but you expect someone to hire you or be paid a fat sum of money before you serve. Such action or behaviour is usually shown by children of perdition. This text does not mention anybody's name but simply says, "that whoever has this world's means for supporting life, and beholds his brother in need." When it says, "this world's means for supporting life," it refers to all possible means for supporting life; **what you have and not what you haven't. What is not valuable to you is valuable to others, and what you have in plenty, is the lack of others. You must therefore seek the welfare of others in order to fulfill the Word of God.**

If you fail to help the poor and needy; if you shut your door of compassion upon others in need; you have denied God of these things. On your way you come across someone with his car tyre punctured; **the service of God would want you to give out that spare tyre of yours; or if he is short of fuel and you have some reserve, you must give out that reserve fuel of yours. Do not think whether your tyre will get punctured on the way or whether you will run short of fuel, you must have hope that the Father will do His work. If you pass by the fellow who is in dire need of assistance, when you have your spare tyre and reserve fuel with you, you are in fact running into hell fire.** This New Kingdom of God requires liberality. Do not wait for invitation to help. Whenever you meet the poor and needy, no matter what family, tribe or nationality they come from, show them that tender compassion as much as is within your power.

You are not told to give more than what you have. You are not required to beg people or to ask God to give you more things in order to assist others. You must understand that there is no child of God that is poor, as long as God their father is not poor. **You must be contented with what you have. All members of your body are valuable treasures and wealth. There are those without eyes; then you who have eyes and can see, will be in a position to help those without sight. Your wealth in this case is your sight. The same thing applies to hands, legs, etc. Good health is another wealth. You can use your good health to help the sick. You may be rich in dreams, visions, prophecies, good voice, songs, wisdom, etc. You must then use all these things to help others**

**who are in need or lacking of them. You are priviledged to have this Truth preached to you. With this your faith is increased, and you are now rich with the message of life. Go out with this Truth and help others to share this same message.** The Bible says, "Whoever has this world's means for supporting life." If you have love, help others who have no love. The world today is looking for truthful and faithful people. Go to them and be of help. For I do not mean that it should be hard for you and easy for others; but that by means of equalising, your surplus just now might off-set their deficiency. You must abound in this kind of giving. No one lights a lamp and place it under a bushel, but is placed on top of the lamp stand. But if you fail to do this to others, it means that you have failed to do it to God Himself; and this will keep you under punishment. May we have the golden text read.

### GOLDEN TEXT:   St Matthew 25 v 45 - 46

"Then He will answer them with these words, truly I say to you, to.the extent that you did not do it to one of these least ones, you did not do it to Me. And these will depart into everlasting cutting off, but the righteous ones into everlasting life."

As long as you have this world's means for supporting life and you fail to share with others, you are under eternal punishment. Now you have seen those who are going to hell, and to everlasting punishment. They are those who shut the door of compassion against the needy; they are the selfish and greedy persons of this generation. There is no one who will say that he has not seen this truth. All mankind on the earth are Brotherhood. God and His Christ are Brotherhood. The animate and inanimate things are all Brotherhood. Therefore show the same compassion and help anyone that you see in need, with whatever means for supporting this life, that is within your reach.

When you see those on the wayside; the blind, lame, crippled, those in hospitals, clinics, prison camps, those in affliction and tribulation; it is your duty to help and assist them. This is your chance to get out of hell fire by heeding to this timely instruction. Use this chance now to erase your name from hell, by practising this gospel. Those who practise this gospel are those who will inherit this Kingdom to eternity. If you are disturbed in mind and you lack peace, it means that you are not liberal, you are lacking love. This is sin on your part and you are definately in hell fire. If you use your wealth to help others you will be compensated with salvation from God. Many people who have money hate themselves. In fact, their children are not cared for, and their wives are not well fed, in the least. That is why such rich persons have no share in this Kingdom for they know not Christ.

This is the time to practise the gospel. If it is a very small child that requires help, give it, for by so doing, you are doing it to God. People suffer because they fail to help others in need. God has abundantly supplied you with all good things. Then share it with others. **This is the order of the day for your eternal salvation. If you are blessed with riches do not think that God loves you more than the one that does not have. If you are given a submissive wife, do not boast as if God loves you more than the one who has a stubborn wife. Use this chance to help others in order to be blessed by God.**

Many people in Brotherhood have peace of mind and enjoy the blessings of God because they are generous, hospitable and liberal; while the avaracious ones are still in hell fire now. If you decide now that all what you have belongs to the Father, then you have no problems at all. You will not be selfish and greedy over them. Therefore brethren, go back and sell all that you have and give to the poor, and then rededicate yourself to this Kingdom. Brethren, those who have ears to hear, let them hear. May God bless His Holy Words, Amen.

# PART FOUR

**FIRST LESSON:** St Luke 24 v 26
**SECOND LESSON:** Romans 8 v 17
**GOLDEN TEXT:** Hebrews 12 v 8

Brethren, it would have been something worthwile if the whole world were present, to listen to this vital revelation as contained in this gospel; because the worldly people think that when they persecute, hate, falsely accuse you or kill you, that they are doing you the greatest evil on earth; not knowing that it is a crown of glory they are putting on your heads. However, if the world had this knowledge they would have stopped persecuting you, how then would you have these crowns of life? Christ said to Peter, "Thinkest thou that I can not now pray to My Father and He can presently give Me twelve legions of Angels? But how then would the scriptures be fulfilled, that thus it must be?"

All those who do not want suffering, persecution, hatred, false accusation and abuses, do not want this glory. The world regard such a condition of humiliation as the worst position in life. From God's point of view it is the gareway to heaven. Therefore those who do not want to pass through this state of life, are in hell fire. Do not rejoice and boast if you have never been persecuted, afflicted, suffered for righteousness sake; because only those who pass through such sufferings are the ones who are in heaven; while the unafflicted and unpersecuted ones are in hell fire.

## TAKE TO THE NARROW GATE.

You are told to get into the narrow gate because the broad way leads to destruction, and those who are going into this broad way are many. The narrow gate is the way, and only a few people take to it. The narrow gate is the different type of tribulations, afflictions, persecutions, false accusations, scandals, etc. If you have come across these situations, rejoice because your reward is great in heaven. If you have not met with these conditions, weep because your entrance into heaven is very remote; you are in hell fire. Christ and other faithful men of old, entered through this narrow gate of suffering. They walked with God and pleased Him; and were rewarded. This is the source of peace and life, it is the way to heaven.

## SUFFERING FOR RIGHTEOUSNESS SAKE

This suffering that we are talking about is not suffering as an evildoer, a thief, a fornicator, adulterer, a liar, a busy body in other people's matters, immorality and lawlessness; not at all. If you suffer under the above conditions, you are suffering for the sins you have committed, you are reaping what you sowed. In the case of Christ, He committed no sin, but He suffered for the doing of good works. He was called Beelzebub, a lawbreaker, a demon and the Prince of demons. Because of these false accusations, they could not regard Him as the Prince of Peace, the Ruler of the Universe. These accusations did not make Him change from His set purpose for the world; to .redeem mankind. Yet they persecuted Him and even put Him to death. People take delight in persecuting others and they think that they are getting away with it, because things continue to be better with them; while with those who do not commit crimes, or who are not immoral; things do not run smoothly. Do not be deceived, the former ones are in hell fire right now.

## WHY DO THE WICKED PROSPER AND LIVE LONGER?

Many people ask the above question today. Such people who are wicked, and take delight in wickedness, are in hell. Do not envy them because they are condemned persons. When you look at the thieves, witches, wizards, liars, fornicators, etc, things are better with them. But you who are trying to do good, things are bad with you. This may disturb you and make you murmur against God. Never be perturbed, suffer for the sake of righteousness, for yours is the Kingdom of heaven; but the wicked are in hell fire. Why should you murmur against God, when you know that immoral persons are in hell fire? **The children of God must pass through sufferings; they must be persecuted, hated, falsely accused, mocked at; but bear in mind that, such actions constitute your passport to heaven.**

Do you see how broad is the way to hell fire? Men of ingratitude, unappreciative persons; people who take delight in doing evil are already in hell fire. In the world today, those who are in high positions of life, are those who are having difficulty in life, and when you ask them, from their heart of hearts, they will confess that they are not enjoying life at all, though they have wealth. Life with them is not what it should be. Why? Because they are in hell fire. These are the people that you look upon as enjoying life because of their wealth, but they are suffering. What seems to you as happiness by the children of the world, is suffering, because they are already condemned. But the children of God must pass through suffering to enter God's glory.

The cross means suffering. You must not flout the instructions of God. The children of God do not have any place in this world. They are looked down upon; in social life, status, government and in the community. They are not of this world, hell is not for them. This Truth is hidden to the world. It is now revealed to you. Jesus knew that the only way back to heaven was for Him to suffer; He endured persecution, hatred, disgrace and shame for the sake of the Kingdom. Read the first lesson.

### FIRST LESSON:   St Luke 24 v 26

" Was it not necessary for Christ to suffer
these things and to enter into His glory?"

Anyone that has suffered for righteousness sake, has separated himself from sin. In the last gospel in this series, you were told that if you have two garments and give one to the person that has none, that you can enter into the Kingdom of God. But I am telling you by the strength of this gospel that, if you should give all your garments to the one that has none but you do not suffer for righteousness sake, you cannot enter this Kingdom of God. The scripture vehemently says: " And if I give all my belongings to feed the poor, and if I hand over my body to be burnt, and have not love, I am not profited at all." When you are praised and glorified for your evil doings, you are in hell.

Pharaoh was great and by the virtue of his position, **he exalted himself and taunted the Most High God. You have heard what was the outcome. He and his hosts were drowned in the red sea.** You have heard of Herod. He was similarly great; he exalted himself but God brought him down.. **King Nebuchadnezzar challenged the Almighty God, only to find himself as an amimal in the bush for seven years. The world is pitiable because the Kingdom of God is hidden from them.**

Christ suffered even in the hands of those whom He has led. They were the first to pick up stones to stone Him. At one instance Christ asked them; "Many good works have I showed you from My Father; for which of these works do you stone Me?" They said that it was not because of His good works why they wanted to stone Him; but for the fact that He being a man, called Himself the Son of God. All those who are for the Kingdom of God must likewise suffer. Keep on blessing those who persecute you, be blessing and do not be cursing. Return evil for evil no more.

Provide fine things in the sight of all men. Do not avenge yourself or yield to wrath. If your enemy is hungry, feed him. If he is thirsty give him something to drink, by so doing you will heap coals of fire upon his head. **See our Lord Jesus Christ on the cross, under such pains and disgrace, yet He pleaded with His Father: " Father, forgive them for they know not what they do." This was an outstanding example set for you.** Consider the example of Job: he said, " I have heard of thee by the hearing ear, but now mine eyes seeth thee." **When did Job see God face to face? Under suffering, distress; God comes near to you during the time of suffering.** May we have the second Bible lesson read.

### SECOND LESSON:    Romans 8 v 17

" If then we are children, we are also heirs,
heirs indeed of God, but joint heirs with Christ;
provided we suffer together that we may also be
glorified together."

All those who do not want to suffer are in hell fire. What will separate us from the love of Christ? Will tribulations, distress, persecutions, hunger, nakedness, danger or the sword? Paul said, " I am convinced that neither death nor life nor angels nor governments, nor things now nor things to come, nor powers nor creation, will be able to separate us from the love of God in Christ Jesus our Lord." This is the yoke that you must put around your neck. Materialism is a snare, and a hindrance to the heavenly glory. All those who are seeking for the glory of this world are in hell fire. Christ said, " My Kingdom is not part of this world, if My Kingdom were of this world, My people would have fought so that I may not be delivered unto the enemies."

**The Jews knew that Christ was innocent. Some of them knew that He was the Son of God. But out of jealousy, they nursed an animousity against Him. Pilate knew this well; he asked whether he should release Jesus to them, but they refused. They wanted Barabas to be released instead of Jesus. They wanted their fellow man who was in hell with them.**

Jesus said, "If the world hates you, know that they first hated Me," Why then do you want the world to love you? Those who are in friendship with the world are in enmity with God. Such ones are in hell. Christ said, "I have spoken these things to you so that you may not stumble. Men will expel you from the synagogue. In fact, the hour is coming when anyone that kills you will imagined that he has done a service to God. But they will do these things because they have not come to know either the Father or Me." Consider what the people did to John the Baptist and to Christ Himself. Thus, must all His followers pass through this suffering to eternal glory. May we read again, the golden text.

### GOLDEN TEXT: Hebrews 12 v 8

"But if you are without the discipline of which all have become partakers, you are really illegitimate children and not sons."

How can one be smoking, snuffing, stealing, lying, fornicating, committing adultry and all forms of abominations, and such ones still boast that things are going well with them? They are in hell. An illegitimate child is never wanted or owned by anyone. No one cares what happens to him. He is just left alone to suffer any fate that comes his way. He is a bastard. And so it is with anyone who does not suffer or is disiplined by God. It means that he does not have God and he is not for this Kingdom.

From ancient times, the children of God passed through sufferings. They were from time to time chastised and disciplined by God. When Saul, who later became Paul, did not see this light of Truth, he persecuted the congregation of God. According to records, Paul testified: "When the blood of Stephen your witness was being spilled, I myself was also standing by and approving and guarding the outer garments of those who were doing away with him." In fact, by then Paul thought that he was doing a righteous work. He at one time, received letters from the High Priests to go and kill all the followers of Christ. When he was later converted, these things turn around against him.

**Today, you may wonder why the world hates the Brotherhood of the Cross and Star. The reason is that Brotherhood of the Cross and Star is the Kingdom of God; while the children of this world are in Satan's kingdom.** It is stated in the scriptures: "Those wearing white robes, who are they and where do they come from? These are the ones that come out of great tribulation and they have washed their robes and made them white in the blood of the Lamb." **Once you get into Brotherhood of the Cross and Star, all hatred mounts up against you because, you no more walk in the same way with the world.** The backsliders, the disgruntled ones, who became inactive and find their way out of Brotherhood, are back to hell fire; a worse condition than when they were not called into the Kingdom.

Do not doubt if you see those who have come in, and yet they have no peace and things are even getting worse with them. They have been cast into hell because they do not have the true identity. Do you remember the illustration of the man that made a feast and invited people to come for the feast? The record stated: When the king came in to inspect the guests he caught sight of a man who was not clothed in a marriage garment. So he said to him, Fellow, how did you get in here, and not having a marriage garment? He was rendered speechless. Then the king said to the servant, bind his hands and feet and throw him out into the darkness, where there is weeping and gnashing of teeth." **That is hell.**

## WHAT IS THE OFFICIAL GARMENT?

It is suffering, tribulation, distress, hatred, etc; all for the sake of the Kingdom. There are those who would not put on this garment, both the Spiritual and physical garments, because of fear and shame. But Christ said, "Anyone who is ashamed of Me, I will also be ashamed of him before My Father." If you die with Him you will also be raised up with Him. If you suffer with Him, you will reign with Him. If you deny Him, He will deny you. This Kingdom requires humility. People like Nicodemus thought of their high positions. You must become a little child. There is no agreement between light and darkness. Brotherhood of the Cross and Star is the Kingdom of God; and all those who have chosen to suffer for righteousness sake, are in heaven, but those outside are in hell fire. Brotherhood therefore must be hated. Paul said, "as for this sect, nothing well is spoken about it."

From Abel onwards, which of the Prophets did people not kill? That was why Elijah prayed for fire to come down and consume his persecutors. But God said that not all His Prophets were killed, for there was a remnant for Him who have not bowed down to Baal. He numbered them to be 7,000. Illustratively, those who are for heaven are not many. **Those who are going to hell are countless. Because of pride, arrogance and this world's showy display of one's means of life, such people would not want to humble themselves; they would not go barefooted; they would not want to bow down and knock their heads on the ground in worship of their CREATOR. Because of their vain position in this life, they would not worship a human being nor give him honour. That is why such people are having a rough time in hell now. Their names have been written in the Book of Eternal Torment, in the lake that burns with sulphur- the Lake of Fire.**

Brethren, those who have ears to hear, let them hear. May God bless His Holy Words. Amen.

# CHAPTER 12

Several Gospels of Leader Olumba Olumba Obu
Summarized by Elder W.B. Smith

# INCARNATION, DECARNATION AND RE-INCARNATION.

**1. St John 11 v 25 - 26**
"And Jesus said unto her, I am the resurrection and the life, he that believeth in Me though he were dead yet shall he live; and whosoever liveth and believeth in Me shall never die."

**2. St Matthew 10 v 28**
"And fear not them which kill the body, but are not able to kill the soul, but rather fear Him who can destroy both soul and body in hell."

**3. Acts 7 v 48**
"Howbeit the Most High dwelleth not in temples made with hands, as saith the Prophet."

The world is populated by means of Incarnation, De-Carnation and Re-Incarnation. As thousands of people die each day, so are thousands born each day. All human beings had existed in " Spirit Form" only, before they were born into this mundane world.

## WHAT IS SPIRIT?

Spirits are humanlike messengers of God, having neither flesh, blood nor bone. Spirits and Angels are the same. Angels inhabit the Celestial planes, while human beings inhabits the Terrestrial plane. Man without the Spirit is mute and negative. Without the Spirit, man would be absolutely useless and worthless. We could not talk, walk, work, eat, sleep, think, reason or do any other thing without the Spirit. It is the Spirit that provides the body with all energy. **The Spirit is God, and without God man cannot do anything.** Whether we do good or bad it is the Spirit at work. We do bad things because we do not listen to the Spirit in us; we rather listen to the flesh. When we do good things, it means that we are listening to the dictates of the Spirit.

**The SPIRIT which is GOD, is in all human beings, and all human beings are the image of God. Many people say that there is no God in a person who steals, fight, murder, etc. This is erroneous. The Spirit which is God is in all human beings regardless of whether they are good or bad.** Moses, Abraham, Isaac, Jacob, David, Elijah, Samson, Solomon, etc, committed murder, adultry, idolatry and other sins; are you saying that God was not in these great men? God is in all human beings regardless of whether they are black, white, poor, wicked or good. It is the Spirit that does everything in the world. The Spirit is the still voice in us, while the flesh is the loud voice. Satan works with the flesh and is always at war with the Spirit. If a person decide to kill, fornicate, steal, etc, the Spirit which is God will advise him not to do it, and also warn him of the consequences if he does it. Because of his greed, burning desire and lust, he refuse to listen to the dictates of the Spirit which is God; and then commit sins in order to satisfy the desires and lusts of the flesh; thus yielding to Satan.

# INCARNATION

Man had existed in "Spirit form" before he is born into this mundane world. The Spirit becomes embodied in flesh, and the process is referred to as Incatnation. Apart from Adam and Eve, all human beings are born through the womb of a woman. We are told that God formed man with the clay from the earth, and breathe into his nostrils the breath of life. The significance of that "breath" is, that God dwelth inside Adam. Adam was the house of God, and so all human beings are the house of God. We are further told that God sent Adam into a deep sleep and created Eve with a rib from his side. The significance of this "deep sleep" is, that Adam actually died. When he resurrected, that's when a rib from his side was used in creating Eve. **It was the same Spirit that Adam had, which caused our Lord Jesus Christ to re-incarnate as a quickening Spirit.**

**Eve was the first mother on earth. It would have been very easy for God to create human beings in the same manner as He created Eve, but if He did, what would be the use of a woman? God created the womb of a woman through which all human beings, Spirits, Angels and God Himself must pass through into this mundane world. Man is the heaven and woman is the earth, therefore all human beings must first pass through the man into the woman; and is then conceived in the womb and be born into the world. It is the Spirit that actually becomes flesh. The Spirit covers itself with flesh. No one can see the Spirit, and the Spirit does not appear by itself; it is embodied in the flesh. The SPIRIT which is GOD the FATHER is in all human beings. That is why no one can see GOD the SPIRIT.**

No human being would go out naked, and so the Spirit would not appear on its own in this mundane world; it must first cover itself with flesh and then be born into the world as a human being. **The Father is the Creator and Owner of all human beings, Spirits and Angels. Every baby, born or unborn is the replica of God.** Since God created the womb of a woman for Spirits, Angels and Himself to pass through into the world, you can now realise what grievious sins human beings commit when they practise abortion, sterilisation and other forms of birth control. **There is no place in the Bible where human beings are told to practise abortion and other forms of birth control; and God did not give man authority to prevent anyone from coming into the world.** A baby conceived in the womb could be an Angel or God Himself. Remember how Pharaoh tried to kill the baby Moses; and Herod tried to kill the Baby JESUS? They destroyed many innocent children in the hope that they would kill Moses and our Lord Jesus Christ, during their mass extermination of children. From these examples you should realise that no one should practise these sins of abortion and birth control. These sins are murders, and this is how human beings are challenging God Who is the giver of all life. As the giver of all life, He is also the taker of all life; therefore everyone sent to the earth by God has the right to exist, until God takes away his or her life.

## DE-CARNATION: THERE IS NO DEATH

**The Spirit becomes a human being by incarnation. After some time on earth the Spirit de-carnates; that is to say, the Spirit is extracted from the embodiment of the flesh.** Our Lord Jesus Christ said, "Fear not him that destroy the body, but rather fear Him that can destroy both body and soul." There is a Greater Being that lives inside every human being; that is the Spirit which is God. **The Spiritual element or Soul in man, is undestructable. Since the Spirit which is God, dwells in man, it means that man does not die because God cannot die. What really happens is that the Spirit is extracted from the body, and is transfered to another place to perform another duty or assignment.** The Spirit comes out, leaving the body or house behind. It is just like a person that takes off his clothes, then walking away and leave them behind him.

Many people believe that when a person dies that it is the end of that person. Others believe that after a person dies he will not give account for all the sins he has committed when he was alive. This is erroneous, because his Spirit is still alive and have to account to God for the sins he committed while he was in the flesh. When our Lord Jesus Christ spoke about death, He is referring to the Spirit. **When the Spirit is destroyed, that is the end of that person.** That is why our Lord Jesus Christ said, that we should not fear him who destroys the body, but rather fear Him who can destroy both body and soul. He further said, that He is the resurrection and the life; anyone who believe in him, though he was dead yet shall he live. Many people believe that when a person dies and is buried, it is the body with the Spirit that is buried in the ground. It is only the body that is buried; but the Spirit goes up to God to be given other duties; since Angels, Spirits and human beings are all messengers of God, and servants and workers in His Vineyard (the world).

**Many people claim that thay build a church or a temple or a synagogue for God. How can one erect a building for God, and it is God who owns everything including human beings? The scripture clearly state that God does not dwell in temples made with hands. Human beings are the temple of God.** The way in which the Spirit leaves the body is very sorrowful. The person may be shot with a gun, or stabbed with a knife, sword, spear, machette, etc; or drowned in water, or killed in a motor accident; or hit by a tree or stone, or died from sickness, old age, etc. These are agents of evolution. The Spirit is the life of the body. It is God who gives life and it is God who takes life. **All human beings are messengers of God, and man may be used for constructive or destructive purposes. It must be clearly understood that all human beings are the property of God; and, whatever He does with human beings He is entitled to do it, and no one should question Him or murmur and blaspheme against Him. That is why no one should weep or keep a mourning house when someone dies. If you do, it means that you are questioning God for the action He has taken with His creation.** The inhabitants of the world pays more respect to a person when he dies than when he was alive. When he was alive, that person may be neglected when ill or in distress or poverty. He may be denied food, clothing, etc, when he was alive and in need; but at death, thousands of pounds may be spent to give the dead person what they call "a decent funeral." Thus, the person receives more attention and respect when he dies, and in many cases may even be honoured with awards of medals and titles. **What good are all these things to a corpse? Other people saved all their money for their funerals, but refuse to help the poor and needy.** The scripture says, that man in his best state is vanity; he heapeth up riches and knoweth not who shall gather them. It further says, that man is but a shadow. When the FATHER withdraws His Spirit from man, all that remains is just a corpse, a lump of clay. All his lust and selfish greed are in vain. When the Spirit is extracted from the body, it is transfered by God to another place, where it again incarnates and is born again as another human being. **This is known as Re-Incarnation. One Spirit re-incarnates as many persons.**

# RE-INCARNATION

Why is it that as thousands of people die each day, thousands are born daily? And why is it that the world is so densely populated today as compared to hundreds or thousands of years ago? The answer is, because of Re-Incarnation. This is the method used by God to populate the entire world. Human beings are messengers and workers in God's Vineyard (the world). When a human being is born into the world, he is given a specific assignment. At the end of his assignment, the Spirit is extracted from his body by God, and he is transferred to another place to carry out another assignment. For example, **a person may be born in Africa as a black man; after he dies, his Spirit is transferred to England where he is born into an English family as a white man. There is no difference between male and female in the Spirit world, all are one and the same; neither is there any racial discrimination as in this mundane world.**

A person may die as a man and be born as a woman at another place, and vice versa. So also, a white person after death, his Spirit may re-incarnate as a black person at another place. This means that one Spirit re-incarnates several times at different places; ie, One Spirit Many Persons. For example, a human being that is born in the world today, could be in the world for the third, tenth or eighteenth time. Only God knows who every human being is. Whether you are in the world fifty or a hundred times, the FATHER knows who you are. You could be Abraham, Nimrod, Jezebel, or one of the Prophets of old; but He knows you. **That is why a human being who is currently on earth for say the tenth time, is accountable to God for all the sins which he has committed during the previous nine times that he was on earth.** That is why our Lord Jesus Christ came into the world to sacrifice His blood to redeem mankind to God. If He had not come, people like Abraham, Moses, David, Solomon and the other great Patriarchs would not be saved.

**That is why, only when you are baptised into the Brotherhood of the Cross and Star ( the New Kingdom of God on earth ), all the sins which you have committed from the time of Adam to the time of your baptism, are forgiven; because you have to repent and confess all your sins; and be immersed in water three times in the name of the Father, Son and Holy Spirit; unlike how people are baptised in the church denominations.** If when people die their Spirits did not re-incarnate, there would only be a small number of people in the world as compared to the present time. It is now a population explosion.

At this end of time, all the people from Adam downwards are here on earth today, to face the Judgement Day. This Great Day will come very shortly. All the Patriarchs, Prophets and Apostles are here on earth today. All the people of old are here. **Jehovah God and His Christ and all His heavenly hosts are now here on earth; and all what you see and hear happening in the world today, are in preparation for the Judgement Day.** That is why the primary teachings of our Lord Jesus Christ and the Holy Spirit of Truth now personified is, that we should love one another regardless of race, colour, creed or status in life. No one knows who the other human being is. A human being may be a Prophet, Angel or God Himself. That is why we are warned to "Love ye one another." The scripture says to "Honour all men, love the Brotherhood, fear God and honour the King." The Brotherhood is God, Christ, Angels, human beings and all things animate and inanimate. The animals and all the animate things are our brethren also. The commandment which says "Thou shalt not kill" applies to all animals, birds, fishes and other living things.

Every animal on earth represents a human being. Every time an animal is killed, a human being dies at that particular time. That is why Abel was killed by Cain soon after he (Abel) had killed the lamb. In this New Kingdom of God (Brotherhood of the Cross and Star) no one is allowed to kill even a fly or mosquito. All human beings must return to that "First Love" that existed in the garden of Eden, where human beings, animals, birds, fishes, creeping things and plants lived together in love. When a human being return to Spirit form, God can send him to carry out certain assignments in the animal, birds, fishes or plants kingdoms.

For example, a Spirit may be called Michael in the Spirit world. By incarnation he is now known as Christopher on the planet earth. Christopher after spending a certain time on earth dies and his Spirit re-incarnates as an elephant in the animal kingdom, and is called Betsie. After a time Betsie dies and her Spirit returns to the Spirit world as Michael. After a time, Michael may be sent to the plant kingdom to become a tree in the forest and is known as Yukon. After a number of years, Yukon the tree was cut down by man, and the Spirit returns again to the Spirit world as Michael. Even prominent trees represents human beings. That is why when a prominent tree in a village falls down, a prominent person in that village dies. All what is happening in the world today is the fulfillment of the Word of God. Our Lord Jesus Christ said, that those who kill with the sword will be killed by the sword. This statement of our Lord Jesus Christ, applies to everything. If you do good you can expect good to be done to you; if you do evil, you must also expect evil to be done to you. Those who take delight to wage war against other people and kill with guns, swords, machettes, bombs, etc, will be killed by these things.

If you discriminate, hate and kill people because of their race, colour or creed, these things will also happen to you; it may not happen in this present life, but when you are re-incarnated you will experience these things. This applies to people who practise abortion or abandon their babies; those who steal, tell lies or deny needy people of food, clothes, etc. The Bible says that whatever you sow that shall you reap. A person who slaughter animals, may become an animal when his Spirit re-incarnates, so that he also will be slaughtered like the animals that he killed. **That is why we should not eat meat or fish, because it is our brethren that we are eating. God did not instruct man to eat meat, fish, etc, for food.**

The manifestation of God on earth is in human beings. Human beings had existed in Spirit form. Spirits and Angels are the same and they are servants of God, and they cannot be seen by human eyes. From time to time Jehovah God sends His Spirits or Angels to the earth, to carry out specific assignments. Their assignments may be constructive or destructive. Spirits may be seen either by (a) Dreams or Visions, or (b) Physical Manifestation.

### DREAMS OR VISIONS

Spirits are seen when the Dreamer or Visioner is not conscious, but they are rather in a state of trance. For example, the visions of John the Divine on the Isle of Pathmos, as recorded in the Book of Revelation.

### PHYSICAL MANIFESTATION

When Spirits are sent to earth they will take on the form of life there; that is, they will appear as human beings. They may be seen for seconds, minutes, or hours and then disappear. **This is called Short Term Manifestation.** Examples, (1) The Angels that appeared to the virgin Mary and to the

Shepherds. (2) The Angels that appeared to Mary Magdalene after our Lord Jesus Christ was risen. (3) The Angels that appeared to the Apostles while our Lord Jesus Christ was ascending to heaven. On the other hand, Spirits may be seen on earth for days, weeks, months or years. **This is called Long Term Manifestation.** The Spirits are born through the womb as babies; they grow up into adults; they then carry out their assignments and after that they depart this world after say, twenty, forty or ninety years, according to the length of time which the FATHER has given for completion of their assignments. All human beings on earth have specific assignments during their life time. For example, a human being may be assigned to a particular family, community, village, town or country to carry out certain assignments. He grew up from infancy, goes to school, college or university; and later become a doctor, farmer, lawyer, professor, prime minister, president, pope or king etc. After the end of his assignment he is transferred in Spirit form by God, to perform other assignments at a different place.

Heaven is God's throne and earth His footstool. When in heaven, God will be in the form of an Angel. On earth He will appear as a Human Being. Jehovah God has visited His Vineyard ( the World ) from time to time, and He reveals Himself to whosoever it pleases Him. Since the creation of the world, God has sent certain special human beings to the earth to carry out " Specific Assignments." Where one has finished another one takes over. It is like building a house. The person who does the roof is not the one who does the floor and walls. The plumbing is done by another person; so does the electrical wiring, carpentry, painting, etc. **Adam, Enoch, Noah, Melchezedek, Moses, Elijah, John the Baptist, our Lord Jesus Christ and the Holy Spirit of Truth- Leader Olumba Olumba Obu, are all GODLY Names. They were all sent to earth to carry out specific assignments, and each one's assignment differs from the other.**

## ADAM'S ASSIGNMENT

Adam came into the world by being moulded from the clay, and God breathed into his nostrils the breath of life. The significance of this " Breath " is that God dwelth inside Adam. Adam is the house of God, and he came into existence for that purpose. If you go to work on your farm, the first thing that you would do is to erect a hut for you to shelter. You are told that God does not dwell in houses built with hands. All human beings are the house of God. Adam was the dwelling place of the Almighty God. The Holy Spirit dwelth in him. It was the same Spirit that Adam had which caused our Lord Jesus Christ to re-incarnate as a " Quickening Spirit." It is the Spirit of our Lord Jesus Christ that re-incarnates as the Holy Spirit of Truth. That is why our Lord Jesus Christ said, " It is expedient that I go away, for if I go not away the Comforter will not come; but if I depart I will send Him unto yiou." One Spirit re-incarnates to many persons.

## ENOCH'S ASSIGNMENT

Enoch came into the world to inspect if all the creations of God were in their respective order as they were created. He was an Inspector, and when he inspected the position of things, he discovered that they were not in the order as God had created them and he submitted his findings to God. That was why God said that He regretted creating man in His own image, and that it repented Him that He had made man on the earth, and it grieved Him to His heart. Enoch submitted his final report that sin had dominated mankind; and God had no alternative than to take the decision to destroy mankind and the world.

## NOAH'S ASSIGNMENT

God remember His promise to Adam; that except a Holy blood was shed, his sins would not be atoned for. In order to fulfil His promise to Adam, God did not destroy all mankind, but He saved eight persons. Noah came into the world to save the remnant of the children of God. He preached repentance to the people for 120 years, but they ignored, taunted and ridiculed him. That is exactly what this present generation is doing. After taking his family along with one pair (male and female) of each kind of animate things into the Ark, the rest were destroyed by the Great Flood. God made a covenant that He would never destroy the world again with flood, no matter how sinful the world might be.

## MELCHEZEDEK'S ASSIGNMENT

The main assignment of Melchezedek was to bless the people who were saved after the flood, and to set all things in order, because despite the flood mankind would continue to sin. He entered into a covenant with God, never to destroy the world again with flood. He had a duty to teach and demonstrate righteousness, peace, love, forgiveness, patience and other Godly Virtues to the people. Melchezedek was God Almighty that became flesh and dwelth among the people. Only Abraham recognised Him. He blessed him, and Abraham paid Him tithes which was the equivalent of one-tenth of his booty in acknowledgement of the Divine Priesthood of Melchezedek. People did not recognised Him as God on earth, just like what the people did during the time of our Lord Jesus Christ; and, like what this generation is now doing to the Holy Spirit of Truth persomified in our midst.

## THE ASSIGNMENTS OF MOSES

Jehovah God and His Christ told Abraham that his seed would sujourn in a strange land, and will remain in bondage for 400 years; and after that God would judge the nation that enslaved them (Acts 7 v 6 - 7). Moses came to deliver the children of Israel out of bondage in Egypt, in fulfillment of God's promise. He led them out of Egypt and disappeared on his way to the promised land. Without the coming of Moses, the Israelites would not have been delivered. Pharaoh was the greatest king on earth with his army and weapons of war. Who was Moses to appear before him and demanded the release of the Israelites? Moses did not possess guns, swords, machettes and other weapons of war; nor did he had an army. Moses was in fact God manifested in another Form to reveal His power and glory (Romans 9 v 17). He appeared before Pharaoh with only a crook staff and perform all the great wonders in Egypt. Many people do not believe that it is God only who kills and keep alive. You have heard what happened to Pharaoh and his army. Moses delivered the Israelites from Egypt, gave them commandments and set them on their course to Caanan.

## THE MISSION OF ELIJAH

Elijah came to punish all those who did not abide by the commandments and ordinances of God, particularly idolaters. Elijah was a Destroyer, and he came specifically to destroy the worshippers of Baal. It is the same God performing His assignments through different persons. When you continue to say that God is Love and cannot kill, and that it is only Satan that kills; who sent down fire from heaven to destroy 400,000 worshippers of Baal? (St Luke 9 v 52 - 56). Elijah came to reveal to that generation that God is Alpha and Omega; and that He is the only power to kill and keep alive. Therefore, all those who do not submit to His government will be destroyed like the worshippers of Baal.

## THE MISSION OF JOHN THE BAPTIST

John the Baptist came in the Spirit of Elijah ( Luke 1 v 17, Malacai 4 v 5 - 6 ). The Spirit of Elijah came back in the person of John the Baptist to perform a different assignment. He came to prepare the hearts and minds of the people to accept Christ.

He preached repentance and purification. Without him, nobody would have accepted or believed in the Deity of our Lord Jesus Christ. He spent most of the time in the wilderness fasting and praying. The scripture says, "Blessed are the pure in heart for they shall see God." John taught the people purity of hearts and minds so that they would recognised the promised Messiah. Peter, James, John and other disciples of our Lord Jesus Christ, were disciples of John the Baptist.

## THE MISSION OF OUR LORD JESUS CHRIST

His assignment was to shed His precious blood for the remmission of sins. He came in fulfillment of God's promise to Adam: that without the shedding of a Holy blood his sins would not be atoned for, and man would not regain the paradise lost in the garden of Eden. Adam had defiled the house of God. That is why our Lord Jesus Christ said, "Foxes have holes and birds have nests, but the Son of man hath no place to lay His head." God's first house in Adam was defiled, and the Holy Spirit could not dwell in him. The shedding of the precious blood of our Lord Jesus Christ gave rise to the purification of the house of Adam, and the arrival of the Holy Spirit on earth ( St John 16 v 7 - 8 ). The assignment of our Lord Jesus Christ is the greatest. Without the shedding of His precious blood, God Almighty would not have come down to earth to dwell with men in flesh and bone. The blood of cows and goats could not atone for our sins and purify us. Through the precious blood of our Lord Jesus Christ, all our sins from Adam till now are forgiven.

## THE ASSIGNMENT OF THE HOLY SPIRIT OF TRUTH

Now that the Holy blood has been shed for the remmission of sins, the Holy Spirit of Truth promised by our Lord Jesus Christ has come for the final assignments. Read St John 16 v 7 - 13. The assignments of the Holy Spirit of Truth are:-
  1. To establish the Kingdom of God on earth; a New Heaven and a New Earth wherein dwelleth righteousness.
  2. To reform sinners and bring them up to the standard required by God.
  3. To teach all nations the ways of God, and rebuke sinners.
  4. To judge all nations; and
  5. To rule all nations with a rod of iron.

**The Kingdom of God on earth is the Brotherhood of the Cross and Star; and its Sole Spiritual Head- Leader Olumba Olumba Obu, is the Holy Spirit of Truth personified. It is only the Holy Spirit of Truth that can reform sinners.** No other person has succeeded in changing a sinner and let him refrain completely from committing sins and vices.

We have now learned that One Spirit re-incarnates several times. Therefore our fore parents whom we claim are dead are in fact alive in new bodies at some other places in the world. The Almighty Father Himself has re-incarnated several times on earth; but the hearts and minds of the inhabitants of this earth are so focused on the carnal things and worldly pleasures, that they fail to recognise Him. It is said that God is in the world but the world do not know Him, but He knows everyone. The Almighty God and His heavenly Hosts are on earth right now.

## SUMMARY

Man had existed in Spirit Form only. All human beings had existed in Spirit. Man and God is One entity. Man is part and parcel with God. The "real man" is SOUL. Soul is a Spiritual Spark of GOD or SOURCE. Soul, Spirit and Angel are the same. All human beings have this Spirit embodied in them. The SPIRIT which is GOD is indestructable. There is no death because God cannot die. The appropriate term for death is "Transfer." The Spirit is extracted from the body and is sent by God to another place to carry out other assignments. One Spirit can re-incarnate several times; ie One Spirit, Many Persons.

The real man is "Soul." Man, Soul, Spirit and Angel are inter-related. They all refer to One thing: ie "SELF" in many Colours or Forms; evolving, evolved and highly evolved. Soul is bodiless, extremely brilliant and highly potent; being a Spiritual Spark of GOD (the SOURCE of Energy and Life). Man is the apex of creation. When the Soul (Spirit) becomes flesh, it is clothed in Five Bodies: (1) Etheric body (Mind), (2) Mental body, (3) Causal body, (4) Astral body and (5) Physical body. The Soul takes on these bodies in that order. When you look at a human being, he has all these bodies, but he can only see the Physical body.

# CHAPTER 13

# AFTER 1999 SOMETHING SPECTACULAR WILL HAPPEN

Everlasting Gospel Delivered by: Leader Olumba Olumba Obu
Sole Spiritual Head of the Universe.

First Lesson: Romans 8 v 14
Second Lesson: St. John 15 v 9
Golden Text: Revelations 2 v 4 - 5

This voice is coming from the highest plane to all parts of the world. All the nations of the world should listen attentively to this Lesson. Let all the trees in the forest, the animals in the forest, the birds in the air, the fishes in the sea, human beings, angels and all created and uncreated things, listen to this message because it is a message for the entire world. The time for the judgement of God is at hand. You have already been told that judgement will begin from the house of God. Let nations, human beings and angels not joke with the time. You have money, children, clothes, houses and other things in the world, but I have one thing against you. You have health, landed properties, children, husbands and wives, and many other things and none of these things are evil. Do not forget about these words: "Heaven and earth and the fullness thereof belongs to God." The man of God asked, "who shall ascend into the hill of the Lord? or who shall stand in His Holy place? He that has clean hands and a pure heart, who hath not lifted up his soul unto vanity nor sworn deceitfully. He shall receive the blessing from the Lord, and righteousness from the God of his salvation." That is why this message is sent to you from the Most High, to all human beings, animals, trees, birds, fishes and angels, so that no person may live to regret.

This message is also directed to the millionaires, professors, judges, highly learned persons, kings, emperors and all sorts of people in the world. Whether you go to church or not; whether you make concoctions or not; whether you are a necromancer or not, whether you are a man or a woman, black, white or coloured; this message is for the entire world. The wrath of God will be visited on all human beings, all animals and all of God's creation which have not walked along the path of rectitude. The time for the judgement of the Lamb of God is at hand. Since God is Love, Mercy, Truth, Patience, Humility, Self-control, Peace, Joy, Lowliness of heart; that is why He has chosen to send this message to the entire world. God is not slow to redeem His promise, but He has long patience and wants every person to become truly repentant. He had sent this same message to the people of Sodom and Gomorrah. When He heard about their transgressions, the attrocities that they have committed, their indulgence in roguery, fornication, adultry, whoremongering, etc, He had to send this message to the two cities. If you like open the book of Isaiah 1 v 10 - 20; when you get home read this portion and you will discover that the message given to you today, was sent to the two cities of Sodom and gomorrah. The world today is the same Sodom and Gomorrah.

You who stay at home building houses and say that you are building a house for God; when you indulge in roguery, you say that you are doing it for God. God has told you as He has told the two cities of Sodom and Gomorrah that the sacrifices of unrighteousness are not pleasing to Him. All that you are doing from day to day are the same things that the people of old were doing. If you read the book of God, you will discover that there is nothing new, everything that is happening now is exactly what happened in the past. The world of Noah is exactly what we have today. When Noah preached for a period of 120 years and the people paid deaf ears to his preaching, this is exactly what you are doing today. As the people of old put the words of Noah into disdain, so are you putting the words of God today into disdain. The Ark which he built as instructed by God, was converted into a public toilet by the people of those days. It also became a place of salvation and redemption when somebody by accident fell into the excreta became well, so also others who had difficulties had to go and swim in the excreta in order to become well. No one has ever stopped to think about repentance. The only thing that prevailed was that whenever anyone was sick he was always directed to go to Noah's Ark and fall into the faeces and he would become well. Look at the world today. What is happening today is exactly what happened in the days of Noah. If the people of old had listened to the voice of Noah which was the voice of the Most High God, then God would not have destroyed the world. If the people of the two cities of Sodom and Gomorrah had listened to the voice of Noah which was the voice of the Almighty God, God would not have destroyed the two cities. Today is the last of all the ages, the last of the era. This is why He has directed this message to all the creations of God, to all the winged creatures, the wind and the hazards of the weather, the rain and the sun, and all the created and uncreated things.

This is the time for the judgement of God; this is the time when all trees must bend and all tongues sing His praises. All human beings, all animals, birds, fishes and creeping things have to recognise God now. Remember that in the begining there was only one flock and one shepherd. Now everybody is staging a return to the Garden of Eden, so that we may all remain in one flock under one shepherd. Remember that at that particular time, there was no wars or rumours of wars, no quarrelling, fighting, drinking, fornication, adultery, concoctions, charms, talisman or any evil was found there during this time. Human beings, animals, birds, fishes and all created things lived together. Together with all of these things, God Himself lived there; our Lord Jesus Christ lived there; all the angels, the good people of God, human beings, animals, birds, fishes, trees and other created things lived there, because they remained in that one love. By what were they led? They were led by the Spirit of God. You are told that all those who are led by the Spirit of God, they alone are the children of God. When we say this to you, it seems as though we are speaking in a strange language to you. What is the Spirit? The Spirit is God. What is God? God is Love. What is Love? Love is Mercy. What is Mercy? Mercy is Humility. What is Humility? Humility is good Conduct. What is good Conduct? It is to serve one another. The sum total of all that are enumerated is what is called God, and that is how to be led by the Spirit of God.

In those days, man did not kill animals or fowls, and man was not bitten by snakes or animals. They all existed in love, and lived together side by side. You are true witnesses to the fact that the animals, trees, etc. did not create themselves, all came into existence by the spoken Word which is the Spirit. After creating all these things, God saw that it was good, and so He sanctioned all of them. You are witnesses to all these good things and you admire the flowers and the green leaves and say how beautiful they are. Sometimes you observe how the domestic animals are very good and beautiful; the goats, hens, sheep, cows and all the others. God created all these things and saw that they were good, because He Himself is good; that is why He created all these things and wanted them to live together in love. At that time, there was no distinction between human beings, fishes and animals, all of them walked according to the Spirit; according to the instructions of God; according to the laws of God; according to the truth, humility, patience and all the virtues of God.

There was no curse, juju, mermaid, fornication and whoremongering, because all of them were led by the Spirit of God, and they complied with the instructions of our Lord Jesus Christ, "Love ye one another." This is what He has said today, "Nevertheless I have somewhat against you because thou hast left the first love." Adam was told to eat all the fruits in the garden, but he should not taste of the one in the middle of the garden, because it was the tree of good and evil. Any day that he would taste of that fruit he will surely die. From the day that they had tasted that fruit, they departed from God. From that day until today, no person walks by the Spirit of God. This is what is used in condemning all human beings, trees, all animals and birds, because they no longer walk in the love of God. It was for this same reason that the world of Noah was destroyed, because the people did not want to live together in love, and love the trees, animals, birds, fishes, creeping things and all the other things, and to remain in the love of God; that is why that world was destroyed.

During the time of Lot, the two cities of Sodom and Gomorrah refused to walk according to the instructions of God; according to His love; according to His grace, humility and His truth; for this reason these two cities were destroyed. It is stated also, that the Father wanted to destroy the world for the third time, and His Son offered to come and fertilise the ground, and put manure around it; and then offer Himself as a supreme sacrifice, to see if man would repent. You have forgotten one thing; He said that "If I go and manure the whole place and if the people become truly repentant, then they should be saved; but if after I have manured the whole place, they still refuse to repent, then they can be destroyed."

**FIRST LESSON: ROMANS 8 v 14**
" For as many as are led by the Spirit of God, they are the Sons of God."

Brethren have you heard what is read to you? That is your only channel of salvation. That was the first instruction that was given to Adam and Eve. He said, "I will teach you everything, you will not listen to the angels, or any other person, but listen attentively to Me, because I will teach you everything." The only thing that we have to do is to listen to the Almighty God which is the voice of the Spirit. If we listen to Him attentively and abide by His instructions which says, "Love ye one another" and we love every person as we love ourselves, then we are saved. Adam was the son of God for as long as he continued to keep the instructions of God, but from the time he ceased to comply with the instructions of God, he was no longer the son of God. God is the Word. The Holy Spirit is the Word. If you do not comply yourselves with the instructions of God, it means that you are not children of God. When you erect a building, to whom do you build this house? When you marry a wife, to whom have you married this wife? My duty and your duty is to walk according to the instructions of God. The same thing was said by our Lord Jesus Christ when He said, "I can on my own do nothing, as I hear I judge, and My judgement is righteous, for I do not seek My own will but the will of He who sent Me." He was the Son of man, the Son of God and God Himself, because He complied with the instructions of God.

Why Abraham and Moses were not the sons of God? It is because they erred somewhere. The reason why our Lord Jesus Christ who was the Son of David, Joseph, Abraham; and who was born by the Virgin Mary became the Son of God was because He complied Himself with the instructions of God. It is irrelevant whether you have one leg or one eye, whether you are a tree or a stone or an animal; once you comply with the instructions of God, you are a child of God. You will be surprised that none of the things which we see is new, healing the sick is not new, raising the dead, making the deaf to hear, or the lame to walk; all these things are not new; what is new is complying yourself and walking according to the insrructions of God. You must always walk according to the promptings of the Spirit. Where you are directed to go is where you go; when God say you must not do a particular thing you should not do it. If you comply with this, then you are a child of God. Sometimes you argue that "I have never committed murder, I have never commited theft and I have never fornicated," but have you never disobeyed the voice of God?

Do you not know that in as much as you do not obey the voice of God, you do not walk according to the Spirit? You do not walk according to His love, and you do not walk according to His truth. His word is life, peace, truth, power and His word is everlasting. You do not have to speak according to your own volition, but you have to speak according to the voice you have heard; and you do not have to do anything according to your own promptings, but you have to act according to the promptings of the Spirit. The only thing that Christ used in conquering the whole world is that He always act according to the promptings of the Spirit. Since the creation of the world there has never been anyone who walked according to the dictates of the Holy Spirit. The only person who has done this is our Lord Jesus Christ. Have you ever heard that He committed murder? Have you ever heard that He committed theft? Have you ever heard that He committed any act of sin? Did He ever hate anyone? Have you ever heard that He quarrelled with any person? Because He was led by the Spirit of God, He was led by the Father. When He was praying, He was always listening attentively to the Father. If the Father said He should run, He would run; if the Father said He should sit down, He would sit down; He obeyed whatever He was told to do by the Father. If you like you can read through the book of St Matthew or the synoptic gospels, and you will see that all the things written in all these pages; that our Lord Jesus Christ had never arrogated anything to Himself; He said that everything came from the Father. He says that the Father said this, that the Father did that; He never credited anything to Himself.

Have you not heard that when the Holy Spirit descended upon Him, that He was led by the Spirit into the desert? Not that He led the Spirit into the desert, but that He was led into the desert by the Spirit. He Himself would not have wanted to go into the desert, but He was led by the Spirit into the desert. Whatever He did was as directed by the Holy Spirit, because He had surrendered Himself as an instrument of the Father. Therefore wherever He was taken by the Spirit, He had to follow. Read all the words of our Lord Jesus Christ, and you will discover that He was referring everything to the Father. He never said that He Himself said anything, but He always said that the Father said or did. He said, " I can on my own do nothing, what the Father tells Me that is what I say because His instruction is everlasting life." God cannot tell you to go and commit murder, or prepare concoctions; He cannot tell you to go and marry a wife or to beat up someone. He cannot tell you to do anything evil. It was spoken by the mouth of the Prophets that God will teach you everything, and that those who learn of Him will follow Him. There is nothing in the world that can lead you to the wisdom of truth, no human being can lead you, no tree, no animal, no bird or fish; nothing at all created can lead you to the accurate knowledge of the truth; it is only Our Lord Jesus Christ Who can teach you and lead you to the truth. Remember when the people said, how can He behave in this way, He has never seen the walls of any classroom;

why is He so intelligent and indulgent? He told them that any person who practise My words will discover whether they come from Me or from the Father. He also continued to say that anyone who speak out of his own volition is looking for his own glory, but whoever speaks the words of He who has sent Him is the truth and there is no guile in him.

Have you not heard His instructions today? "Continue ye in My love as I have continued in My Father's love." God is Love; our Lord Jesus Christ is Love, and He has taught us how to love. We should therefore continue to abide in His love. No children does anything apart from what their father does, and no servant can do anything apart from what he has seen his master doing. As long as the son does not do what the father is doing, such is no longer the son. Any slave that does not listen attentively to the voice of his master is not a good slave. When you say that you are building a house for God, when did God actually tell you to build a house for Him? It has been spoken by the Prophets that God does not dwell in houses made with hands. "What type of building will you erect for Me, did not My hands create all these things?" Oh ye disobedient and heady fellows who do not believe in the words of God. You continue to resist the will of the Holy Spirit, even as your forefathers did. When you kill someone you say that he does not walk according to the instructions of God; or you see somebody who belongs to another church, you cast him into prison or beat him up and say that he is causing confusion everywhere. I ask you, is this how to preach the words of God? If you are not led by the Spirit of God, what are you? Can you see how pitiful we are? Do not boast in any wisdom of this earth. But boast in this wisdom of truth. He has brought love to us because He Himself is Love; the Son is Love; the Holy Spirit is Love; therefore it is a must that we love one another. We have no other instruction at this end of time, the only instruction is that we should love one another and continue to abide in this love as He has loved us.

Adam departed from the love, that is why the world was visited with wretchedness. Our forefathers departed from this love by committing murder, stealing, committing fornication, whoremongering, concoctions, charms, talisman and doing all sorts of things; that is why they fell from the way of rectitude. Go and read all the records of our Lord Jesus Christ, about His life and teachings; He did not teach anything apart from love. What do you think it is to walk by the Spirit of God? It is to comply with the teachings of our Lord Jesus Christ, because His teachings constitute life, love, and it is God. It says, love your enemies and pray fervently for those who persecute you, so that you may resemble your Father who is in heaven, because He causes the rain to fall on the just and unjust, and the sun to shine on both the just and the unjust. If you love those who love you, and hate those who hate you, what spectacular thing have you done? Abraham, Moses and Adam did the same thing. We should be perfect even also as our heavenly Father is perfect. You should not eat any animals, nor kill the birds or fishes, for this reason also you should not tell lies, commit murder or whoremongery, beat any person, or cast anyone into prison. If you read Genesis chapter one, you will discover that after God created man and every other thing; He prescribed the type of food that man should eat. He said, "You should eat from all the trees bearing seeds and fruits; these seeds and fruits shall be your food." He gave man the superintendency over the animals in the bush, the fishes and birds, over all the creeping things; that he should superintend over all these things and love them. He did not give him the instruction to kill the snake, lizard or any animal, or to cut down any trees. God Himself does not commit any atrocity, therefore He cannot direct any one to kill anything. Now that it is said that a goat and cow is sacrificed to a mermaid or for concoction; I want to ask you whether any of these things have goats or any animals? All these things are created by God Himself.

Now that you say that you are indulging in the preparation of concoctions, or that you are worshipping nermaids, charms, talisman, concoctions, etc; I tell you that all the things that you find, whether they are bark of trees, roots or herbs, sand and gravel or any other thing; are these things not created by God Himself? How do you know that when you say woe unto this tree that you have not abused God? How do yuo know that when you say to animal, woe unto you, that the animal you have cursed is not God Himself? You think that God is as stupid as you are. When you remain and have nothing wrong with you, for no reason you begin to fight and struggle with one another. He has divided Himself into all the things that you see in the world. Some parts in the ground, these are the Spirits, some in the animals, some in the trees and all the other things that you see. All these things are created by the Spirit of God, and these are God Himself. All these things are human. The sand, stones, trees, animals are humans and all of them are your brothers. It is therefore encumbent on all the human beings to love the trees, animals, birds, fishes and creeping things. He has not directed that you should go and worship a tree, or pluck leaves and pound them into concoctions and rub them on your body. As He is protecdting you, so is He protecting all the other things; as He loves you, so He loves all the other things. As He directs you, so does He direct all the other things.

## SECOND LESSON: ST JOHN 15 V 9
" As the Father hath loved Me, so have I loved you; continue ye in My love."

Have you seen what it is to walk by the promptings of the Holy Spirit? There was love in existence from the begining of the world. That love was with God, and that love was with the Son and the love is with the Holy Spirit. How many categories of love do you have? It is only One Love. Christ said, "As the Father has loved Me, so I love you, abide ye in My love." You have no other city or country in which you live; your country is Love. The country of the fishes is Love; the country of the trees and animals is Love, and we have to live inside this Love. What is the Father? The Father is Love. What is the Word? The Word is Love. What is the Holy Spirit? The Holy Spirit is Love. What is Love? Love is you. If you do not love the person that you see with your eyes, it means that you have no love. You have to love Me and I will reciprocate and all of us have to love one another, because we are members of the family of God.

Whosoever love God must love his brother also. If you love God you must love the fishes. If you love God you must love the animals. If you love God you must love the grass. If you love God you must love the trees, the creeping things, the winged creatures and all the other creations of God, because He Himself is found in all of these things. If you abide in His love you will never be annoyed, you will not quarrel with anyone, you will not steal and you will not commit any of the other sins and vices. If you steal money in order to build a house, or cast someone into prison, it means that you have no love. Do not look for God anywhere else; look for Him in Love. Do not look for our Lord Jesus Christ somewhere else; look for Him in Love..Do not look for the children of God somewhere else; look for them inside Love, because Love is the begining and the end. That is why we are told today to continue in that love. Paul asked, "What shall separate me from the love of Christ? Is it hunger, sickness, imprisonment, wretchedness or death? Nevertheless nothing can separate me from the love of God which is Christ Jesus."

If we love the brethren, it means that we are walking according to the promptings of the Spirit; it means that we are walking with the Father, the Son and the Holy Spirit. Everything will pass away, but love will never pass away forever. God loved the Son, but He surrendered the Son to come and die in order to redeem Me and you. The Son loved the Father, that is why He accepted to comply with these instructions, and because of the love He has for us; He accepted to come and shed His precious blood for your redemption and Mine. We must therefore reciprocate the love which our Lord Jesus Christ has for us by loving the Father, the Son and the Holy Spirit. Whoever love his brother has passed completely from death to life. Knowledge will pass away, prophecy will cease, visions will vanish and all other things will pass away but love will endure forever. Knowledge is man made, but love comes from God. Love is not grievious to anyone. Love is the fulfillment of the law. Love does not tell lies, is not annoyed, does not hate, fornicate, commit adultry, steal or deceive anyone. It is because man departed from the first love that death, sickness, poverty and all the encumbrances came into the world.

Go and tell all the people in the world, the angels and all the creations of God; because I am declaring this from high heaven, that whoever does not have love is in death. So brethren, obedience is better than sacrifice. Since Adam departed from this first love, do you not see what has become of the world? Send someone to a university to study medicine and let him return to cure all sicknesses; I tell you that this is nonsense because if you have no love, you will always be faced with difficulties, problems, sickness, wretchedness, death, hunger and all other things. What is the wisdom behind your killing of somebody in order to get money; or casting someone into prison in order to get money; or fighting with somebody in order to get money; or doing any other thing to acquire money, when you know that by doing all these things you will continue to be wretched? Sometimes you say, I want to be a millionaire, a traditional ruler, a great man or to have prominent children. Have you not heard what has been read to you, that whoever does not have love abides in death? Have you not heard that the wages of sin is death? That the gift of God is eternal life in Christ Jesus? Do you not want eternal life? Whoever hates his brother remains in death, and he has no share in this kingdom of God. It is because the Father does not want you to perish, and the whole world, that He has sent you this last message. This is an everlasting gospel which will never be preached again, and you will have to comply yourself with it, in order to have everlasting life. This gospel must be preached to the entire world, that is why we have to tape record it and have it produced in pamplets, and then distribute it throughout the world, so that no one will be able to say that they did not know about this gospel.

When you argue that you have not paid tithe, and because of this you have annoyed God, that is useless because God does not want your money. When you say that you have no child, therefore when you die there will be nothing to remember you by; do not think about such things because God is not interested. When you complain that you have not built a house like those of your age group; God does not want any building. Any day that He wants a house He will build one for Himself. God only want one thing from you, and that is that you must go back to that first love. When you argue that you cannot attend service, you have no white garment and you cannot go barefooted; God is not interested in your white garment. There is only one thing that He has used in condemning you from the time of Adam. The punishment besetting the world today is not such that you should bear, but because your fore fathers and all of you have departed from the first love, that is why you are visited with all these tribulations. It is prophesied that you should not be puffed up. Any day that you are puffed up, the candlestick will be removed from its place.

What is there in the world that you can boast of? You cannot boast about anything apart from love. When you have love, you have life and you have everything. Of what use it is for you to be a king, a president, a governor, a minister, a millionaire, a learned person, or that you have wisdom? All these things are useless. Sometimes you argue that you want to serve your country, constituency, church and your community. Which are you going to serve in? Or you say that you want to establish a government and leave the leadership to your children. With what are you going to do all these things? Do you know where you and your constituency and church will go? Since God does not take pleasure in the death of an evil person, that is why He has directed this message to you, so that you may become truly repentant and enter into everlasting life.

*After 1999, I have told you before and I am repeating now, that Something Spectacular will happen. All the Gospels preached and tape recorded and written, will come to pass at that particular time. The testimony of our Lord Jesus Christ is the Spirit of prophesy. There has never been a time that the Word of God touches down and return empty handed.*

**GOLDEN TEXT: REVELATION 2 V 4 - 5**
"Nevertheless, I have somewhat against thee, because thou hast left thy first love. Remember therefore from whence thou hast fallen, and repent, and do the first works; or else I will come unto thee quickly and will remove thy candlestick out of his place, except thou repent."

Brethren, have you seen how great the love of God is for us? Have you any argument to put forward, because I see the whole world as people who do not have love. No church denomination, no black man, no white man, no coloured, no facet of society, no institution have love. That is why you are overshadowed with darkness. This gospel must be submitted to Me, if not today, by tommorrow. This gospel must be written and circulated to all the children of men in the world. If you have no children, money, work and relations you cannot be condemned for these things. There is only one thing used in condemning you and that is, you have left that first love. If you perish today it is not because you have no husband, wife, children, a job, or that you have not administered to the poor, but you will perish because you have departed from the first love of God. Compare this gospel with the writings in Isaiah 1 v 10 - 20, summarised in the Revelations, "Nevertheless, I have somewhat against thee, because thou hast left thy first love. Remember therefore from whence thou hast fallen, and repent and do the first works; or else I will come unto thee quickly, and will remove thy candlestick out of his place, except thou repent."

This gospel serves as the final stage of the changeover. Therefore you have been given a commission to go and preach this gospel to the millionaires, governors, kings, presidents, emperors and principalities. Tell them that if they do not return to the first love and repent, the candlestick will be removed from its place. Go and preach to the Pope, Archbishop of Canterbury, Pastors, Reverends, Evangelists and Apostles; and all those who have formed their own churches and have many branches. Tell them that if they do not return to that first love of God, God is prepared to remove the candlestick from its place. You realise that He searches the hearts and reins, and that He does not look at things on the surface, but looks deep inside. He searches your heart and brain. He does not look at these beautifully decorated cities and their high standard of civilisation. If you do not repent, then the candlestick has to be removed from its place. If anybody ask you why the world is beset with problems and difficulties, tell them that the world has departed from the first love of God. God does not look for your money, wisdom, houses, or anything at all. He wants you to have that love, and extend that love to all His creations. He says that we should not steal, fornicate, indulge in whoremongery, make concoctions and you should love every person as you love yourself.. Love is not clothing, food or building. It is that you should not impute sins on anyone; think evil about anyone, or speak evil about anyone. Do not disregard anyone, despise anyone or sow the seeds of discord. Take everybody as yourself. It is said that the children are not the ones to provide for the parents, but it is the duty of the parents to provide for the children. God does not look for your wives, children, money or clothing, but He does not want you to perish.

Remember when Peter took up the sword to cut off the ear of one of the servants of the high priest; our Lord Jesus Christ told him to put away his sword, because whoever lives by the sword must surely die by the sword. Whoever kills with the sword must be killed with the sword. Evil men will wax worse, deceiving and being deceived. Refrain completely from all manner of vices, because no vice can serve any useful purpose to any person. From now to December you must completely change your lifestyle. You must withdraw all your court cases, and be reconciled with all your adversaries. You must not indulge in any vice. You have to look for the black goat when it is not yet dark, because when it is dark it will be impossible for you to find it. Right now there is nothing like concoctions, juju, money, or houses in existence. All these things are regarded with disdain. If God had not loved us, He would not have given us such a large lattitude in order that we may become altogether changed. You all know that you are all instruments in this Vineyard, and when you complain that you have pain in your waist, head, back, stomach, etc; this is erroraneous. The problem is because you have departed from that first love, and you have no love towards another person. This is the cause of your problem. You ask what is the cause of the trouble in your family, it is because you do not have love. When you ask what is the cause of the trouble in Nigeria; the cause of the problem is because Nigerians have no love. When you ask about the cause of the trouble in Africa, it is because of lack of love. The trouble in the Western World is because no white man has any atom of love in him. When you ask about the trouble and tribulations in the whole world, it is because of lack of love.

You always say that God is your witness that you have love. Today after this gospel, can you say that God is your witness that you have love? Today after this gospel can you defend yourself? God is no respector of person. After hearing this gospel, go and give it to the Pope, Archbishop of Canterbury, and find out if any of them have love. The Pope has no love, the Archbishop of Canterbury has no love, the Army Officer who says he want to defend his nation give him this gospel to read and he will see whether he has love. If he had love, he would not have committed murder by killing people. When you stay in the court and say that you are a judge or magistrate, and you condemn someone to death or send someone to prison, have you got love? You say that you are working for the government, you are a policeman and you arrest somebody because he has committed murder or stolen, for this reason you throw him into prison, have you got love as a policeman? Is it possible for satan to cast out satan? Can you use sin to take away sin? God says that He does not look on any other thing that you have done, but He has looked at one particular thing, and that is that you have departed from the first love.

I do not condemn Abraham, Isaac and Moses; all of them committed murder. Were they directed by God to go and kill any person? Abraham, when he heard that his nephew Lot was abducted by soldiers; he went to that community and destroyed everything, and then return home with spoils of war. When you claim that you are a friend of Abraham, because he was a friend of God, do not go to that aspect of being a friend of God. When you claim to be a disciple of David, I will warn you not to be a disciple of David. This gospel is intended for every person in the world. It is the last gospel, the everlasting gospel, and therefore you have to comply with the contents of this gospel. You have to go back to that first love of God. If our Lord Jesus Christ did not come to redeem mankind, how do you think that Abraham, Moses and David would have been saved? After all these things have been done, have you seen any peace in the world? The changeover symbolises your returning to that first love of God which you have departed from. Every person has to return to that first love. We are retracing our steps back to the Garden of Eden. Many of you are still hunting animals, killing birds and animals; and afterwards you scratch your head and say, "God forgive me," it is too late.

When you kill your goat; looking left and right you dont see anyone you say, "Let us quickly eat up this thing and go away." When you capture a goat in order to slaughter it, it begins to bleat because it is trying to help itself, but you do not want to let it go, you chop off its head. These animals that you are killing, have instincts; it is only that they have no reasoning faculties. The only thing which man has used to outwit animals is that man has reasoning faculties. If you want to kill an animal, it knows that you are going to kill it, but it has no reasoning faculties to know how to escape from you. When you are going to steal, you have reasoned with yourself that maybe those people will have prepared for you with guns, swords and machettes. You also will prepare yourself and be armed. You will have your disciples lay ambush around the house as you go in and steal. You have already prepared yourself well.

So brethren, take this gospel and preach it to your wife, and to the angels. I know that every person is listening right now. Even the angels are listening. The angels who do not comply with these instructions, stand to perish. The significance of the changeover is for everyone of us to confess our sins and become truly repentant, and return to that first love. The only way to changeover is to be completely reborn, and become reconciled to your adversaries; those you are quarrelling with, those you have been speaking evil against; you have to become truly reconciled; and then refrain from stealing, fornication, preparation of concoctions, whoremongery, and then go back to that first love.

This gospel will be taken to the whole world; it will be preached in all the nooks and corners of the world, before the end comes. Do not preach about the church denominations or man, but preach about love. Tell them that no person in the world has love. Tell them that God has revealed that love to us and that God wants us to return to this first love. All those who has love are the children of God. The whole world is languishing in the hands of the evil one, because all the people in the world are now dying out. I have no intention of being tedious unto you, one stroke of the cane is sufficient unto the wise. Let those who have ears, hear; may God bless His holy words, Amen.

# CHAPTER 14

# THE UNIVERSAL LEADER IN THE YEAR 2001 IS BORN OF A WOMAN

**Bible Class lecture delivered by the Sole Spiritual Head,
Leader Olumba Olumba Obu, on the occasion of
the Queen Mother's Week.**

**BIBLE TEXT: REVELATION CHAPTER 12**

This is the time of the fulfillment of the revelation of John the Divine, which is found in the book of Revelation Chapters one to twenty two. If you read the Bible from Genesis to Malacai, you will not find the name of our Lord Jesus Christ. This is because it is the Old Testament, and the Old Testament speak about the things of old. Here the Prophets prophesied about His coming, and these prophesies were fulfilled from St Matthew to Jude. If you read through these chapters you will not see Brotherhood of the Cross and Star in its full context. When you read the book of Revelation, you will understand that Brotherhood of the Cross and Star is the New Kingdom of God.

Today, it is my intention to reveal to you the mysteries concerning Jehovah God and His Christ. I have come to reveal to you, the second advent of our Lord Jesus Christ. I want to reveal He, Who has brought salvation to the sons of men, and has saved them from ruin. We have been told that Adam was created from the clay of the earth. It would have been possible for God to make Adam descend from the sky. There had never been a time since the creation of the world, that a human being had descended from the sky into this mundane world. Adam was first created from the dust of the earth. Apart from him, all human beings are born through the womb of a woman. All of you know that Eve was the first mother on earth. It would have been possible for God to cause Eve to descend from the sky, but you have been told that she was created from the rib of Adam; during which time, God sent Adam into a deep sleep, and a rib was taken from his side to create Eve. At no time has any human being flown down from above like a bird into this earth plane; if that was to happen where would such a person land?

Before Moses was born, his mother was pregnant for nine months. There were numerous prophecies about his birth before he was born. The prophecies said that he was going to be a Prophet greater in power and glory than even Pharoah. When Pharoah heard this, he sent his soldiers to kill all the small children aged from three months downwards. This was the first massacre of the innocent children. During this massacre Pharoah hoped that Moses would be killed. All the prophecies were about this great Prophet. You are all aware of the mysteries surrounding the birth of Moses. Immediately the mother knew that her child was going to be killed, she quickly made a basket and placed the child inside it, and carried it to the riverside. There she placed the basket by the river, and instructed her daughter to watch the basket and see what would happen. Suddenly a miracle happened. Pharoah's daughter came to take bath in the river and discover the basket with Moses inside it. Moses's sister then emerged and asked Pharoah's daughter if she needed a maid to care for the child. She accepted, and Moses's sister went and told her mother, who came and took charge of nursing Moses.

### ST MATTHEW 1 V 22 TO THE END

"Now all this was done, that it might be fulfilled which was spoken
by the Prophet saying; behold a virgin shall bring forth a Son, and
they shall call his name Emmanuel, which being interpreted, is God
with us. Then Joseph being raised from sleep did as the Angel of the
Lord had bidden him, and took unto him his wife. And he knew her
not till she had brought forth her first born Son; and he call His name Jesus."

When you read about the nativity of our Lord Jesus Christ from St Matthew Chapter One verses 22 to the end, you will discover the prophecy of Jeremiah. All this time, David and the other Patriarchs were not yet born, but there was a prophecy about the birth of our Lord Jesus Christ. The statement that the Angel made- "God with us," means that our Lord Jesus Christ is God Himself. It would not have been so easy to say that Mary delivered God. This was a way of camouflaging Him. The real truth is that our Lord Jesus Christ is the Almighty God. Just as a sensible person cannot go out naked, in the same way God cannot appear naked. He must cover Himself with human flesh, so that He may not be easily identified. Can you see how people are confused? We are told that a virgin will conceive and bring forth a male child, and His name shall be called Emmanuel.

### ST LUKE 1 V 28 - 31

> " And the angel came in unto her and said, hail Mary, thou art highly favoured; the Lord is with thee, blessed art thou among women. And when she saw him she was troubled at this saying, and cast in her mind what manner of salutation this would be. And the angel said unto her, fear not Mary for thou hast found favour with God. And behold, thou shalt conceive in your womb, and bring forth a son, and thou shalt call his name Jesus."

This vision was given to Mary during her service in the temple. At the age of seven, God revealed Himself to her. Mary had taken the vow of a Nazarite, which is a period during which a person devotes his or her time to serving in the temple. It was during this time that Mary had the revelation that she would give birth to God. If Mary conceived and gave birth to God, who do you think will descend from the sky? If Moses who was a brother of Aaron, was born by a woman how do you expect anyone to emerge from the sky? It is a very simple thing for a host of people to come down from the sky, but the result would be that all of us would run away. Even if one was to descend from the sky, knowing that the earth is owned and occupied by certain persons, where would such a person stay since everywhere has been occupied? What would be his clan? To which family would he belong?

When man is in Spirit he is like a flame of fire by nature, that is why he passes through the womb of a woman which is an antidote. This is the reason why God has created the womb of a woman as a passage through which all individuals, angels and God Himself passes into the world. There is no other way through which human beings, angels, Spirits, and God can pass into the world except through the womb of a woman. Man is the heaven and woman is the earth. Therefore everybody has to pass through a man into the woman, to be born into the earth plane so that God may be glorified. God can cause human beings to be born through a man but then, what would be the usefulness of the woman? Just as Eve passed through Adam, it is also possible for human beings to enter the world in the same way. If it happens this way, what would be the usefulness of women? A person who emerges from the sky would not like to take any instructions from anyone. God Who is knowledgable in all aspects of things has caused human beings to come down through a mother and father, who will control them and who they will respect.

### ACTS 1 V - 9 - 11

> " And when He had spoken these things, while they beheld, He was taken up; and a cloud received Him out of their sight. And while they looked steadfast towards heaven as He went up, behold two men stood by them in white apparel; which also said, ye men of Galilee, why stand ye gazing up into heaven? this same Jesus which is taken up from you into heaven, shall so come in like manner as ye have seen Him go into heaven."

**The passage read out to you has confused the whole world. The explanation of this is that, He will come back as a Human Being.** The world interpret it to mean that He will emerge from the sky and come down to the earth. It appears to Me that the people of the world have ears but cannot hear. It is for this reason that I want to explain and expatiate on these things, so that you can know the theme of our lecture this evening; **that the person who will rule the world is born of a woman.** Two Angels have borne eloquent testimony that our Lord Jesus Christ will come back as a Human Being. There is no other way that God can come down on earth except by passing through the womb of a woman. Who can endure the Spirit, and which Spirit can tolerate you? If you were to see the Spirit, would you be able to withstand it? Would you say that Spirit has patience? I want to point out to you, and I have not added nor subtracted from the words of God that are written in the scriptures. I want to make it quite clear to you that if there is any person among you, who is still looking at the sky to see someone descending to earth, he is wasting his time, because until doomsday such a thing will not happen. What happened is exactly what had been prophesied by the Prophets, that a virgin would conceive in her womb and bring forth a child who will be called Emmanuel.

### ST LUKE 2 v 5 - 9

" To be taxed with Mary his expoused wife, being great with child. And so it was, that while they were there, the days were accomplished that she should be delivered. And she brought forth her first born son, and wrapped Him in swaddling clothes, and laid Him in a manger, for there was no room for them in the Inn. And there were in the same country, Shepherds abiding in the field, keeping watch over their flocks by night. And lo, the Angel of the Lord came upon them, and the glory of the Lord shone round about them, and they were sore afraid. "

Now that Mary has brought forth a child called Jesus, Who has saved us from all troubles and encumbrances of the world; the ruins we were in, and has taken dominion over death and taken the keys of hades; is it not that small child called Jesus who was crucified on the cross and on the third day rose from the dead? Is this not that small baby who was born as Jesus? Have you yourself the ability to resurrect from the dead? Was our Lord Jesus Christ the only child of His mother? I want to show you that eggs are eggs, but some are rotten and everybody is not the same. The main reason why the Jews started to ask questions, and disputed among themselves was because they said, "Howbeit, we know this man whence He is, but when Christ cometh, no one knoweth whence He is." When the Jews saw the child Jesus, they regarded Him as an ordinary human being, because He had been born through a woman.

It had already been said, when Adam disobeyed and fell short of the glory of God, that he pleaded with God to return to him. **God told him that unless a holy and precious blood was shed He would not return; and the signs of Gold, Frankincense and Myrrh would mark His return.** When our Lord Jesus Christ came, all these signs were seen. **Therefore our Lord Jesus Christ was the real God Who came down on earth.** He created man. Can Angels do it? Who else has the power to create man? He is the person who has the power to create. When Adam and Eve defiled themselves through the sin of fornication, God left them, and they were driven away from the garden of Eden. There was therefore no way for them to atone for their sins. They used the blood of sheep, cows, etc., but they were not made perfect. He had made a promise that He would only return when a holy and precious blood was shed; and that Gold, Frankincense and Myrrh would be the signs of His coming. He stated that He would be pierced with a sword, and the signs would be the Water, Blood and Spirit.

When He came as the Son of man, the Son of God and God Himself, the Jews stoned Him because He called Himself the Son of God. Had He told them that He was God Himself, they would have laughed at Him and told Him that He was a demented person. How sweet does it sound in people's ears, if anyone says that he is God. As you are all sitting down here, if anyone call himself God, even your child will laugh at you and say, "Papa I think you are mad, because man is created in the image and likeness of God, therefore you cannot equate man with God." Since the creation of the world, can you mention one person who has been able to accomplish the work that our Lord Jesus Christ had done? Melchezedek, Moses, Enoch, Elijah and all the other Patriarchs came; I want you to mention any one of them who was able to do exactly what our Lord Jesus Christ did. Our Lord Jesus Christ said, "No man take it from Me, but I lay it down Myself. I have power to lay it down, and I have power to take it again." It is impossible for anyone to kill God. He Himself surrendered His life.

### ST JOHN 10 v 17 - 19

" Therefore doth my Father love Me, because I lay down My life, that I might take it up again. No man taketh it from Me, but I lay it down of Myself. I have power to take it again. This commandment I have received of My Father. There was a division therefore again among the Jews for these sayings."

When our Lord Jesus Christ was on the cross, He said "Father into thy hands I commend My Spirit." He surrendered His Spirit into the hands of the Father. What actually was nailed on the cross were the sins of the whole world. After three days and three nights the Spirit returned into the body of Jesus. Since then He has continued to exist. Erroraneously the Church denominations which have not yet come to the accurate knowledge of the truth, claim that our Lord Jesus Christ was taken up to heaven, to sit on the right hand of His Father. If you look at the firmanent, you will not find a dwelling place there. Our Lord Jesus Christ's ascension into what they call heaven can be likened to a person who boards a plane from Calabar to Lagos. On his return he may decide to travel by bus or taxi; but you will be convinced that he is still in Lagos, since he has not returned by air. Who actually took away the life of our Lord Jesus Christ? Would you say that it was Pilate or the Jews who killed our Lord Jesus Christ? It was the sins of the whole world that our Lord Jesus Christ crucified on the cross, and not Himself. After His death the sins of mankind were atoned for, so that man may be perfect and remain undefiled, so that Christ may come in and dwell in man, since man is the temple of the Most High God. **That same sin which defiled you, and made it impossible for God to dwell in you, is what you have gone back to commit.**

**When you begin to shout on top of your voice that Olumba Olumba Obu is God, I know that some of you are deceivers, because I know your thoughts, movements and deeds.** Philip asked our Lord Jesus Christ to show him the Father, this meant that Philip regarded our Lord Jesus Christ as an ordinary human being. You always shout, "Wonderful Leader," I say shut up your mouth, because you do not know the type of Being that you are dealing with. **Forget about who I am, and put My teachings into practice because this will give you salvation.** Do not give Me any name. I am not a Prophet, Moses, Elijah or Jesus Christ. **I am a Supernatural Teacher; I want you to put into practice the teachings which I give you, and this will reveal to you who I am.** The lessons that I have brought to you are supernatural. It surpasses all the wisdom of the whole world put together. Had you humbled yourselves to take in these lessons, you would have found yourselves where you did not expect.

### ST JOHN 14 v 8 - 11

"Philip said unto Him, Lord shew us the Father and it sufficeth us. Jesus said unto him, have I been so long time with you, yet thou hast not known Me, Philip? He that hath seen Me hath seen the Father, and how sayest thou shew me the Father? Believest thou not that I am in the Father, and the Father in Me? The words that I speak unto you, I speak not of Myself, but the Father that dwelleth in Me, He doeth the works. Believe Me that I am in the Father, and the Father in Me, or else believe Me for the very works sake."

Do you really understand this statement? Philip had been with our Lord Jesus Christ all the time, and yet he went and asked Him, "Shew us the Father and it sufficeth us." Our Lord Jesus Christ said, "Have I been so long time with you, and yet thou hast not known Me, Philip? He that hath seen Me hath seen the Father, and how sayest thou then, shew us the Father? Believest thou not that I am in the Father, and the Father in Me? The words that I speak, I speak not of Myself, but the Father that dwelleth in Me, He doeth the works." This means that our Lord Jesus Christ is God Himself, Who created heaven and earth. But when you pray and say, "Our Father which art in heaven, hallowed be thy name;" it is possible that you think that God is living in the desert, or in the moon, the sun, the stars or in a secret chamber. Our Lord Jesus Christ had said, "He that hath seen Me hath seen the Father."

### ST JOHN 3 v 11 - 13

"Verily, verily I say unto thee, we speak that we know, and testify that we have seen, and ye receive not our witness. If I have told you of earthly things, and ye believe not, how shall ye believe if I told you of heavenly things? And no man hath ascended up to heaven, but He that came down from heaven, even the Son of man which is in heaven."

When I tell you that I am delivering this gospel from the high heavens, you begin to contemplate in your mind, what type of statement is this? No person has ever come down from heaven, except He who is from heaven. When He speaks here on earth, you can hear His voice everywhere in the universe.

### ST MATTHEW 17 v 2 - 6

" And was transfigured before them, and His face did shine as the sun, and His raiment was white as the light. And behold there appeared unto them, Moses and Elias talking with Him. Then answered Peter and said unto Jesus, Lord, it is good for us to be here, if thou wilt, let us make here three tabernacles; one for thee, and one for Moses and one for Elias. While he yet spake behold a bright cloud over shadowed them, and behold a voice out of the cloud, which said, This is My Beloved Son in whom I am well pleased, hear ye Him. And when the disciples heard it, they fell on their faces, and were sore afraid."

Who can understand these things? This is another aspect of the mysteries of this kingdom. Mary the mother of Jesus Christ was told that she would be over shadowed by the power of the Holy Ghost, and that which would be born of her will be called the Holy Son of God. When John baptised Jesus, the Holy Spirit descended in the form of a dove, and a voice in heaven declared, "This is My Beloved Son in whom I am well pleased, hear ye Him." **Is there among the members of Brotherhood of the Cross and Star and the public, anyone who has not seen Me Spiritually and physically in their houses and everywhere? Yet you continue to doubt. Eventhough you have seen Me in your dreams you are still doubting. One person who thousands and millions of people see Spiritually and physically at the same time, and hear His voice distinctly.** Here is a person that can appear to millions of people at the same time. Sometimes when you doze off you see Him. There is no place where you cannot see Him. This is why people conclude that He is not an ordinary man.

They say that He has been a member of several secret societies. **I ask you, am I the only person in these secret societies?** When you read St Matthew 17 v 2 - 6, tell Me who were the two persons appearing there? Before the bright light were Moses, Elijah and our Lord Jesus Christ. In St Matthew chapter 16, He had already told them that some among them will not taste of death. At that time the disciples did not understand Him. After six days all these things came to pass when they were at the mountain of transfiguration. It has already been said, that there is nothing that our Lord Jesus Christ said, which will not be made manifest. If He tells you to go there and you will find two persons; when you reach that place, you will find two persons. If He says it will rain by four o'clock, the rain is bound to fall at that time. This is because all the words proceeding out of His mouth will come to fulfillment.

### REVELATION 19 v 1O

" And I fell at his feet to worship him. And he said unto me, see thou do it not; I am thy fellow servant, and thy brethren that have the testimony of Jesus; worship God, for the testimony of Jesus is the Spirit of prophecy."

Whatever He says must be fulfilled. He told His disciples to go to the upper chamber and there they would find a girl with a pot of water; when the disciples went, they found the girl exactly as our Lord Jesus Christ had said. He told His disciples to go to the village and they would find an ass tied to a stake; when they went they found exactly what our Lord Jesus Christ had said. There was nothing that He said, which did not come to pass. In spite of the fact that the Bible has been written in various dialects and languages; it has been produced in countless volumes after the departure of our Lord Jesus Christ in the flesh. Since He has not re-appeared, the Bible has been thrown away. **I will not say that there is any church denomination which has been able to put into practice the words in the Bible. They cannot even interpret it. The Roman Catholics cannot interpret it, how much less the Protestants. No one has been able to interpret the Bible.** Until now, there has been no person who knows anything about the Bible. People simply look at it without understanding what it contains. Finally the best thing for them to do is to throw it away.

### ST MATTHEW 28 v 18

"And Jesus came and spake unto them saying, all power is given unto Me in heaven and in earth."

Who is the person to whom all power in heaven and in earth has been bestowed? Who is this person? If this is what has been done, what power is left? Who is this person to whom all power has been given? There is no one who can understand the statements of our Loed Jesus Christ. It is only our Lord Jesus Christ who understands Himself.

### ST JOHN 17 v 4 - 5

"I have glorified thee on thee earth; I have finished the work which thou gavest Me to do. And now oh Father, glorify thou Me with thine own self, with the glory which I had with thee before the world was."

Interpret this passage for Me. Who is this Man? When the world was not created, our Lord Jesus Christ was in existence. If He has existed before the creation of the world, who is He? Are you deceived by the name which He has used to camouflage Himself? You want Him to be called God? Is it because He was called Jesus? No precious thing can be presented before swines. Have you heard what has been said in St John 17 v 5? "And now oh Father, glorify thou Me with thine own self with the glory which I had with thee before the world was." Can another pernon's wife rub your back down to the waist? Which man would have accepted to come and die for your sake? **For what reason would he have come to die? What would have been his benefit?**

Those of you who are present here do not behave in the same way with your child, as you behave with your brother or wife. Your behaviour towards each and everyone of them is different. The way that you behave with your friend and your concubine is quite different. Your girlfriend will try to dupe you because she is not certain of her future. But the moment that you come out plainly and say, "I am going to marry you," she will no longer waste her time in going out to buy and borrow certain things, because she is now certain of her future. The man himself will be compelled to write her letters confirming that he will marry her. Remember one thing, that is, that the letter can be withdrawn at anytime. Men are so cunning and crafty that they deceive women.

### HEBREWS 2 v 8 - 9

"Thou hast put all things in subjection under His feet. For in that He put all in subjection under Him, He left nothing that is not put under Him. But now we see not yet all things put under Him. But we see Jesus who was made a little lower than the angels, for the suffering of death, crowned with glory and honour, that He by the grace of God should taste death for every man."

Brethren, have you heard that? Now that you are running to trees, rock and every other things for help; none of these things can help you, because He had already said that all powers in heaven and earth has been given to Him; which means that everything is under His control. You cannot find power anywhere. Who else can have all the powers in heaven and earth except the Son of man? **Now you say, "I cannot worship man, I want to worship the real God;" I want you to go around the whole world, and when you find the real God, worship Him.** You will also find that it is man that God gives all powers over all the creations of God. This is going to be proved in Hebrews chapter 1 v 5 - 6.

## HEBREWS 1 v 5 - 6

"For unto which angel said He at anytime, thou art my Son, this day have I begotten thee; and again, I will be to him a Father, and he shall be to Me a son. And again, when He bringeth in the First Begotten into the world, He said, and let all the angels of God worship Him."

Look at this type of man, who, when He comes as the First Begotten of God, God will say that all the angels in heaven and earth should bow down and worship Him. What kind of man is this? Dont forget that Raphael is an angel; Michael is also an angel; Hell and Hades, the Stars, the Sun, the Moon, Rain, Fire, Thunder and so on are all angels. It has been said that when He will bring down the First Begotten of the Father into the world, all the angels must bow down and worship Him. Who then is this man to whom all angels must subject themselves and minister? If this Phenominon is a tree, stone, or human being, then it is time you take stock of yourselves. It was only one angel, Michael, who was able to remove Lucifer from heaven and cast him into a bottomless pit. The angels outnumber all the human beings on earth. As you are all sitting down here, the angels who are also here number more than one million. Consider this type of Man who all the angels in heaven and earth must bow down to worship.

## ST MATTHEW 13 v 40 - 43

" As therefore the tares are gathered and burned in the fire; so shall it be in the end of this world. The Son of man shall send forth His angels, and they shall gather out of His kingdom all things that offend, and them which do iniquity; and shall cast them into a furnace of fire; there shall be wailing and gnashing of teeth. Then shall the righteous shine forth as the sun in the kingdom of their Father. Who hath ears to hear, let him ear."

Brethren, have you heard that? Just as the Government, the Armed Forces, the Police, Institutions such as Schools, Colleges and the Courts are arranged in the world; so also are they in the Spiritual world. The same situation exists among the Angels. They have assignments from God to go and arrest all those who break the law and indulge in abominations. Such people are brought before the courts. Consider within yourselves what type of person this is? One who gives an order and all the Angels obey. He can order an Angel to go and arrest a particular person. At another time He can order that such person should be released. What I am telling you is, that all the Angels that are all over the earth and in heaven, are under the control of our Lord Jesus Christ. The Angels are so powerful, that one Angel is able to destroy the whole world in under one second. Lucifer who you have been hearing about, has been arrested. Do you not see that you are now able to walk freely in the darkest night without anything happening to you?

**All the principalities have been brought under subjection.** Go to the areas where crocodiles and other wild animals have been causing people to be drowned, or to completely disappear. Such things no longer happen. If you like, you can go to the northern part of the Cross River State of Nigeria where elephants have been a constant threat to human lives. Today such threats no longer exist, because the power of the Holy Spirit has overwhelmed everything in the whole world. The thing that the world are saying is that, now that the members of Brotherhood of the Cross and Star are fully protected by the Holy Spirit personified, they will exercise their power over you when He dies.

The king of Assyria boasted to Hezekiah that he should not be deceived by his God that he would march to Israel and destroy all the soldiers, the inhabitants and Hezekiah himself. King Hezekiah placed this letter before the altar of the Lord. Only one Angel was sent to destroy the Philistines. If only one Angel was able to destroy a whole army, what do you think of this person who when He will come into this world, all Angels in heaven and earth will bow down and worship Him? Had you known yourselves, you would never have referred to our Lord Jesus Christ as a human being. **All the punishments and afflictions besetting the whole world, are as a result of all the blasphemous words that the world are speaking against thus Human Being.** There is no doubt that our Lord Jesus Christ is a human being as we are, but He is God Almighty. When He came into the world, all the Angels had to bow down and worship Him.

During the last election, many people contested for the post of President, but eventually only one person emerged as the President. Even if he was formerly your friend, you cannot play with him as you like, because he now has the power to deal with you as he likes. This does not mean that he is the most intelligent person, but so far as he has been chosen to be the head of state, you have to give him the honour and respect due to him during his term of office. If this power and authority is vested in a human being, who can be tossed about by sickness or death; imagine One who is the King of Kings and Lord of Lords, who has control over sickness, death and everything created, both seen and unseen. Look at this Supernatural Man, that all Angels in heaven and earth must bow down and worship. It is very unwise for you to speak evil words or joke with such a Human Being.

### GENESIS 1 v 26 - 29

> "And unto Adam He said, because thou hast hearken unto the voice of thy wife, and hast eaten of the tree of which I have commanded thee saying, thou shalt not eat of it; cursed be the ground for thy sake; in sorrow shalt thou eat of it all the days of thy life; thorns and thistles shall it bring forth to thee, and thou shalt eat the herb of the field; in the sweat of thy face shalt thou eat bread, till thou return unto the ground; for out of it wast thou taken; for dust thou art, and unto dust shalt thou return."

What do you think He is? you say that you regard Him as God. When people ask you why you regard Him as God, you reply by saying, "My wife was barren and He made her become fruitful;" or you say, "I was sick and He made me well." The people will ask you, "Is that the reason why you accept Him to be God?" If you go to a necromancer he will heal your sickness and perform many miracles. It is for this reason that people stick to necromancing, secret societies and other diabolical powers. Adam came into existence by being moulded from the dust of the earth, and God breathed into him the breath of life. The symbolism of that breath is that God dwelth inside Adam. We have been told that Adam was sent into a deep sleep. **This actually means that he died.** When he resurrected, that was when a rib was taken from his side and used to create Eve. It was the same Spirit that Adam had which caused our Lord Jesus Christ to re-incarnate as a quickening Spirit.

Have you not heard our Lord Jesus Christ when he said, "It is expedient for you that I go away; for if I go not away the Comforter will not come unto you; but if I depart I will send Him unto you." Do you mean to tell Me that another person was going to be sent? Was that Comforter not our Lord Jesus Christ Himself who was going to re-appear? You always claim that you cannot worship a man. Whether that person is your mother or father, a governor, a president, a commissioner or a permanent secretary. Whatever his status might be in life, he is a human being. How will you not worship man, when at your different places of work, you are placed under superior officers. Eventhough you claim that you cannot worship man, it is a man who is placed in a position to promote or punish you. Sometimes you claim that your promotion has been witheld. This is because you refuse to worship man. When the time for promotion comes, yours will not be given to you, while a much junior officer is promoted.

At the moment, is the world not filled with Angels and Spirits? Are you able to see these invisible beings? No matter how great an Angel or Spirit is, since they are your servants, you can dismiss them or ask them to go away from you. This is because, it has been ordained by God that man must rule over Angels and Spirits and all the creations of God. The passage says that, you must love the brethren and honour the king. This is the position in which I find Myself. Apart from that, I would not say that I cannot respect man. I would like you to interpret this passage for Me:

### 1 PETER 2 v 17

> "Honour all men. Love the Brotherhood. Fear God. Honour the King."

Who is man that you should worship him? A woman, a man, an old man, a thief, a native doctor and a sick person; are all these not human beings? You do not regard man as a precious thing. Rather you always complain, "I cannot worship man, I am worshipping the real God." The fact is that man is a precious thing and must be honoured and respected. Honour all men. Love the Brotherhood. Who are the Brotherhood? Are they not human beings? You are ask to fear the King. Who is the King? Is He not a human being? You have been told to fear God, Is God not Human Being? What are you doing now?

### REVELATION 5 v 1

" And I saw in the right hand of him that sat on the throne a book written within and on the backside, sealed with seven seals."

Have you heard what has been read to you? Why is it that there is no other person worthy to open that book and read it? The Bible which you have been reading every day: **the point is that there is no Angel that can open it, read it and put its contents into practice; there is no white man or black man who is able to practice the word of God.** Why is it that He is the only person who is able to open this book, remove the seals and read the contents of the book? The reason is that He was the one who was killed, and His blood was used in cleansing all human beings in the world. **This same Jesus has returned and you have no regard for Him. He is the only one who is able to open this book.** Compare this statement with the earlier statement in which He said, "Whom shall I send, and who will go for Me?" Heaven and earth remained silent. It was only our Lord Jesus Christ who offered to come. Is this the same situation in Revelation 5 verses 1 - 12?

### REVELATION 5 v 1 - 12

" And I saw in the right hand of Him that sat on the throne a book written within and on the backside, sealed with seven seals. And a strong angel proclaiming with a loud voice, who is able to open the book, and to loose the seals thereof? And no man in heaven, nor in earth, neither under the earth, was able to open the book neither to look thereon. And one of the Elders said unto me, weep not; behold, the Lion of the tribe of Judah of the root of David, hath prevailed to open the book, and to loose the seven seals thereof. And I behold, and lo, in the midst of the throne, and of the four beasts, and in the midst of the Elders, stood a Lamb as if it had been slain, having seven horns and seven eyes, which are the seven Spirits of God, sent forth into all the earth. And He came and took the book out of the right hand of Him that sat upon the throne. And when He had taken the book, the four beasts and four and twenty Elders fell down before the Lamb, having everyone of them harps, and golden vials full of odours, which are the prayers of saints. And they sung a new song, saying, thou art worthy to take the book, and to open it and remove the seals thereof; for thou wast slain, and hast redeemed us to God by thy blood, out of every kindred, and tongue, and people and nation; and hast made us unto God, Kings and Priests, and we shall reign on the earth. And I beheld and I heard the voice of many angels round about the throne, and the beasts and the Elders; and the number of them was ten thousand times ten thousand, and thousands of thousands; saying, worthy is the Lamb that was slain to receive power, and riches, and wisdom, and strength, and honour, and glory and blessing."

There was no one in this case who could open the book and read the contents. Somebody said, do not weep because the Lion of Judah is able to open and read the contents of the book. He is worthy to open the book because He was the one who was slain.

## REVELATION 12 v 5

*"And she brought forth a man child, who
was to rule all nations with a rod of iron; and
her child was caught up unto God, and to His throne."*

Ponder over this and tell Me who this man is? Who is this man child? Is this Moses, Abraham, Isaac, Jacob or John the Baptist? Compare the words in Revelation chapter 12 verse 5, with the message that angel Gabriel gave to Mary; that a virgin will give birth to a male child and His name shall be called Jesus. If a virgin is to bring forth Jesus again, this would be a repetition. You will also observe that Jesus is an old name. In the book of revelation we are told that a woman, not a virgin this time, will bring forth a male child who will rule the world with an iron rod. **The Iron Rod signifies the Kingship position. He is the King of Kings and Lord of Lords.** There are many Lords, therefore if you refer to Him as a Lord, you will be chastised by the Angels. He is above all the Lords, therefore He is Lord of Lords. If you refer to our Lord Jesus Christ as Jesus, you will be chastised by the Angels. He is the King of Kings and Lord of Lords. It is an insult and blasphemy for people to refer to our Lord Jesus Christ as Jesus. The 144,000 virgins who will be redeemed from the earth are the kings. They will rule under the King of Kings and Lord of Lords.

## REVELATION 19 v 12

*"His eyes were as firm as a flame of fire,
and on His head were many crowns; and
He had a name written, that no man
knew, but He Himself."*

Look at the glory which our Lord Jesus Christ spoke about in St John Chapter 17 verse 5. Does it mean that when He comes back as the King of Kings and Lord of Lords, He will go about from house to house and from village to village? He will have to be the Pillar of the Church, and maintain His position as the King of Kings and Lord of Lords. Revelation chapter 12 verse 5 says that this male child was caught up unto God and to His throne. He does not go anywhere. He remains in the throne to give His commands. **If He goes out anywhere in the flesh, He is not the One. Unless the Father reveals this revelation to you, you will not understand the meaning. All Angels, Human beings, Spirits and all the Created things, both visible and invisible are under His control. If you say that you do not know Him, He certainly knows you. Everything is under His control. He has come to rule over death and hades, and He is born of a woman.**

Have the white people or the Africans, elected anybody as a King? The Africans have Chiefs, traditional Rulers and Clan Heads. Throughout the whole world, there is no particular person who is to rule the whole world. **This male child born of a woman, with an iron rod has come to assume His reign on this earth plane.** Why is it that the people of the world are so rich in the mundane things of this world? While those who worship God go about in tattered clothes. The priests say that their reward is in heaven. The church goer is unable to obtain any mundane things. People always ask, why is it that when a person goes to the Brotherhood of the Cross and Star, he become very wealthy? He is blessed with all the mundane things, plus he is given the Holy Spirit. People always complain that Brotherhood of the Cross and Star is not a place where God is worshipped. Others will confront you, and say that you go to the Brotherhood of the Cross and Star for the sake of material wealth. People believe that it is only beelzebub and secret societies that can provide material wealth. Those who come to the Brotherhood of the Cross and Star are accused of looking for money.

I am saying that the glory which you see now, is one that you have never witnessed before in its true perspective. **When it is fully manifested, you will realise that this is the Kingdom of God which our Lord Jesus Christ prayed for when He said, "Thy Kingdom come, Thy will be done on earth as it is in heaven." Do you all know that you are Lords and Kings? This is the reason why, whenever you go anywhere, people are afraid of you. All the Angels and Spirits bow down and worship you. I have not yet bestow full power on you, so that you might not misuse it.**

When the Bishop pays homage to the traditional Rulers, he bows down to them. He will kneel down and say that he has come to offer him prayers. The personal guard of the traditional Rulers will say, "Reverend please go and wait for some time, because the King is resting." If the Governor or Head of State goes to visit a traditional Ruler or the Emir, he has to bow down and worship him. The Emirs and traditional Rulers are the permanent Rulers, while the Governorship is temporary.

Let My peace and blessings abide with the entire world. Amen.

# CHAPTER 15

# WHEN GOD BECOMES MAN HE IS WATER, BLOOD & SPIRIT.

Everlasting Gospel delivered by Leader Olumba Olumba Obu
Sole Spiritual Head of the Universe.

First Lesson:   St John 10 v 30
Second Lesson:  St John 14 v 10
Golden Text:    1 John 5 v 8

Brethren, where are your papers and pens to take note of these gospels? If you are posted to India, America or any of the European countries, how are you going to relay these gospels as students of the Christ Universal Spiritual School of Practical Christianity? The reason why you do not come with your writing materials is because you are coming for prayers. These lessons are what the whole world needs. When you are asked by the people outside whether you are being taught, or whether you have been to a Seminary you say no. If you are not taught and if you have never been to a Seminary, how do you understand the scriptures? Now examine the lesson just read to you; if I do not reveal them how would you understand? It is the revelation of these lessons that teaches you the scriptures. I could have taken this lesson very lightly, but at this time I want to reveal the hidden mysteries of God to you. I do not know the resaon why I am exposing these mysteries to you. These mysteries have confounded the wisdom of the whole world. My hope is on the tape recordings beaause these are going to be translated, and compiled into booklets which will be used in teaching the whole world.

If all of us here had come to receive the recondite teaching of the Holy Father, by now all of you would have refrained from all manner of sins. Since you regard Brotherhood of the Cross and Star as a prayer house, that is why you continue to sin. My mission on earth is not to establish a church or prayer house or healing home, but I have come into the world as a Supernatural Teacher, to reveal the things that had never existed in the world. Our Lord Jesus Christ said, "I have yet many things to say unto you but you cannot bear them now. Howbeit, when He the Spirit of Truth is come, He will guide you to the accurate knowledge of truth, for He shall not speak of himself, but whatsoever He shall hear, that shall He speak and He will show you things to come." I have come into the world because of this statement of Christ, that He will come and lead you to the accurate wisdom of truth. When people ask you where you have learned these wonderful gospels that you are delivering; it had been written in the Prophets that God will teach them everything. The world will come to the Christ Universal Spiritual School of Practical Christianity to learn everything.
Now I want to reveal this statement in the scriptures that says, "I and my Father are One," to all of you; so that you will realise that all the words of God do not fall to the ground and return empty handed. You will discover that any passage that you read in the scriptures which refers to Jesus, is incomplete. If you say God or Jehovah you have failed. When you say Jehovah God and His Christ, then you refer to God and His Christ. The Father and the Son are one entity. Wherever you find our Lord Jesus Christ, is where you will find God the Father. Wherever you find the Father, you will also find our Lord Jesus Christ. Wherever the Carcass is, there you will find the vultures. People do not believe that the Father and the Son are One, because they feel that God is separete from man. Now somebody can ask you where is that your God? Who is that human being before you is that not God? It had been written in the Prophets that ye are gods; ye are children of the Most High God. Since people do not believe that they are the children of God and nobody had revealed it to them, that is why I have come to reveal these hidden mysteries to you. Many people make mistake when they call only on Christ to come and save them. The truth is that the Father, the Son and the Holy Ghost are One. Always call on God the Father and the Son.

Have you not heard that "I and my Father are One?" Christ represents the Father. Jesus is flesh and blood, while the Father is the Spirit. Jesus is flesh and blood, He is an Angel. When He is in the flesh, He is flesh, blood and Spirit. What was used to identify Christ as the King of Kings and Lord of Lords, was not because He raised the dead or open the eyes of the blind or all the miracles that He performed. The likeness of God here on earth is Water, Blood and Spirit. That is the reason why whenever water is removed from your body, your life ends. When there is no more blood in your body, that is the end of your life. It is said, "For there are three that bear record in heaven; the Father, the Word and the Holy Ghost, and these three are One. There are three that bear witness on earth, the Spirit, the water and the blood and these three agree in One."

**When God is personified here on earth, there are three things that you can use to identify Him, that is Water, Blood and Spirit.** Water cannot say that he alone is God. Blood alone cannot claim to be God, nor the Spirit. The Trinity God is Water, Blood and Spirit. There is never a time that Spirit will appear before you. It is only water and blood with Spirit that can appear before you. That is why it is said that I and my Father are One. Whenever God comes into this mundane plane, He will appear as a Human Being. In the Spirit He will appear in the form of an Angel. That was the reason why angel Gabriel said, "I am Gabriel who stands before God." Our Lord Jesus Christ also said, "I and my Father are One." This is the hidden gospel that confounds the whole world. When people keep on saying that man is not God, what is man? The three witnesses- Water, Blood and Spirit, bears witness that man is God.

When He was nailed to the cross He said, "Father into thy hands I commend my Spirit." As soon as the Spirit left Him, He gave up the ghost. When the soldier came to inspect whether He was really dead, he used his sword to pierce His side. What came out was water and blood. It is that water and blood that is used to wash away our sins, and the sins of the whole world. Every work done on the surface of the earth until the end of time, is done by water, blood and Spirit. Water, Blood and Spirit does not exist alone, the three of them are One. That is the reason why our Lord Jesus Christ, when He speaks, He uses the word "We" and not "I.". The reason why we fail in our prayers is that we always excluce the Father in our prayers. Sometime when we mention the name of God, we either exclude the name of the Father or the Son. When you give glory to the Spirit, you must also glorify the flesh. Since man is of a dual nature, the water, blood and the Spirit are One. You will never find the Spirit standing apart from man. Wherever you find our Lord Jesus Christ, you will find the Father, Son and the Holy Ghost. That is the reason why Christ said "I and my Father are One." At anytime you say that you are responsible for doing this work, you have disgraced the Spirit. When you say that it is the Father that is doing the works, as you give glory to the Spirit, you also give glory to the flesh. You all are living witnesses to the fact that we always respect what we see with our naked eyes more than what we do not see.

Brethren, if you place two plates on the table and say this plate belongs to God, and the other belongs to the Leader; the plate that belongs to the Leader will be full with money. The one that belongs to God would be empty, because you are looking for the things which you can see with your eyes. In the same way if you have committed a serious crime for which the government can imprison you, when you meet the person who is responsible for the case, after you offer him a bribe he will be satisfied. He that does not fear anybody is a useless person because it means that such a person do not fear God. This is the advise we receive from God, that whosoever love God must love his brother. Christ said that anyone who respect Me, honours Him that sent Me; any person that does not hear My words, it is not My words he despises, but the words of the One who sent Me. That was the reason why the disciples of our Lord Jesus Christ, when they saw weeds and maize growing together, they requested from their Master whether they should remove the weeds. He told them that both should grow together until the harvest. At the time of harvest the Angels would come and separate the maize on one side and put the weeds into the fire. Any person that says "I do not respect any man, I fear only God," he fails. Where will he find God? God and man are one person. Man and God are One. There has never been a time that God separated Himself from man. The trouble that exists with human beings, is that they do not know that once you see man, you have seen God. Our Lord Jesus Christ also said to His disciples that in as much as you do these things to any of these little ones, you have done it to Me. In what way did our Lord Jesus Christ do the work? When you are doing some service to man you are serving God. That was the reason why He washed the feet of His disciples, because He knew that He was doing it to God. When you punish the flesh, you are punishing God. Anything that affects the flesh also affects the Spirit. In the same way anything that affects the Spirit also affects the flesh.

As we are told that we should not steal, tell lies or fornicate, if you commit any of these vices, it affects the Spirit. As we are warned that we should not drink, we should not inject things into our body; as soon as you do these things it affects the Spirit and the flesh also. In the Spirit God is an Angel; in the flesh He is a Human Being. The Angels are the Spirits and man is the flame of fire, and both of them go together. Wherever man exists there you will find God. The manifestation of God is in human beings. Wherever you call somebody to come and see God, if the person comes and looks around, and he does not see any human being, he will not see God. But if you come here and see a huge man sitting on a magnificient chair with a long beard, you will conclude that you have seen God. Man and God are one entity. Man is not God, and God is not man, but God and man are One. Wherever you may go, if you do not see man, what do you see? Will you find a Church, School, Hospital or Government there? Will you hear songs, find food or music? What social amenities will you find at that place? In spite of the fact that you do not find anything there, there is God; but there is no manifestation because God manifests His glory through man.

When Stephen was stoned, he said he looked up and saw our Lord Jesus Christ at the right hand of God. What he saw was a human being. Any time in your visions if you do not find a human being saying, "I am Jehovah God" you will not believe. Jacob in the early morning wrestled with a human being, he did not fight with an angel. Neither did he fought with God or Spirit; he fought with a man. Believe Me that Word and Spirit are One. The Words and God are One thing. Water and blood form man, the Spirit is God. Add the three together and they form man. There is no way you can separate God from man, both of them are One and the same thing. Your own failure is that when you go to do a particular thing, you will say that this is not the business of God. You cannot succeed. On the other hand, if you go to a place and say that as you are going there, whatever you are going to do is not the business of man, but that of God, you will also fail. If you brought somebody here and ask that everyone should come and bow down and worship him; nobody will accept to worship a human being like himself. When you take God away from anything, that thing becomes negative. In the same way when you remove man from any business, it also becomes negative. When somebody is caught stealing and you say that God will punish him, he will continue to steal because he knows that God will not come and punish him. In one way or another, it will be a human being who will appear and arrest him. God always operates through man.

God will glorify all those who give honour and glory to His name. Whatsoever you do always attribute the deeds to the Father, and this will please God very much. Flesh and Spirit are together to do the work and receive honour and glory. God does not have servants to serve Him, because people expects to receive reward for their services from God in heaven. All those that say they do not worship man, they worship the true God are enemies of God. All those who honour and respect God, must also honour and respect human beings. Whenever something is given, the giver must realise that it is God who is receiving that gift. This attitude will give glory to God. Whenever you go to a place and you are given something, if the giver says "take this thing to God, but as for you let God be with you," next time you will not go again; you will say let God go alone. It has been made clear to us that God and man work together to do the work of God. Any kingdom divided against itself must fall. Therefore you are not separated from God. You cannot pay gratitude to God without paying gratitude to man. Man does not know that he and God are One; that is the reason why man claims all the glory for himself. Any conversatioin that you do not bring in God cannot work. If you say that tommorrow I am going to do this or that for yourself, you will not succeed because the Father has not signed it. The Spirit can go to Lagos to offer prayers to people, but if a human being does not accompany Him to show the physical presence of the Spirit there, the work will not manifest in the flesh. When God revealed Himself to Saul, He had at the same time revealed Himself to Annanias; so that Annanias could go and offer prayers to Saul. Tell me, if Annanias did not go and offer prayers to Saul, how would that work manifest in the flesh God has glory and bestows glory to man, but man want to enjoy all the glory by himself and forgets about God. It pleases God when man attributes all the work done to Him. The child that the Father gives you, you claim to be your child, tell Me why you will not suffer at the hand of God. This house that you and God built, if you claim ownership of that house, you do not give glory to God. When you include God in your business, that business will succeed, but if you take God away from your business it will not function. This is the wisdom which our Lord Jesus Christ used to conquer the whole world, because He said "I and my Father are One." You and the Father are One. Now people begin to say that God is on high; if He is in the sky, who is sitting here? Some people say that God does not exist; who is that person talking, sitting and walking about? is it not God? There is much work to be done in you before you realise that you and God are One. Wherever you find yourself, you are with God. All of you sitting here, and the people in the entire world are with God and God is in them. As from today do not speak on your own volition, always say I and my Father are One. When you speak on your own volition, you have put God to disgrace.

### FIRST LESSON; St John 10 v 30
### " I and my Father are One. "

Have you now realise why whatever you do, does not succeed and whatever you say does not come to pass? It is because you have separated yourself from God. Most people do not succeed in their undertakings because they attributed whatever they do, to themselves. In doing this they have excluded God from their business. Always say it is the Father doing this, or it is the Father who is speaking; then you will find that you will succeed in all your business, and God will be pleased with you. The work of God does not end in singing, dancing or giving of visions, but you must include God in every activity that you do and in every word that you speak. You will then see the glory of God in whatever you do. You have been told to give unto Caesar what is Caesar's, and unto God what is God's. Caesar is the flesh, and God is the Spirit. Give the glory that belongs to man to man, and give the glory that belongs to God to God, because God and man are One. Do not cause any division.

When somebody is sick and he goes to the hospital to be examined, if there is no water in him his life will pass away. The limited knowledge that medical doctors have, is to give drips. As soon as they put water into the person's body, the body springs up again. As we are sitting here, it is the water, blood and Spirit that does everything; when one is missing, that is the end of your life. The medical doctors know that when there is no blood in you, that is the end of your life. Whenever it is found that a person is lacking of blood, as soon as blood is put inside him, he will recover from his sickness. The failure of all the scientists, medical doctors and the entire world is that they do not know the Spirit; they do not know the Father. They know the Son and the Holy Spirit, which is Water and Blood. The Father is the Spirit, the Son is the Water and the Holy Spirit is the Blood. Whenever you have God in human form, you must always have the Water, Oil and the Word. When the Spirit departs from a person he is dead, but as soon as you sing a song such as, "Father send down thy power," that person wakes up again. This is a mystery to the world. That is why when you are sick you cannot eat solid food, you keep on drinking water only. There is nobody who knows where water comes from, and where it goes, nor does anyone knows where blood comes from and where it goes. That is the reason why you are warned not to eat blood. When you find somebody dead, all the blood in him goes out of him; the water is drained out of him and the Spirit goes away. The Trinity means, God in Water, Blood and Spirit. As we move about it is the Water, Blood and Spirit that keep us alive. These are the three things that keep us alive. You will see water and blood with your naked eyes, but you will not see the Spirit. That is why it is said that God is in the world, but the world does not know Him. The Father is the Word. You have heard that Spirit is the Word. That is the reason why when a person is dead, the Spirit goes away but the water and blood are there. When you call his name, he will stand up because the Spirit has re-entered into him. The on-lookers will say that you are a very powerful person; what do they mean by powerful? When you call his name you invoke Spirit into his body again, as soon as it enters into his body, he rises up. We claim to know God, but in our conversations we exclude Him. When you keep on saying, "I am alone, I do not have any relations," you are not honest with yourself. When you claim that you cannot do that particular thing, you have also failed. You have been warned not to make plans for tomorrow. When you say that tomorrow you will do this or that, you do not know what tomorrow have in store for you. Man is nothing but the dust of the earth. If you knew you would have said, if God wills I will do this or that. When the speaker begins to say that tomorrow he will do this or that, it is an insult to God. When you begin to make plans or proposals for tomorrow, you are speaking in the flesh, the Spirit is not involved.

Sometimes you hear a voice within you, telling you to do one thing or the other. Sometimes it tells you to fall in love with a girl. It is the water and blood in you that is speaking. The Spirit which is the Father; if He does not sign it, it cannot happen. Have you now found the reason why people have been saying that Brotherhood is not a church, but the highest Society in the world? The reason is because of the type of lessons that you receive here, such as this one delivered to you today. This gospel, if you were to write it and give it out to the people who are very advanced in secret societies, they will wonder where this doctrine comes from. You do not understand what is meant by the past, present and the future. The life you live now is directed by the flesh, but it had been written that the Spirit will lead. The water in your body has got his own assignment. The future is the Spirit, or God or Chairman, anything He does not sign cannot happen. It had been written that the Spirit of Truth will lead the world. If you act according to what the flesh tells you to do, you will never succeed. The flesh is blind and deaf; it is God who is the Spirit that is Omniscient, that controls the whole body. It had been written that flesh and blood will never inherit the kingdom of God. We must realise that God exists in dual nature. You will see another human being saying that he is a Prophet, or the Son of God. You will observe a human being coming up to you and say that he is God Almighty. When you are united with the Spirit, he will reveal all things to you.

If you have two people, you must have one who is the head. In the midst of five people there must be one who is at the head. Of the three entities; Water, Blood and Spirit; the Spirit is the Leader. That is the reason why when a doctor operates on a person, he will find water and blood. He will not find the Spirit, because the Spirit is God. Always include God in whatever business you do, because God is the Father. He is that Spirit. You will find that the flesh will tell you to go and steal, fornicate, hate, etc; rebuke the flesh; tell him that he should allow the Spirit to direct you. Water will also direct you to sin and look for mundane things, rebuke him. Allow the Spirit to direct you. Water and Blood are the instruments which the Spirit used to cover Himself. When our Lord Jesus Christ said, "I and my Father are One," the people did not understand the implications of this statement. They always took His words to be that of a mad person. A person having known the truth will not speak lies about what he knows to be true. Nevertheless the truth is better, and the world regard people who speak the truth as mad people. Ever since I told you that you are gods, and that God is in you, there is not one person that believe Me. There is no person that knows where water goes when it leaves your body. You are eating but you notice that blood is getting less in your body; where does it go? You discover that water is no more in your body, eventhough you may drink up to four or five cups daily. Now that water has left your body, where has it gone? Water and blood go with the Spirit. Water and Blood cannot do anything by themselves. When the three of them are combined they can work together. If there is no water in you, the Spirit can give you water. If there is no blood in you, the same Spirit can give you blood. When there is no water and blood in a person, call the Father, and the Spirit will be sent to provide water and blood. The blood leaves your body, when you have disconnected yourself from the Spirit. I am giving this gospel to the whole world; those who have ears will hear.

### SECOND LESSON: St John 14 v 10
**"Believest thou not, that I am in the Father, and the Father in Me? The words that I speak unto you, I speak not of Myself; but the Father that dwelleth in Me, He doeth the works."**

From today all your conversations should be with the Father. The Father is in us, yet we do not know Him. You are moving with the Father, carrying out your assignments with Him but you do not give glory to the Father. You give glory to yourself only. When the master goes in the company of his servant on an assignment, having completed that assignment, how can the servant claim all the glory for himself? God is a God of hosts, He does not move alone. He wants us to fully know Him as the Father. We have to know God and identify Him as He identifies us. At all times, God calls us His own children, but when you speak you disgrace God by excluding Him from your conversations. God teaches us His nature, that is why our Lord Jesus Christ said, "I am in the Father and the Father is in Me." This is a new language which all of us ought to learn. When somebody dies, with what do you ascertain that he is dead? A person can have water and blood rushing out of his body, but as long as he is speaking, he is still alive. A person can be living normally, but when you call him he does not answer. He is dead because the Spirit which is God has left him. Our Lord Jesus Christ said, "Father into thy hand I commend My Spirit." He bowed His head and the Spirit left Him. As soon as the Spirit goes out of you that is the end of your life. Water and blood can dry out of you, yet you are speaking because the Spirit is still in you. Since the Spirit is present, and He is the controller of water and blood, He can again cause water and blood to enter into your body.

Brethren, from today let us realise that we are the Christs of God. If we are not the children of God, why did God send the Spirit of His Son to dwell in our hearts to enable us to call God "Abba Father?" When people keep on asking you, where is that your Father, why do you not say "I and my Father are One?" Even if people keep mocking you and say that you are worshipping man. Remember that our Lord Jesus Christ said, that whosoever is ashamed to confess His name before men, He will also be ashamed to confess his name before the holy angels. I have introduced you to the whole world as the children of God. God is not at Biakpan or 34 Ambo Street, but He dwells in you. Go and tell everybody in the world that you and the Father are One; that you move hand in hand with God. Why people hate to see you knocking your head on the ground, is because they do not know that you do not knock your head to any person, but you knock your head to the person that is the Greatest who is inside you. Even if you have the smallest servant, know that you and that servant are one. No matter how old a person is, know that the old man and God are one.

It is not until a person comes to 34 Ambo Street, before God dwells in him. wherever you are, He is inside you. All we have to do is to believe that God is in us and we are all in Him. Do not go to Lagos in order to see God, or read a certain book in order to know Him. He is in you. It is not the flesh and blood that is God, but it is the presence of the Spirit in you that is God. When you pray to God saying, "Oh God come and save me; as you pray you will find a human being coming to help you with your problem. Who is that person? Is he not the same God you prayed to, to come and save you? Sometime you have no money and pray to God to come and give you money; then you find some one coming along and give you a thousand Naira. It is God that gives you that money. When you say that you do not need anything from anybody, it means that you will never have anything, because God and man are One. If you operate on a person you cannot separate God from him. I want to ask you, who is wrong or right? Is it Christ who says "I and my Father are One? The words that I speak I speak not of myself, but it is the Father who dwells in Me that speaks." And you who says, "I own myself, I speak my own words, and what I do I do it on my own." Who is right, is it you or Christ? Upon all the gospels which I preached to you from January to December that you and God are One, you do not want to believe. Do you not believe that when you see a human being, you have seen God? Whenever you see man, do not want to know where God is, look at yourselves because you are gods. As you are sitting here, God directs all your thoughts, movements and proposals, but if you do not call Him, you will not succeed. People thought that what our Lord Jesus Christ said, was exclusively about Himself alone. Since He is a Human Being, whatever He said includes all human beings. Do not say, I am not Jesus I am a human being; was our Lord Jesus Christ a tree or a stone? Do you not remember when He told Mary to go and tell her brethren that, "I have not yet ascended to My Father and your Father, and to My God and your God?" God is a universal God for all His creations. In as much that you do not know that you are in God and God in you, you will not fail to suffer.

Many of you keep on praying to God of Olumba Olumba Obu; some of you say that I am God, Spirit or Prophet or our Lord Jesus Christ; alright, what do you say about yourself? Give a testimony about yourself. Have I not declared that you are the Christs of God? You are spirits and gods; God dwells in you and you dwell in Him. I am going to prove how God dwells in you. If I dont prove to you how you and the Father are One, do not believe; if I prove it believe that the Father is the Spirit and the Son is the Water. When there is no water and blood in you, the Father who is the Spirit will supply both. This 1983, I have opened your eyes, ears and minds to hear the word of God and practise it. Our Lord Jesus Christ was ordained to speak in parables. That was why He spoke in parables; but the scripture said that when the Holy Spirit will come, He will reveal everything to you. That is why I have revealed everything to you, because I am the Supernatural Teacher, and I have the authority to teach and lead all the creations of God to the wisdom of truth. When this gospel is written, let it be sent to all the institutions of higher learning. Whoever he may be let him argue over this gospel. You will find that no one will argue. Have you ever come across people who argue and refute about the gospels delivered by the Holy Father? Whoever hears of the Father's gospel, must submit to it. I am not preaching, but revealing God to you; His nature, His likes and dislikes. Why did our Lord Jesus Christ say, "Love ye one another as I have loved you?" If you were not God the Trinity, why should our Lord Jesus Christ say, "Love one another as I love you?" Why did He also say that whosoever love his brethren loves God? Why did He also say, "I was hungry and you feed Me, I was in the hospital and you came to see Me?" The person answered, "When did I do all these things unto you?" He said that as long as you did it to these little ones, you have done it to Me.

When God is here in the mundane world He is a Human Being. If water, blood and Spirit are not in you, it means you are not God, for the three of them bear witness here on earth. Whenever God comes into the world, He is that Water, Blood and Spirit. Did you know that the Father, Son and Holy Spirit are in you? Therefore when somebody kneels down or bows to you, he is doing it to the Spirit that dwells in you. When you are bowing down, it is not you that bows but the Father, Son and Holy Spirit. God must respect Himself at all times. He never disgraces Himself, and He always honour His words. Why does He say in 1 Peter 2 v 17, "Honour all men, love the Brethren, fear God, honour the King?" Honour all men; who is man? is he not God? All the brethren are God. God is a Human Being. Who is the King? He is a human being. That is the reason why if you do not honour and serve men, you do not respect God, and you do not believe in God. This is not the era when you should boast that God knows your heart that you really love Him. At the same time you hate, quarrel, fight, and then you profess that God knows your heart. At the moment who knows himself? It is the Father passing through and doing every work. The Father constitute Water, Blood and the Spirit. When the medical doctors examine your body, have they found God in you? If the native doctor injects charm and black powder in your body, does he see this God? All the scientists, occult masters and astrologers, have they seen this God that I am revealing to you today? All of you sitting here and in the whole world, is there any person that has seen this God inside himself? It is said, "you shall know the truth, and the truth shall make you free." If the whole world would no more indulge in sins, they would be able to conduct themselves as gods. You would be able to say like our Lord Jesus Christ said, "I and My Father are One." Have you not heard that statement, "until the end of the world," but the world has no end; they say, world without end. People believed that God destroyed the world of Noah, I am saying that God did not destroy the world of Noah. Noah and his family that were saved, were they not water, blood and Spirit? If God had destroyed all the people in the generations of Noah, God would no longer exist. That would bring an end to the world. This lecture is greater than all of you. You are in the elementary school, some are in class one or class two. These lectures are meant for the great intellectuals of the world.

### GOLDEN TEXT: 1 JOHN 5 V 8
**"And there are three that bear witness on earth, the spirit and the water and the blood, and these three agree in one."**

Have you now seen the Trinity God? You sitting here are you not these three properties? When God is on earth, He is the three persons, Water Blood and Spirit. There is no other form God can take in the world, apart from water, blood and Spirit. Whenever you see a human being, do not ask about God, that is God before you. You own yourself, but you do not know what is within you. Anything can manifest in your body at any time, and you will not know. There is another person living inside you that is greater than you. That is the reason why, sometimes you may make up your mind to carry out a certain assignment, but cannot do it. It means that the Father has not signed it. Why is it that when something happens, everybody will congregate together with different ideas and opinions so that the situation may be corrected, but at the end all their plans and ideas will fail? It is because the Father was not there. When the Father is in heaven there are three things that represent Him, that is the Father, Word and the Spirit. When He is on earth, He is represented by water, blood and Spirit. Since we are looking for God with pride and arrogance, we cannot see Him. You believe that God is in the sky, and vow that you will never worship a human being. Have you gone to heaven to see God there? you can now see how ignorant human beings are. They keep on looking at the sky to see when our Lord Jesus Christ will come back. Christ when He was nailed to the cross, did He not say "Father into thy hand I commend My Spirit?" As soon as He said that, the Spirit left Him. When that soldier came to see if our Lord Jesus Christ was actually dead, he pierced His side with a spear and water and blood came out. These three properties, water, blood and Spirit, prove the deity of our Lord Jesus Christ.

Tell Me which human being that has this wisdom in the world? God has no other form but Water, Blood and Spirit. The fact is that you do not believe in Him. He said, "Let us make man in our own image." The trouble is that you do not worship God, neither do you respect anybody, because you cannot worship a human being. When you are beating somebody, how do you know that you are not beating God? Do you push God aside and slap that person? When somebody is hungry and you do not feed him, how do you know that you have not denied God food? If this house begins to leak and you do not repair it, it will affect the person who lives inside. That is the reason why, when God created man He said let your food be vegetables and fruits, because He knew that these things will supply water and blood to the body. Then God said, let the water bring out fishes, animals, etc; these are His body. Man attaches importance to eating meat, fish and other things not ordained for food. What drives water and blood from human beings' body is fornication. When you are intimate with a woman, at that one second the small sperms which pass into the woman is equivalent to the quantity of blood that will sustain your life for fifty years. Now that women cannot do without sexual immorality, and likewise men, when the blood is exhausted, they collapse and die. Then they attribute the cause to witchcraft, juju or other causes. If a man or woman stays without being intimate with one another, their blood remains pure, and they will not taste of death. The wines that you drink; the medications that you take, defiles your blood. It is exactly as if you bring fresh palm wine from the tree, and add water to it. You have adulterated that wine. You have heard that Adam lived for 930 years. The reason is that after Eve had three pregnamces, Adam prayed to God to remove the desire for sexual intercourse from him. They lived as brothers and sisters from then on; that is why they lived for 930 years. In your case you jump from one woman to another; when the blood in you is exhausted you drop dead. The snuff that you take dries up the blood from your body. Do you not know that you are the temple of God, and the Spirit of God dwells in you? Whoever defiles this temple of God will be destroyed. You defiles the temple of God when you do not believe that God dwells in you. As a result you begin to drink, smoke, fornicate, tell lies and live an abominable life. For this reason the Spirit leaves you.

All these buildings that you see are only to reveal God's work. God dwells in you and He will never abandon you. He said, "I will not leave you comfortless nor forsake you." Why did our Lord Jesus Christ ordered Peter to feed His sheep? Who are the sheep of the Lord? they are human beings. How does he care for them? It is by imparting all the teachings which Christ gave to him to human beings, in order that they should not adulterate the body of Christ by committing sins. Any person that does not believe that He and God are One; that he does not exists alone, but with God, is a child of perdition. Do not say that you are God, but that you and God are One. Have you not heard the statement, "I and my Father are One?" This means that you are one entity with God. It is said that when God is here on earth, three things identifies Him, they are water, blood and Spirit. Have you not found these three things in you? It is the Trinity God that you have been hearing about. The water and blood has power, but it is the Spirit that controls. What has caused all the confusion in the whole world is flesh and blood. This is what induces you to tell lies, steal, fornicate, drink and eat fish. Both the water and blood know that they are under the control of the Spirit. This is the reason why you must always subject yourself to the Spirit, who is Supreme. Brethren, anyone who loves God, must always love a human being that he can see. What is the work of God? It is to refrain from offending one another, because both man and God are One.

Never say that you are alone. Wherever you are, you are with God. The water cannot say that it is not Spirit, and therefore not from God. The blood cannot say that since it is not water, it is not from God. Nevertheless, the three of them have different assignments, but the Trinity is composed of Water, Blood and Spirit. This signifies the presence of God on earth. When our Lord Jesus Christ resurrected, He showed Himself to His disciples, but they were afraid because they thought He was a Spirit. He asked them to touch Him because He was flesh and bone, for Spirit has no flesh and bone. Whenever you call man, you must always include God. When the word of God is given to you, that is Spiritual food. When you eat feast such as bread, etc; this is to feed the flesh. You are witnesses that when we undertake the three days dry fasting, by the third day you become very weak. If you fast for longer period, the skeleton of your body begins to show; that is to say that the flesh is demolished, but the Spirit is still very strong. Do not forget that both of them are one. In the same token, when you steal, fornicate, drink and indulge in vices, the Spirit is affected. When the Spirit leaves, the flesh also colapse. You have to give to the flesh what belongs to the flesh, and give to the Spirit what belongs to the Spirit. When I give this gospel, it is for the Spirit. I then in turn give the body food. All the material things belongs to the flesh; while the Spirit requires the Words of God. Right from today, this gospel has opened your eyes. Wherever you go and people ask you, "where is that your Father?" tell them that you and your Father are One.

Worship God in you. Do not look for God in the Churches or in the sky. Worship God by refraining from sins. Some people say let us go to the Bethel; or I have made an altar there to worship God. Do not bring such foolishness into the Brotherhood of the Cross and Star. John the Divine said, "And I saw no temple there, fot the Lord Almighty and the Lamb are the temple of it." All things come from the Father and come out of you, so that you and the Father are One. We must know right from today, that we are one with the Father. If you believe that you are always with the Father, converse with Him at all times and you will never have any problems again. It is said that where your treasure is, there your mind is. If you know that the Father is in you and you concentrate all your attention on Him, you will no longer have problems. Since your mind is wandering; when you go on ministry work you claim that you have forgotten to take the Holy oil. Does it mean that the Holy oil is your God? Eventhough the Father is always with you, unless you call Him into your affairs, He will not say anything. Rememder when the disciples went out with our Lord Jesus Christ in a boat? When the boat was about to sink, our Lord Jesus Christ was watching them, when they called out to Him to rescue them. All the people in the whole world including the native doctors, juju priests and the churches, keep on saying that God is in the sky; whereas God is within you. He said call upon Me in the time of troubles and I will answer you. In the time of difficulties call upon Him, and He will answer you.

When Peter called out, "Master, master, we are going to perish." Our Lord Jesus Christ stretched out His hand and the sea became calm. The father is My witness that I have never told you that God is in Calabar, Lagos or America. I have told you that God is within you, and that you and God are One. Right now speak like our Lord Jesus Christ spoke, when He said "I and my Father are One." From today, do not exclude God from your activities. When food is put before you, call on the Father to bless it. As soon as you include the Father in all that you do, all is well. When you remove Him, you will have problems.

Brethren I do not want to be tedious unto you. It is said that a stroke of the cane is sufficient unto the wise. Let all those who have ears to hear, let them hear. May God bless His Holy Words, Amen.

# CHAPTER 16

# WHOSOEVER WANTS TO BE GREAT MUST FIRST BE A SERVANT

Everlasting Gospel delivered by Leader Olumba Olumba Obu
Sole Spiritual Head of the Universe.

First Lesson:    Romans 9 v 11
Second Lesson:   Romans 8 v 30
Golden Text:     1 Peter 2 v 9

Brethren, that is the revelation of our lesson this morning. Many people say that the way of God is straightforward. He is not like a human being, He makes no mistakes, and in Him is found no guile. He does not take the advise of any human being, nor does He take directives from any human beings. He does everything according to His wish. You will realise that whatever happens here, does not depend on what you can do; it does not depend on your righteousness; but rather right from the begining when the children were not yet born; when they had not done anything good or evil, it had been nominated that the elder shall serve the younger.

**Everything happens according to the will of God.**

This goes to show when you sometimes lament, and say that it is because of the sins which you have committed why you find yourself where you are, I tell you that this is irrelevant. It does not depend upon how much you conduct yourself, or how much you protect yourself against the enemy. God does not do anything to please any human being. He does not do anything for any specific reason. He has no reason and no conditions to comply with. He does His Things simply because He is the Almighty God. It does not show that He likes you more than the other person, or that He loves the other person more than yourself, but He does everything for the fulfillment of His own will. Many people say that God loves them, while others say that God does not love them. People complain that God has done something for the other person, it does not mean that He does not do anything for them. And God says, "Those people who were not my people, I will call My beloved children;" who knows where these people would come from?

**The Words of God only fulfills in man:**

He further said: "At the fullness of time those who were not called My beloved children, would be called dearly beloved wife; " who are not the beloved children of God? The trouble is that we do not fully grasp or believe the words of God, because they cannot touch down on the ground and return empty handed. When they come down, they would break the mighty rocks, and when they rise they would fulfill His will. The words of God can never be manifested in trees, rocks and other inanimate things. They must be manifested in human beings. If there are any words of God that are to be fulfilled in the trees, they would certainly be fulfilled in the trees. But the majority of the words spoken by God are fulfilled in human beings.

### The identity of God is not easy to recognise:

Sometimes ago it was prophesied by the old Prophets that a young virgin would conceive in her womb, and would bring forth a child who would be named Emmanuel. No specific name was given; no particular village was mentioned; it was just spoken in a blank checque form of description that a virgin would be conceived in her womb, and would bring forth a child whose name would be called Emmanuel. No person bothered to know what was prophesied about Christ or what would happen, but at the birth of somebody and at the fulfillment of all the predictions and prophesies, it was clear that He was the one who was prophesied about. This is the reason why we must search the scriptures. Once you are able to search the scriptures, all the things written by God will be understood by you. That was why, when Andrew saw our Lord Jesus Christ, he went and told his brother Simon saying, "Come we have found the Messiah who was written about." If people were to read the bible they would have understood what is right. Your merely looking at somebody's facial appearance will not just indicate to you what that person is. Immediately you are able to search the scriptures, then whatever you are able to deduce from the scriptures, you will be able to identify Him.

### The First shall be Last, and the Last First:

On the prediction that the elder will serve the younger, very many people regard Jacob as a very cunning and crafty person, as if it were not the prediction or prophesy of God. If you regard him as a cunning fellow, you should go and play that kind of prank with people and see whether you will succeed. It was not only in the case of Esau and Jacob; you also heard the passage read in the scriptures, that the first shall be last and the last first. Our Lord Jesus Christ also indicated that all those who came after Him are thieves and robbers. These words have been made manifest. Why the people believed that the Son of God had made His visitation on earth, was that all the predictions that were made and written had been fulfilled at the fullness of time when our Lord Jesus Christ came to the earth in the likeness of man, but He was God on earth. He came down and people saw the manifestation of His Deity.

### The will of God is Supreme:

Whatever you execute in this life which does not comply with what has been nominated on the pages of the scriptures, are null and void and without effect. That is why the scientists and all the learned men of the world, have endeavoured to get the Bible burnt so that they can write their own scriptures which will comply with their own teachings. You will see newly written version of the bible from America; some of them are called the Revised Standard Version; others are called the Duoy Version.; various names are given, distorting the salient facts in the Bible; but have you seen nominated on the pages of the Bible, the name America, Britain or London, Lagos, Madrid or Paris? You can never see Nigeria, Ghana or indeed any other city in the Bible until Doomsday, but something has been written about a particular place which shows itself when you look carefully on the situation of things.

Our Lord Jesus Christ gave this parable; He said that a certain man had a farm; He kept in the farm some husbandmen, and from time to time He had to send some men to inspect the farm. Each time they went, they were tortured, beaten up and some killed. He again sent another set of people to inspect the farm and they were treated the same way. At the end he sent his only begotten son, thinking that when he appear before the husbandmen they would fear him and regard him as the Son of God, but as soon as the only begotten Son of God arrived on the farm they said: "Look at the person who is heir to the inheritance, let us kill him;" and so they communed together and killed the Son of God. That was the reason why He asked, " When the owner of the farm comes what shall he do to .those wicked husbandmen?" They answered that when the owner of the farm would come, he would bring his soldiers to exterminate all the wicked husbandmen, and the whole farm would be handed over to a righteous nation. Our Lord Jesus Christ said, "Yes you have rightly answered, have you not heard that the stone which the builders rejected have become the chief corner stone?"

### Righteousness alone exalts a Nation:

He concluded by telling them that this kingdom of God shall be taken away from them and given to a nation which will bear good fruits. He did not mention Calabar, He did not mention England, He did not mention Nigeria, He did not mention any particular place, rather He said," This kingdom shall be taken away from you and given to a nation which will bear good fruits." It is an act of foolishness for any person to say that he is going to Jerusalem, Bethlehem or any other place. What purpose will it serve you to go to such places? Have you not been listening to the words of God? Some people claim to have gone to the place where our Lord Jesus Christ was buried, and went into the sepulchre. In all these, you are wasting your precious time and energy.

Have you not heard what the scriptures have told you that this kingdom will be taken away from them and given to a nation that will bear good fruits? You may be the one, it may be any other person, any continent or any community.

### Jerusalem is no longer a Holy City:

Any time you want to go to Jerusalem, you say you are making a pilgrimage to the Holy City; Why do you describe it as a Holy City? Abel was killed there; our Lord Jesus Christ and many others were killed there. You would rather call it an evil city; a city where people commit all kinds of atrocities, and the Father would never go there. Sometimes I hear people say that they went to Jerusalem; what have they gone to do at a place where God has rejected? Sometimes you say that you have gone to Egypt, Jerusalem or Bethlehem and I ask you: what did you go to do in those rejected cities? He had said that this kingdom will be taken away from them and given to any nation, the emphasis is on "Nation" and I ask you: Is that nation Calabar? They have not mentioned Nigeria, they have not mentioned Ghana, Britain or America, but any nation that bears good fruits.

### The Way of God is like the Pilgrim Progress:

If you find any city where the inhabitants do the will of God, that would have been the city that is referred to by this passage. You have also heard: that many shall come from the East and West, and will sit down with Abraham, and Isaac and Jacob, in the kingdom of God; but the children of the kingdom shall be cast out of the kingdom. It is the height of foolishness for you to say that this kingdom emerges from the black man's country, or from my territory, or it does not come from the white man's country; have you not listened attentively to the scriptures? The ways of God can be compared to the Pilgrim Progress. Have you not heard what the people said? They asked:" Who is Jesus? we have known His father, His mother, brothers and sisters, and where He comes from; but when the Messiah will come, no one will know His father and mother, and no one will know where He will come from." Is that not a stupid type of statement? Another person asked: Have the children of Israel stumbled that they should fall? God forbid; but rather through their fall, salvation is come unto the Gentiles. Ponder over that statement: that the elder shall serve the younger; it is just as if you have water inside the canoe and when the boat rows the water goes backward and forward. Now that he has first elected the second born, what do you think will happen to the first born, will He bestow His blessing on him? Prophecies will pass away, languages will vanish, but love will abide forever; that first love which He had for the first born, do you think that first love had eluded him? He will continue to show that expression of love for the first born.

### Africa is the Cradle of Civilisation :

The two children you heard about were Esau and Jacob. Abraham begat Isaac, and Isaac begat Esau and Jacob, and these two were twins. It was prophesied before they were born, that the elder shall serve the younger. In order to fulfill the scriptures, you have been hearing stories about Esau, how he was toiling and labouring all throughout his life. Esau symbolises Africa and the black race, and Jacob symbolises the white race. I want to make it quite clear to you that Africa is ever known as the cradle of civilisation. Whatever inventions and discoveries you can think of today, all came from Africa. God Himself was born in Africa. All what the Europeans are struggling for now, are in vain, since it has already been written, signed, sealed, stamped and delivered; the whole thing tends to tilt towards Africa. The irony of it all is that the Africans do not even believe in this; they believe that the whites have gone very far, and that there is no possibility of catching up with them. What they do not know is that Africa is the land of Salvation. God was born in Africa, and all good things must come from there; therefore the whites must come down and worship God in Africa. Can you, therefore, see the type of manipulation that the Europians have adopted to outwit you? Can you definately say that our Lord Jesus Christ was born in Britain, America, or that He was a white man? Was He really an english speaking person? Did He know how to speak the English language? He had never been to Britain, He had never been to America, but He had gone on a ministry work to India. This is just to indicate to you, that God does not behave the way human beings behave. No matter what Jacob did to usurp the first position of the brother; he struggled and did everything, but since God had written, He had signed, sealed and delivered it, no person can expunge the episode from the annals of Bible History. What God had documented must remain forever. It actually means that the older will first of all toil, and moil before he takes his rightful position.

### Whoever wants to be Great must first be a Servant:

Have you not heard the statement of our Lord Jesus Christ that whosoever wants to be great amongst you must, first of all make himself a servant, and messenger? If you want to gain an important position, you have to serve diligently in order to establish your position as a big man.

Whoever wants to be a leader, the primus inter pares (first among equals) must, first of all, enslave himself to others. The way of God is very narrow and difficult to pass through; it is filled with all sorts of thorns and incriminating weapons. If you find somebody trying to meander through, such a person would always complain that heaven and earth are against him. If you see somebody sitting at akimbo, enjoying himself, you feel that he is in heaven. It is not so, the situation cannot be a bed of roses. Our Lord Jesus Christ said: "As the Son of Man did not come to be ministered unto, but to minister, and give His life a ransom for many." Have you seen the manifestation of this statement in the world today? Have you observed the manipulation of words, when in another passage He says: "And again when He bring in the First Begotten into the world; (He did not say when He will bring in His Second), He says: when He will send down His First Begotten into the world, He will say: let all the angels of God worship Him." This shows you how flexible the words of God are.

### The Words of God are not Contradictory but Complimentary:

When, in another statement He said, that the people who were not My people will be called the beloved children of God. To what place did He refer? Is it not Africa? What I am telling you is fully understood by the whites. When they will come in, if you are not careful yourselves, they will so enjoy the activities in Brotherhood, that you will be surprised. What remains is that since God has promised to give this kingdom to all of you, there will be no way of His taking it away from you. Have you not heard what is said that, whether there be prophecies, they shall fail; whether there be tongues they shall cease; whether there be knowledge it shall vanish away; all things will pass away, but Love will endure forever. Have you no ears to listen to this type of language? It is a very important statement. You will realise that the World Wars were meant to usher in something into the world; the First World War of 1914-1918, and the Second World War of 1939-1945; all that we have learnt is the ushering in of the visitation of God into the world. Every spectacular situation that has been created, is in preparation for the arrival of God, and for the manifestation of the Holy Spirit.

### Not to him who wills, but to God Who has mercy:

Considering the period of time that the Children of Israel were enslaved in Egypt for 430 years; what sort of weapons of war could they have acquired for themselves in order to fight and liberate themselves and move from Egypt? In all these years that the Africans were under the slavery of the Whites, the colonial rule, what impliments of war could they have acquired for themselves in order to fight against the Whites to liberate themselves? If it were a matter of war, Africa would not have had anything to use in fighting against the whites; because if you talk of money, it is produced by the whites; if you talk of the manufacure of weapons, they stand foremost and we always go to buy from them; you will not be able to manufacture your own in order to fight against them. Have you seen the way God has used to liberate You? That is the same way God has used in liberating the children of Israel from the land of bondage. Do you realise that all what obtains in the world, are the fingers of God in action?

### Birth place is incontestable:

There is nothing like satan, apparition and mermaid. There is nothing like disappointment. Whatever you see from day to day is the fulfillment of the will of God. The First Lesson will now be read.

### FIRST LESSON: ROMANS 9 V 11

"For the children being not yet born, neither having done
any good or evil, that the purpose of God according to
election might stand, not of works, but of him that calleth."

I now ask the question: Does it now mean that Jacob has become the first born? Eventhough the first is serving the second, has Jacob taken the position of the first son? Once you are the first, you continue in the position of the first forever. The first has really to serve the second, but the position of the first born is incontestable, but continues to remain for the rightful owner. As it was written about our Lord Jesus Christ that people would persecute Him, kill Him, and He would rise from the dead after three days; as the people had taken such steps against our Lord Jesus Christ, did they remove from Him the position of the Messiah, the Christ of God? All that has been written about you, that people will persecute you, hate you, kill you, punish you, torture and torment you; these things have been written to be fulfilled in you.

These situations cannot cause the promise of God, not to be fulfilled in you.

### Birth Place Lost Now Regained:

If you search the scriptures, you will discover that Jacob was not wealthier than Esau. After he had sojourned in a strange land for a long time, he came back and when he met his brother, he (Jacob) bowed down, showing that Esau was still his senior. He divided some of his wealth to his brother, but before he did this, Esau had already established in the land. The relationship between him and his brother was just the fulfillment of what had been written. Esau was the first born, he served his father day and night, that was why Isaac wanted to give him the blessing; but because of the mother's manipulation, Jacob received the blessing instead of Esau, thus fulfilling what was prophesied that the elder shall serve the younger.

### God Is Unchangeable:

The whites have known this, but they are struggling in their own way. Because of the low position which the Africans have occupied, they are struggling in their own way. It has now dawned on them that God has arrived. They now have to take their rightful position. God has never forgotten His own promise. What He has promised stands forever. Do you think that God can forsake His first son and replace him with the second? That prophecy has now been set aside, but the glory of God must continue to be manifested. It was also prophesied that our Lord Jesus Christ would be persecuted and crucified, and that prophecy has now been put aside. Right now there is no such thing again, He has now come to rule over the whole universe. When you hear of any prophecy, do not begin to quake, stand firm because God is unchangeable, there is no variableness in Him. You are advised that you should not be weary in well doing, for in due seasons you will reap good fruits if you faint not. Since God has elected His First Son to take over the superintendency of the entire world, no matter what others do, it is man who has been elected to rule. After God had created every other thing including animals, birds, fishes in the water, trees and creeping things, He then give man the superintendency to rule over His creations. It is said that the Spirits of all those who prophesied, will continue to remain under His rule.

### Arfica Is The Kingdom Of God:

That was why that Centurian told our Lord Jesus Christ, "For I am also a man set under authority, and I say to one go and he goes, and to another come and he comes; You are also a man set under authority, you can say to the Spirit go and he goes, and if you say to another come, and he will come." From the begining God had not said that Angels should rule. No matter how weak man may be, no matter how stupid man may be, God can never regret the position that He has given to man, that position he will continue to nurture and glorify. In the same token, since God has made the proouncement as regards the city of God, the Kingdom of God is Africa, and God germinated in Africa. That has been written, it has been signed, sealed and delivered, there is no running away from it. It has come to stay; and when the name of the Father is mentioned the people laugh, arguing that there is nothing you can do, you have no money, you cannot invent anything, what can you do? The visit of our women to Great Britain, was the handwork of God. God is doing His work in a marvelous way, under the ground, in the air and everywhere.

God gave the worldly people the opportunity to open universities, departments of religion, seminaries, bible colleges, trinity colleges to study the bible, theology and religion; but within the twinkle of an eye, He turned the table and things have appeared in a way they would not have appeared. If it were said that the black man would go and teach the whites how to manufacture aeroplanes and motor cars, that could have been acceptable to them. If it were said that the Africans should open universities in order that these people should come and learn, it would have been acceptable to them; but to say that the whites should come and receive the Words of God and be taught by an African, that is what they think is unacceptable to them.

### The Incomprehensibility of God's Ways:

The Americans feel that should God have to come back on earth, He would be born unto them and so they have started making preparations. I wonder whether they have been reading the scriptures to know what was written about this particular time? These people rather than look for Christ, are looking for riches; and people will accumulate riches for a time, and after a short time they disappear. The ways of God are incomprehensible. If there is any person who argues that he cannot fear God, let such a person think about himself. Up till now you are still doubting; why should such a thing happen here in Calabar; not in any other place, but in Nigeria, indeed in Africa? God has never forgotten you, He has not failed to fulfill His promise, but He exercises long patience. May be many of the white men have been conjecturing why things are found the way they are; no person has been able to know why things are happening the way they do.

I am going to tell you the reasons today. Why you are doubting, is that you think that there is no good thing that has come from Africa to the European countries; and no person has known the reason why things are happening the way they do. The reasons are what I am going to give to you this morning.

### Can Any Good Thing Come From Africa?

You are witnesses to the fact that you are all poor people, you are all stricken with abject poverty; you have no money, you have no wisdom, you have not attained any height in education, and you do not know anything at all; why should this type of thing happen within you? All Church denominations originated from the European countries; all monies came from the European countries; languages came from there; wealth were brought from there; but just look at us here, we do not know anything; we cannot do anything, but many spectacular things have happened. You are still doubting and do not believe yourselves, you rather depend so much on the whites. God has never forgotten the black man. He had already made His promise. It does not depend on how rich you are; it does not depend on how educated you are; it does not depend on the good things you can do, but He has redeemed His promise by allowing His wishes to be fulfilled in you.

### God's Wisdom Hidden From The Wise And Prudent But Revealed To Babes:

You would see why it has been possible for women to travel to overseas countries; children and illiterates have travelled to European countries. This is not because you are going on your own volition, but it is the fulfillment of the will of God. You do not find millionaires, governors, princes and princesses, kings, emperors and principalities of this world here; you do not find presidents, and uniformed personalities in the society here; you have no money and you have nothing at all, but you continue to doubt why these things should happen in your midst. You have not gone to school, you do not know how to speak any language, but you see how things are moving in a mysterious way.

### Brotherhood Manifested:

Brethren, many people look astonished at what is happening in Brotherhood of the Cross and Star; they become so bamboozled because when they ask you which Bible College you attended but you did not read the bible; how many years you spend at university but you did not attend any university; it is very surprising to them. Another surprising thing is that if you went anywhere, you would not hear any news about any person, you would hear about God. Go to the streets in London, America, or Nigeria, you cannot hear any other thing apart from Brotherhood. If you go into the midst of people, you constitute yourself as an object of fear to people, they do not come near you; even in your families, people look at you with surprise. So, brethren, when you read the scriptures, you should be very careful. Read between the lines, the words spoken by God. That is the reason I ask you why do you look at Me as if I use My power to do all the things you see; it is the fulfillment of the prophecy of God, and whenever you see the manifestation of what God has promised, which will come to pass in this last age. God does not forget the destitutes and the afflicted, what He has chosen He has chosen, what He has loved He has loved. Already people are complaining that when the whites come they will take over their places from them, and I ask: with what will they take your places from you? Will they take them away from you by wealth or by attainment in education? They can never take your places away from you. And so, brethren, I do not intend to take you further than this, I do not preach but I am revealing. You have to listen attentively to the second lesson which is going to be read to you.

### SECOND LESSON: ROMANS 8 V 30

" Moreover whom He did predestinate, them He also called; and whom He called, them He also justified; and whom He justified, them He also glorified."

You have been reading through that passage, have you ever understood the meaning of the passage? Those whom He first predestinated, He called, justified and glorified. Because He first called the Africans, He kept them in the position which He first called, but you feel that you are a rejected race. How has He rejected you? He has predestinated you and has called you back to give you that glory which was yours. Have you not seen the position of the elder, even though it was said that the elder shall serve the younger? Lately that prophecy has been fulfilled, but the position of the first born is still there. He first of all justified him, and has kept him in the position of the first born to glorify him.

### The Stages of World Civilisation:

If you read the history of the world, you will see the various stages of civilisation. After the Egyptians, you will see the land of the rivers Tigris and Euphrates, the Middle East, the Europian countries and the African countries. All these places were there. That position of the first born was given to Africa. That is why, as He has come back, eventhough you must have been cheated in the past; eventhough you must have been relegated now He has come and on His arrival, He has first called you and predestinated you; He has justified you now; He has given you the glory.

### Your Sonship is based on Predestination:

If any person should ask you why these things should happen, open that passage to him, let him see the evidence for a proof, because God does His things according to His will. It does not depend upon how righteous you are, or what you can do, but once He has destined you for any position, He must have to fulfill His promise. The whites have gone to the Moon and to all the planets; they have learnt all forms of disciplines and subjects, but since God has given this glory to you, have you not seen His appearance? He has first of all predestinated you, and has kept His promise for you; He has now fulfilled that promise by calling you and placing you at your rightful position. He has blessed you, justified you and has glorified you. He has given you a commission to march into all parts of the world, and to liberate them. It does not consist in the knowledge of science and technology, or in any other thing, but He has emphasised that those whom He first predestinare, He first of all call them; and since He had first called them, He has justified them; and since He had first justified them, He has glorified them. He has not considered others yet, but has first of all predestinated you, called you, justified you and glorified you.

### Calabar the City of God:

Why do you find London and America the theatres of christian religion this day? This is because these two countries feel that they are the only cocks to crow, therefore, no other country should introduce the idea of christian religion to any part of the world. That is why they are taking the lead as God has made His visitation to this part of the world, they have sent their spies to all parts of the world. Why is it that the City of Calabar has been the greatest theatre of Brotherhood of the Cross and Star? This particular place, as its name implies according to the local interpretation: "If you are capable then you can live in." Of all the towns and cities in Nigeria, and indeed West Africa, the first place where the first missionaries arrived was Calabar. Why is it that Calabar has become the headquarters of the City of God? People from various tribes of this country are here. Nothing has ever had its root in Calabar, no matter what it is, the people of Calabar will uproot it. They had sworn that no white man would preach the word of God in their land. They would pay deaf ears to the whites, not to talk of a black man. No person can give any type of instruction here and it will be received by any person.

### You are not Elected because of your Righteousness, but because you had been Predestinated:

Brethren, I want to ask you, is it because we are good, or because we are righteous, or because we are looking for God; is it because we have good conduct, or that we have served Him rightly, that we should be lead into this kingdom? All these times did you know that you were the people selected and kept from the begining of time, and you were the persons to whom God had kept this promise? Many people have asked this question: why is it that God has first of all selected me? He should have first of all selected the important personalities and those who have good conduct. It had been laid down by God according to His divine plan, before the foundations of the world were laid, your name has been nominated in that register. Do you realise that God has justified all of you? you have no case to answer. Have you realised that God has glorified you? He has bestowed unto you that glory which you had from the begining of the world.

### Africa a Holy Nation:

That is the crown He has placed on your head. Are you not surprise that you who were not known anywhere, but now everywhere you go, every person takes cognisance of you, and wherever you go people cowtow on the ground for you? They now know you but in the past no person had known you. You had never been known in your family. Whenever any person mention your name, no person recognised you, but now you are the narch of all the surveys. So brethren, have you now realised why God has first of all come down to the Africans? This is because He had kept this glory for Africa, and has predestinated Africans. This glory is bestowed on them because it was kept for them before the foundations of the world were laid.

### A Prophet is not Without Honour Save in His own Country:
The emphasis is that those whom He first predestinated, He has first called them, and as He has called them He has justified them, and as He has justified them He has glorified them. It does not mean that others will not come, but He will first of all consider you. Very many educated and highly placed Africans come into Brotherhood first of all in London or America; if you call them at home, they would say, "Ah, who is your Leader, is He educated, how many degrees has He, I have had up to four degrees." When they go to Britain or America, that is where they would embrace Brotherhood. Have I not told you that work has not yet started in earnest? When it shall start, you will travel to all parts of the world, you will travel to all nooks and corners, and will reach even the utmost parts of the earth. You will go to India, Asia, China, Czechoslovakia, and everywhere. Have you realised that the power God has given to Adam, to superintend over all of His creations, to name them and take control over everything; that glory which was lost has now been regained; that paradise lost has now been restored to him?

### Man was Destined to Rule:
He did not say that animals, birds, fishes, trees, sticks or any other thing should superintend and take dominion over the creations of God. He had appointed Adam to superintend, to control and have dominion over all the things that He has created. God has never used the animals, birds, fishes, trees or any other thing to reveal His glory. He uses man to reveal His own glory. That is why God said: "Let us create man in our image and likeness." It is this man that He uses to reveal His glory. This is not something that somebody should ask you to gird your loins. You should get yourself fully prepared because you have never seen such a thing in Africa, or Nigeria where people gather and donate handsomely. Have you not seen how God has worked mysteriously, do you not see how things are working smoothly here?

### Ethiopia Shall Rise Again:
A black man does not go to church because he wants to listen to the words of God, he goes there because he is hungry. The white man would bring money to feed him, and out of this he would not contribute one Kobo; and so the upliftment of the work of God in that particular church will not grow. Now you will hear them ask you whether the headquarters of that church is in Britain or America. This is because the church denominations of which they are members, come from either America or Britain. The white missionaries used to give them money, and so when you say that Brotherhood is from Calabar in Africa, they feel that there is no rich men there who can give them a Kobo. Brethren, do you not see what has happened? This is the fullness of time. God can even use the rocks to fulfill His own promise. He is sending you out, this would not have happened in the past, but right now being the fullness of time, He has commissioned you; and you will be able to enter into all facets of society to give people the words of life and the words of comfort.

### If these were to hold their Peace the Stones would cry out:
You will see what is going to happen. Every person is thinking about evangelism, you want to enter into all parts of the world, and into all facets of the society and to the utmost parts of the earth, to preach the word of God. This has been the pre-occupation of every person now. During our Lord Jesus Christ's triumphant entry into Jerusalem, the people were shouting "Hosanna to God in the highest," the people asked our Lord Jesus Christ to tell people to keep quiet, but He told them: "If these people should hold their peace, the stones would immediately cry out." So brethren, you have to be watchful because no person is responsible for what is happening, it is the fullness of time.

### The Vision of the Nuns, Concealed by the Pope:
Anything done by the finger of God will be fulfilled at this end of time, and it must be consummated. First, have you known that you are one of those for whom God had kept this kingdom? In the second place, have you known that you have been elected by God? Thirdly, have you known that you have been justified and you have no case to answer? In the fourth place, have you known that God has bestowed His own glory on you? You have been given the commission to rule over the creations of God. If it were something to purchase with money, you would have boasted, but now everything is in the hands of the Father. He is the only person who knows, even if you are told you wiould not understand. Most of those who are members of Roman Catholic Church have been converted here now. Have you not heard about the vision of the three nuns, and what has happened at this end of time? This vision has been given to them, it was written and given to the Pope in a sealed envelope.

After seeing what it contained, he sealed the envelope and refused to disclose the contents so that people might not know that an African was going to rule. People have been pestering the life of vatican officials to release the vision of the three nuns, but no person want to release it. If you were the Pope would you have released it. After reading that the person who will rule rhe world would be a black man, an African, would you have released it? That means He will rule, including every person.

**It is a Tabu to Read the Bible in some Church Denominations:**

Have you seen the behaviour of the whites? But the Bible says: "There is nothing hidden that would not be revealed, and there is nothing hidden inside the house that would not be brought on top of the roof." What they had tried to conceal, has it not been disclosed now? Those of you who are members of certain church denominations knew that in the past you dared not open the Bible, otherwise you were committing a grievious sin. No person from the catholic church reads the Bible; what was read was the extracts from the Bible and the small missal, but recently they said that they would not continue to conceal this, they have started to read the Bible; and since they have seen that their doctrine does not comply with the teachings of the Bible, some of them have withdrawn and others have revolted. So brethren, no person can conceal what is kept by God, when the fullness of time comes, it would be laid bare before the public, and every person would know its manifestation. Do not glorify yourself, rather give glory to God because all what He has spoken has become manifest. The Golden text will now be read, you will see what was written about, and you also see the fulfillment.

### GOLDEN TEXT : 1 PETER 2 v 9

"But ye are a chosen generation, a royal priesthood, a holy natioin, a peculiar people; that ye should shew forth the praises of Him who hath called you out of darkness into this marvelous light."

**Africans are Chosen People:**

Brethren, have you heard what is read to you? He says that you are a chosen people, you have been chosen by Him. You are a royal priesthood, a holy nation which you have heard about; a peculiar people who have been called out of darkness; then you should go forth and show the marvelous light. That is why you are referred to as wonderful people. It is impossible that you can determine what you can do, you are not living unto yourself again. As you are sitting down here, you are thinking about so many things; how to project the image of God throughout the whole world. Until you get to Russia or the Netherlands, you would not know, others will travel by plane, others by motor car, some by ship or submarine. You will reach all parts of the world, declaring the words of God. And when you are elected into this kingdom, you have no other work to perform apart from showing this marvelous work to people; converting your offices into Bethels; everywhere you go, you have no other duty to perform apart from preaching the words of God.

**Brotherhood is a Royal Priesthood:**

This is why they complain that Brotherhood members leave their offices and go on ministry work. This is the fulness of time, and so these things must come to pass. Your whole minds have been filled with the thoughts of God. You have no other things to pre-occupy your minds. You have to think about Him, and you have to go about working for Him. A Brotherhood member was appointed a pilot, and when he entered into the plane he turned the plane into a Bethel. If he is appointed captain of a ship, he will convert the ship into a Bethel; it is not his own making, it is the handwork of the Father. If you appoint a Brotherhood member on the staff of any school, he would convert the school into a Bethel; whether he is a police, he would convert the police barracks into Brotherhood Bethel and would preach Brotherhood in the whole establishment. No man is responsible for all these. It is because you have been glorified and commissioned to go and preach; and where people were in darkness you bring them out into the light.

**Africa is a Holy Nation:**

You are a chosen people, a royal priesthood, you are a holy nation, a peculiar people, wonderful sets of people. That is why whenever you go close to people, they try to keep you at arms length. As you are sitting down here, some people are going inside the forest, some to towns, cities, villages and hamlets, preaching to people. You cannot sit down at your place of work, in your market stall, you cannot stay with your husband or wife in the house. People continue to complain that I am responsible for all these things, I have not done it. Have you ever seen Me sitting down in one place? It is the handwork of God.

Do not say that you are tired and that you are going to rest, but continue to preach day in and day out, throughout the year. Do you consider that this work is done by man? Have you ever seen a married woman, a Mistress, abandoning her matrimonial home and her husband and going on ministry work to America or Europe: do you think that she has done it out of her own volition? No person is responsible for it, it is the handwork of the Father. Have you ever found a government official leaving his place of work, sometimes without permission, taking his Holy Bible on ministry work and preaching the words of God, and not fearing that he would be disciplined? Are you not surprised that you can leave your office for one month for ministry work, and on your return no person queries you nor disciplines you, but at the end of the month you are paid your correct salary, without any complaint against you?

**Where the Spirit of God is, There is Liberty:**

Are you not surprised that even if you are in the Governor's office, you would stand up to preach and people would gather around you to hear the words of God, and no person would raise an eyebrow; rather they would open their mouth and listen to the words of God; do you think it is the handwork of man? It is the handwork of God, that at the fulness of time such a thing would happen. It is because you have been called and assigned to go and do this work; that is why He has called you, He has justified you and glorified you. He has called you a chosen people, the royal priesthood, a holy nation, a peculiar people. That is why He wants you to go out and proclaim His wonderful works. Where there is darkness, you bring about a marvellous light.

**Show the Light and People will Follow:**

If you go to a place where it is said that people should not say anything about Brotherhood, you would be prepared to back away from such a place. So brethren, that is what is before you. That is the job you have to perform. You have to go out and show people this light. Go and sing His praises, go and magnify His name that you have been brought ffom darkness into marvellous light.

Brethren, a stroke of the cane is sufficient unto the wise, those who have ears let them hear. May the Lord bless His Holy Words, Amen.

# CHAPTER 17

# MURDER

**Everlasting Gospel Delivered By: Leader Olumba Olumba Obu,
Sole Spiritual Head of the Universe.**

FIRST LESSON:      St Matthew 5 v 21 - 22
SECOND LESSON:  St Matthew 26 v 52
GOLDEN TEXT:      Revelation 13 v 10

"To some of us it appears that there are many men of God in this world; and we begin to wonder why in spite of all these men, there is still all that much sin in the world today. Our first lesson shows that from the begining of the world, the supposed men of God were really not what they claimed or what people thought them to be; because they were all guilty of murder. We know that of all the sins, murder is the greatest; " And ye know that no murderer hath eternal life abiding in him." The greatest commandment ever given by God is, "Thou shalt not kill." This commandment is the main reason why others are given.

### Most Precious:

Man is the most precious handiwork of God, and the destruction of man's life in whatever way or by whatever means, compels God's anger, and His justice of "measure for measure" against the destroyer and the killer. Therefore, anybody who does not want his own life to be pestered or destroyed, should not pester or destroy another person's life.

### Murderer:

But if a man of God is a murderer, what remains of him to turn to satan? As a murderer he is already dead, and his work of God is also dead. So are they all dead, who claim to be doing the work of God but who have all committed murder. And since they are dead, those who are supposed to destroy sin; sins live and abound. Therefore, the sin of murder makes it impossible to find one man of God ever since. To be a murderer, one needs not necessarily shoot with gun, cut with machette or slay with the sword. There are several other ways in which murder can be committed: broadly by thought word and deed. If you kill with the word of mouth, it is the same murder as poisoning, beating with stick, bombing or slaying with the sword. If you bear grudge against anybody, or say to somebody "Raca" you have committed murder in your heart and by your speech. Whenever you speak any type of evil against anybody you have committed murder.

### Murder By Intention:

If you have any intention to kill; if you sharpen your knife, prepare your gun or other weapons of war with intention to attack and destroy life; even without making the attack yet, you have already committed murder. Apart from the actual preparation, the intention is sinful enough to be the offence. If you have any secret meeting to plan how to attack and kill any person, you have already committed murder by the mere planning. Yet, today what appears to be the universal handiwork of everybody is, the piling up of weapons of war to attack, kill and defend; and defence is our lame excuse. Before you say that a man is a real christian, have you examined him to see that he is not in any way guilty of murder? If we commit murder and deserve to suffer as murderers, why then should we doubt the way things have been going wrong with us? God does not want us to suffer. In this wisdom He knows that any person who commits murder either by thought, word or deed; must suffer exactly the same way and die exactly the same way that he has caused others to suffer and die. That is why He has given us a commandment that we should not kill.

### Self Defence:

If anybody kills in self defence, he is a murderer before God, eventhough the world may acquit him by the law court. All the military tactics used by soldiers to kill in attack or defence, amounts to murder. In anger most people speak without restraint, trying to defend themselves or revenge. If somebody offends you and you utter some threats like, "I am going to show you," you have committed murder. If your properties are stolen, and you have in mind or actually go to a sorcerer to find out who is the thief to harm him, you have committed murder. The native doctor who tells you, "come, let me kill that thief for you," is guilty of murder. If you accept his proposal you are guilty of murder together with him. If you place juju on anything to prevent thieves from stealing your things, you have committed murder. If you invoke the juju to harm the person who has touched or stolen your property, you have committed murder.

If in the law court you pass judgement that somebody should be hanged, you have committed murder. The person who prepares the gallows commits murder the same as the executioner. Why then should we still doubt the way things are happening to us daily? We are suffering like murderers; we should not blame it on God or neighbours, enemies or juju. We are reaping what we sowed. When you give somebody medicine to drink or inject him; if that medicine or injection kills him, you have committed murder. If you commit abortion, or consent or aid the abortion of your daughter simply because you would not like her to be dismissed from school, you are a murderer.

### Suicide:

When you say that things are not good with you and go to kill yourself, the sin does not end in your committing suicide; you have committed murder, you are guilty of murder. No matter what way you commit the suicide; by hanging, drowning or poisoning, you are a murderer. Even if you think or say that life does not favour or that life is not good with you, and that it is better for you to die, you have committed murder even by the mere nentioning of these words. If you think like this in your heart it is the same murder that you have committed. In these things we have sinned and the wages of sin is death. Do all you can to ensure that your fellow human being has life. It is in this that Brotherhood of the Cross and Star has taught you to bless those who curse and persecute you, and pray for them. Agree to be accused falsely; carry every burden and accept to suffer for the sake of the Cross and the glory of God, and in the end you will earn eternal life. This is the meaning of Brotherhood of the Cross and Star.

### Revenge:

There is no need for us to revenge. Our forefathers revenged and they are all dead today. You may say, "Let me do whatever I like, for whatever a person does he must die;" but I disagree with you. You cannot kill as you like. Whoever kills must die. Whoever does not kill will not die. If you should say that because Abraham, Moses, Joshua, David and Solomon all died to support your statement, you are mistaken. Did not Abraham, Moses, Joshua, David and Solomon kill? Were they not all warriors? And if they were, what sort of God's work could they have done? What sort of man of God could any of them make? Did they not deserve to suffer and die as murderers which they were? Because they suffered and died as murderers, their children are therefore bound to suffer as a result of their parent's sins for the scripture says, "........For I the Lord thy God am a jealous God, visiting the iniquity of the fathers upon the children, unto the third and fourth generation of them that hate Me."

Any person who commits murder hates God. We are suffering today because of the sin of murder which our ancestors committed. In Acts 7 v 6 - 7, is recorded what God said to Abraham: "And God spake on this wise, that his seed should sojourn in a strange land; and that they should bring them into bondage, and entreat them evil for four hundred years. And the nation by whom they shall be made bondage will I judge, said God; and after that they shall come and serve me in this place." Pharaoh and his subjects who committed murder against the children of Israel, finally perished in the Red Sea. We have seen how all men of the past suffered because of murder. Today almost everybody is suffering because of the same sin. Yet even those who are converted christians today are very often heard saying to somebody who offends them, "Were it yesterday when I was of the world, I would have done you something." This also is committing murder by word of mouth. But my christian friends do not know this, though they go about with their Bible preaching and calling themselves men of God.

Since the world began have you ever seen a murderer with his family living in peace? Whoever takes the sword must perish by the sword. It is by committing murder that we lose all our blessings and earn ourselves eternal curse and damnation. Jacob said to Simeon and Levi: "Simeon and Levi are brethren; instruments of cruelty are their habitations. Oh my Soul, come not into their secret; unto their assembly, mine honour, be not thou united for in their anger they slew a man, and in their self-will they digged down a wall. Our seed be their anger, for it was fierce; and their wrath, for it was cruel; I will divide them in Jacob and scatter them in Israel." Again, since Cain killed his brother Abel, the whole world seem to have no other work than killing themselves; the punishment of our fathers who committed murder before us, is on us already. Yet we are seeking to add to this by committing more and more murders ourselves.

If our parents died, vanquished in war, why should we go and plan revenge to wipe off their shame? Revenge is murder, whatever the reason. The person who is guilty of it should die as a murderer. If our parents had suffered because they did not know God or know how bad it is to commit murder in any form, how much greater will our punishment be, who now know all this and still commit murder. In St Luke it is written: "And that servant, which knew his Lord's will, and prepared not himself neither did according to his will, shall be beaten with many stripes. But he that knew not and commit things worthy of stripes will be beaten with few stripes. For unto whomsoever much is given, of him shall much be required; and to whom men have committed much, of him they will ask the more." If we commit murder again this day, it is deliberate and we deserve greater punishment.

### Stopping Death:
See the numerous churches and prayer houses on earth today; yet death does not stop. Why? As long as we continue killing with our thoughts, words and actions in the ways mentioned earlier in this gospel, we continue to set in cycle death that goes and comes back to start again with ourselves. But, it would be possible to stop death if we would stop killing. If we would accept to bear the cross and suffer wrongs without complaining and die for love without resisting, we would pass from death to life eternal. But all those who kill will be killed, and their children too will suffer death from the same sin, unless somebody from amongst them sacrifices himself to suffer wrongs and death without resistance, for the coming generation to live and have peace. So whatever you suffer do not commit murder, and you and your children and grand children shall live.

**GREAT:**

Remember Christ's remark, that of all that are born of women, there is none as great as John the Baptist. Why is John the greatest of them all? Remember also that David, Solomon, Moses and Joshua were regarded as very great men before John. Why did Jesus not confirmed that these men were so great, but instead acclaimed John the Baptist as the greatest of all men born of woman? The reason is that John did not commit murder in any way. He killed nobody by thought. He did not pronounce any evil words against any person. He did not listen to anything said against him by people. He was accused and imprisoned by Herod. He did not care to defend himself or say any evil word. In the prison his head was sent for, chopped off and brought in a plate to Herod as his birthday gift to his daughter. John died without resistance or commotion. Supposing you were John the Baptist, would you not begin to defend yourself by killing and being killed? What we call self defence is not known to God.

Why then do most of us resist instead of surrendering ourselves to God, to use us as He likes, even if it pleases Him to make people illtreat us? After all it was not David or Moses or Solomon who were warriors defending themselves, that Christ proclaimed great. It was John the Baptist who yielded meekly to persecution and death, for the sake of the Kingdom of heaven. The same John did not commit murder. Self defence has never saved any person. It is the sympton of fear. But Christ said, "Fear not them which are not able to destroy both body and soul in hell." If we were christians and workers of God, really trusting in God alone to keep or destroy our lives; why should we fear and try to defend ourselves so much, so that we kill? Let us examine all those whom we call the men of God of old, whether they did not kill in war using either weapons, word of mouth or thought.

### FIRST LESSON: St Matthew 5 v 21 - 22

> "Ye have heard that it was said by them of old time, thou
> shall not kill; and whosoever shall kill shall be in danger
> of judgement; but I say unto you, that whosoever shall
> say to his brother, Raca, shall be in danger of the council;
> but whosoever shall say thou fool, shall be in danger of hell fire."

Perhaps you may say, "Since I was born I have never killed anyone." By this you may only mean that you have never used a gun, sword or stick to kill any person. But you may not in any way deny that you have killed so many thousands with your thought, word and look. When you said thou fool to that brother the other day, you have committed one murder. Since then you have repeated the same killing word to even a hundred people. Are you not a murderer? If you are jealous of the other girl because she is more beautiful than you, and say in your jealousy that she is too proud, just to condemn her, you are a murderer. If you are annoyed with anybody simply because he is more talented than yourself, you have committed murder. If you suspect and say that our rich brother acquired this; if you try to block anybody's way to deprive him of his means of livelihood; you have committed murder. If you pray like David and say, "Oh Lord........fight against them that fight against me," you have committed murder. David prayed like this when he did not see the light; he was a warrior.

When the Light which is Christ came, He did not utter anything even when persecuted. The scripture says of Him, "He was led as a sheep to the slaughter, and like a lamb dumped before his shearer, so opened He not His mouth." We have seen this Light. Why should we kill again with our prayers? Whoever prays like David is not a man of God; instead he is a murderer. We should be better men of God than those of old who committed murder; otherwise we are not fit to be called christians. Christ said to His disciples, "Except your righteousness shall exceed the righteousness of the Scribes and Pharisees, ye shall in no case enter the Kingdom of heaven." Where then lies the wisdom of the people of this world who do not want to disarm and live as brothers, when they know that every sin that you commit will be used against you on the day of judgement.?

**SECOND LESSON: St Matthew 26 v 52**

"Then Jesus said unto him, put up again thy sword
into its place, for all they that take the sword shall
perish with the sword."

After Christ has commanded Peter against taking up the sword; any christian who takes up the sword against anybody under any circumstances, stands condemned. We have other swords which are more dangerous than that of steel. Bad words are bad swords. The evil thoughts we nurse against another person is a bad sword. Our eyes which look dangerously at people are bad swords. With all these swords we commit more murder than those of old. Not many people will, like Peter see Christ face to face telling them to put down their swords. God Himself will not tell us more than what we are hearing in this gospel. If you care to take up your sword after hearing this gospel, God will not interrupt you until you have finished doing your heart's desire. Then you will die by the very sword that you took up against someone else. When you lodge a complaint to the police requiring that you should be given a constable, you will be given one. But when it is discovered that you have given false information, you yourself will be in big trouble, because the police will turn round and prosecute you.

Christ feared this repercussion, that is why He did not call upon His Father to send legions of Angels to defend Him, when the Jews arrested and killed Him. And that is why He was free from the sin of murder, and God raised Him up to life again on the third day. This fulfils God's promise in Luke 9 v 24: "For whosoever will save his life shall lose it, but whosoever will lose his life for My sake, the same shall save it." Who among us today that has succeeded in saving his own life? Is it not time for the whole world to put up their swords, seeing that they cannot be saved by defending themselves or by committing murder? Some people boast that God has helped them to win a war. If they had known that God does not wish anybody to be killed even in battle of war, they would have no reason to rejoice; especially as it is now quite clear that when we kill others we also will be killed by others.

### Soldiers Are Murderers:

If you are thinking that soldiers as fighters, are doing the work of God, you are wrong. For how could they be doing the work of God by murdering? No matter how much a person may be preaching, no amount of patriotism warrants anybody to kill a fellow human being. If you had been making mistake in considering a murderer as a man of God simply because he preaches the gospel, or claims to be defending his country, don't do it again because no murderer is justified before God. Soldiers are murderers, they are always fighting and killing. They are paid to commit this havoc. And are the governments who paid them not murderers? Every minute of the day soldiers are busy thinking and planning how to attack or defend. As murderers they themselves are dead already. In 2 Timothy 3 v 13 we read: "But evil men and seducers shall wax worse, deceiving and being deceived." That is why soldiers today are killing and being killed.

### Our Duty:

We owe a duty to preserve life, not to destroy it. For instance, Christ humbled Himself unto death. He preserved His good works and committed no sin, so that He may be able to preserve the life of sinners and make them partakers of eternity.

## GOLDEN TEXT: Revelation 13 v 10

"He that leadeth into captivity shall go into captivity;
He that killeth with the sword must be killed with
the sword. Here is the patience and faith of the saints."

This faith made the Saints to be patient in suffering all things with the full knowledge that if they would never kill even their enemies with thought, word or action, they will live eternal life. Like Christ, they choose to die instead of attacking anybody or committing any sin against humanity. For this reason Peter was crucified head downward. He knew exactly what he should have done to defend himself, but fighters will not stop fighting until they shed their blood because of sin. Anybody who uses the sword to kill, will also be killed with the sword. This gospel is given to all those who use to say that they wish they could see God to ask Him a question why men should die. This gospel is meant to answer the question by telling them, that the reason why people die is that they commit murder either in thought, word or deed, or by any of the other ways mentioned in this gospel. For, "With what measure ye mete, it shall be measured to you again."

### Faith Of The Saints:

Faith of the Saints means having no gun; keeping nothing whatsoever with which to protect yourself; but surrendering yourself completely to God to take care of you. If you have such faith you would not say as many people are fond of saying, that while God is protecting them, it is necessary that they should protect themselves also. What a foolish statement! How can a man protect himself, if God alone does not protect him. We suffer most when we use ungodly means to protect and defend ourselves. It is then that we commit murder and die as murderers, because defending ourselves means killing ourselves. Then we start to suspect our neighbours of poison, witchcraft, juju and such-like things. We deceive ourselves. These things in themselves have no power for they do not exist at all. What exists which works to our detriment and death, is the murder that we commit every day by thinking evil, doing or speaking evil, thereby committing murder and dying away every day.

### What We Have Done To Others:

So let nobody again, say anything against God for whatever happens to him, for whatever evil we brought on ourselves is as a result of what we have done to others. As our gospel has revealed that anybody who kills will be killed just the same way and by the same means that he used; whatever we sow is what we must reap. God is a righteous Judge. If we hear His word in this gospel and do it we shall have life everlasting. Whoever wants life must preserve the life of others. Whoever kills shall be killed. Who has ears let him hear; may God bless His Holy Words. Amen."

# CHAPTER 18

# AN OPEN LETTER TO THE WORLD
# THE END OF TIMES: THE LAST CALL

### Everlasting Gospel delivered by Leader Olumba Olumba Obu
### Sole Spiritual Head of the Universe.

## *"Beloved,*

### SALVATION IS FROM CHRIST

There is no other source of love, salvation, peace and power other than Christ. Whoever believes and calls on His name shall receive salvation. He alone knows how to deliver from temptations, all that fear Him. Do not be ashamed to repent and call on His name. Do not be afraid to seek and worship Him. He is the same yesterday, today and forever.

No mundane thing can save mankind and no Lord - spiritual or temporal, can deliver the world from its present predicament other than Our Lord Jesus the CHRIST. I beseech you all to forsake sins. Whoever had hardened his heart should change now. Christ is the Noah's Ark and He has arrived at your door post. Believe in Him, seek Him and follow Him for He has come to search for the lost sheep and mankind constitute the lost sheep.
What we observe in the world is wickedness, all forms of vices and evil. Be consoled for the Saviour is not on His way, but is already in our midst. He is the King of Kings and Lord of Lords; the Lord of peace and life.

### SEEK HIM

This is not the time to seek mundane things. This is the time of the Kingdom of God and the right time to seek God with our whole heart, body and soul. Look for Him while it is still possible because a time is coming soon when the opportunity will not be there. As this divine call is extended to you, I urge you not to hesitate, resist or harden your heart. He can call you through sickness, court case, hatred, hardship, enemies, accidents and in various other ways. His ways are different from those of man. He is long-suffering and it is not His wish that any should perish but that all should repent and be saved.

Look at governments, churches, various communities, nations and individuals all over the world and you will see that they are in a precarious and pitiable state. The world should turn to and worship the Almighty and Living God.

### THE END IS AT HAND

All that is presently happening in the world merely represent "police action." The real time of judgement is fast approaching. People are crying and shouting that life is so hard and things are so tough.

This is yet the tip of the iceberg. Tougher conditions and harder times are yet to come. All the inhabitants of heaven and earth should seize this wonderful opportunity to turn to and serve the Lord. Do not deceive yourself that He is the God of love, mercy and grace and so you continue in your sins. This is the time to make peace with God.

### THE TIME OF NOAH.

It was the same situation during the time of Noah. People were going about buying and selling, marrying and giving in marriage, doing business and enjoying the pleasures of life to the total neglect of God and His Message. Noah preached for 120 years, yet nobody listened to him. Instead they mocked him and ridiculed him and called him an idle and crazy fellow. In the end the flood came and Noah was vindicated. BROTHERHOOD OF THE CROSS AND STAR is the Biblical Noah's Ark.

### THE TRUMPET

The trumpet is sounding everyday. The words we preach, the songs we sing and the testimonies all constitute the blowing of the trumpet to the world to repent of their evil ways. All individuals, churches, associations and nations must unite in love to foster peace, prosperity and eternal life in the world. If the whites refuse to abide by this call they will not be saved. If the blacks refuse this call they too will perish. Your colour, religion or sex cannot save you. Live in peace with your parents, children, friends, governments and all the inhabitants of the world. The Christ has come to rule us in peace and unite all peoples in love, therefore this is the time for fanatics and warmongers to think again; this is the time for the arrogant wealthy class to surrender to the rulership of the Almighty Father so that peace and prosperity may return to earth.

Do not live under the illusion that afterall God has been planning to destroy this world since the time of our great, great-grandparents yet up till now He has not done so. Remember that a thousand years is like one day to God. The Lord knoweth how to deliver the godly out of temptations and to reserve the unjust unto the day of judgement to be punished. Remember the time of Noah and the time of Lot. As the Father did not forgive the erring angels but detained them till judgement, so shall it be in these days. As He did not forgive Sodom and Gomorrah, as He did not forgive the people during the time of Noah, He shall in no wise forgive this generation. All sinners should repent. Refrain from stealing, fornication, adultry, idolatry, killing, anger, disobedience and all vices. Only God can bestow peace and life to us; and life, they say, is greater than food and good health better than raiment.

### THE DAYS OF GRACE

"Peace I leave with you, my peace I give unto you; not as the world giveth, give I unto you. Let not your heart be troubled neither let it be afraid."

We are yet living in the period of God's grace. If He is given cause to withdraw the grace, mercy, and love, then the whole world will be destroyed.

"After these things I saw four angels standing on the four corners of the earth, that the wind should not blow on the earth nor on the sea, nor on any tree. And I saw another angel ascending from the east, having the seal of the living God: and he cried with a loud voice to the four angels to whom it was given to hurt the earth and the sea, saying, hurt not the earth, neither the sea, nor the trees, till we have sealed the servants of our God in their foreheads."
That is the plan God has for mankind. Let us therefore embrace the peace that Christ left with us so that we can extend it to our friends, neighbours, churches, governments, husbands, wives, children and all inhabitants of the world.

### THE LAST CALL

This is the last call and golden opportunity for those who want salvation. Those who delay will have themselves to blame. Those who reject this call reject life, for Christ is the path, the truth and the life. This is the time for Jehovah God and His Christ to reign and rule; and all individuals, governments and institutions are in His hands. The blacks, whites, men, women, young and old, animals, fishes, birds, trees and all creation must return to their Creator. A spiritual song says- "Come, oh come, come my children, I do not want you to be destroyed. Come and make peace with me." About Christ it is thus written- "But this man because He continueth ever, hath an unchangeable priesthood, wherefore He is able to save them to the uttermost that come to God by Him; seeing He ever liveth to make intercession for them. For such an high priest became us, who is holy, harmless, undefiled, separate from sinners, and made higher than the heavens."
Christ is our only saviour and hope. He has come to lead us to salvation.

## CONCLUSION

To be fore-warned is to be fore-armed. There is no life, no glory, no truth, nothing in the world but sorrows and woes. Whoever accepts this message is saved. This same letter was written to Sodom and Gomorrah:-
"Hear the word of the Lord, ye rulers of Sodom; give hear unto the law of our God ye people of Gomorrah. To what purpose is the multitude of your sacrifices unto me? saith the Lord. I am full of burnt offerings of rams and the fat of fed beasts; and I delight not in the blood of bullocks, or of lambs, or of he-goats. When you come to appear before me, who hath required this at your hand, to tread my courts? Bring no more vain oblations; incense is an abomination unto me; the new moons and sabbaths, the calling of assemblies, I cannot away with; it is iniquity, even the solemn meeting. Your new moons and your appointed feasts my soul hateth; they are a trouble unto me; I am weary to bear them. And when you spread forth your hands, I will hide mine eyes from you: yea, when ye make many prayers, I will not hear; your hands are full of blood. Wash you, make you clean; cease to do evil. Learn to do well; seek judgement, relieve the oppressed, judge the fatherless, plead for the widow. Come now, and let us reason together, saith the Lord: though your sins be as scarlet, they shall be as white as snow; though they be red like crimson, they shall be as wool. If ye be willing and obedient ye shall eat the good of the land: but if ye refuse and rebel, ye shall be devoured with the sword: for the mouth of the Lord hath spoken it. ( Isaiah 1 v 10 - 20 ).

If Sodom and Gomorrah had heeded God's call that they refrain from iniquity and love one another, they would not have been destroyed. If they had accepted to make peace with their Creator, He would have forgiven them and washed them clean. Christ is here on earth. The Father is here too. They are calling us to come and be saved. Do not follow any group, individual or denomination. Follow Christ and Christ alone, for He has come to gather all the sheep so that there may be one flock and one shepherd. Let us refrain from war, hatred, stealing, killing and every act that destroys man. Let us live in peace and love one another and be humble and merciful.
He that hath an ear let him hear. May God bless His words. AMEN."

# CHAPTER 19

# PRAYER FOR THE WORLD

### Daily Prayer by Leader Olumba Olumba Obu
### The Universal Leader & Sole Spiritual Head
### of the Universe.

*" Let thanks, praises, honour, dominion and power be given to the Father, in the Name of Our Lord Jesus Christ. Let thanks, praises, honour, dominion and power supremacy be given to the Father, in the Blood of Our Lord Jesus Christ. Let thanks, praises, homour, dominion and adoration be given to our Father, now and forever more, Amen. Holy, Holy, Holy, Lord God Almighty who reigns and rules in heaven above and on earth below, we your poor children have come before your throne as woeful sinners. We fall at your feet as the prodigal son, as Mary Magdalene and as the felon on the Cross. We have sinned against you in heaven and on earth. We have sinned against you through unholy utterances, untoward movements and unseeming behaviour. To this end, we are not worthy to be called your children. But because of the Cross on which divine Emmanuel your Son was nailed, and His precious Blood was spilled for the redemption of humanity; you have on account of this turned your back against our wrong doings. You have forgiven and blotted out all our sins, in the Name of Our Lord Jesus Christ, Amen.*

*We thank you, because you have forgiven and wholly blotted out all our sins, not minding how numerous our sins are before you. Daily, you continue to teach us to have love for one another; and to love you with our whole hearts, soul, mind; to love our neighbours as you love us. Let thanks and praises be given to you in the Name of Our Lord Jesus Christ, Amen. We thank you because you have washed us clean in our flesh, soul and spirit. You have endowed us with good and sound health and peace in Spirit and flesh. You have bestowed your love, peace, joy, happiness, hope, meekness, understanding, truth, faith, goodness, gentleness, patience, humility and temperance on all your children, and teach us to be truthful and honest in our lives. Let thanks be given to you Father, in the Name of Our Lord Jesus Christ, Amen.*

*Come, oh! Holy Spirit, come with your mighty power. Come as thunder, come as lightening, come as flood and torrential rain to wash away our sins. Come as consuming fire to burn away our filthiness, guilt, fleshly desires and all carnal desires in us, in the Name of Our Lord Jesus Christ, Amen. Come as the Supreme Doctor to heal us in spirit and in flesh. Visit the mental patients in the psychiatric homes and right in the leprosy hospitals, in prisonyards/detention camps, the epileptics, those with whooping cough, visit the maternity homes and the welfare homes. Enter the depths of the oceans, the Atlantis, and into the four corners of the universe, the East, the West, the North and South. Protect those who believe and have faith in you, and those who do not. Thank you Father, for you have taken away suffering and death within this prevailing hour from your children, in the Name of Our Lord Jesus Christ, Amen.*

*We have surrendered all sinners, mischief makers, lawbreakers, murderers, thieves and robbers, bribe receivers, fornicators, avaricious people, and those who harbour or nurse others grudges. We have surrendered the false prophets who mislead the masses into your powerful hands. Those who pretentiously honour you with their lips only, but their hearts have left you a far off. Those who receive your divine counsel but would not put it into practice. Those who do not pay tithe, freewill offering and charity. Those who give no help to the poor, the widows and the destitutes. We have surrendered those who have not spread your Gospel of good tidings to the four corners of the world. And those who spread the Gospel but do not practise what they preach, those who do not answer "Amen" when the blessed Name of your Son, Our Lord Jesus Christ is mentioned.*

*We have surrendered those who do not sing songs of praises to glorify your Name when they are happy; and those who do not kneel down to say their prayers when they are distressed or sick. We have also surrendered those to whom the secrets of life are revealed to them, but they refuse to herald them to the people concerned. Those who add or subtract from what they are spiritually shown, those who do not believe in vision and prophesy as being the truth. Even those who get angry when visions and prophesies are revealed to them.*

*We have equally surrendered drunkards, juju doctors, sorcerers, necromancers to you. We further surrender those who had been learning and have never come to the accurate wisdom of the truth. Those who have never entered, and do not allow others to enter. We earnestly plead with you Father to forgive them in the Name of Our Lord Jesus Christ, Amen. Thank you Father for the devastating spiritual powers you have poured on your children in the entire world within this hour. Thank you God Almighty for the spiritual backing which you have bestowed on your children at this end of time.*

*We have surrendered the governments, all heads and functionaries of governments into your most powerful hands. All the traditional chieftains, emperors, kings and queens have all been given into your merciful hands for protection and guidance.*

*We have, in the same vein, surrendered all the principalities and powers into your most powerful hands; the orthodox churches, prayer houses, service centres and healing homes and the higher institutions of learning. We have surrendered all the elders, prophets and the prophetesses, spirited children, visioners, pastors, apostles and evangelists, Christ's students, Christ's witnesses and Christ's servants, choiristers, all ordained ones, the children, congregation, men and women. We have surrendered the out-stations, from the eldest to the smallest into your most powerful hands. All your disobedient children and backsliders, and those who listen to your counsel but do not put it into practical realities. Do your work! Do your work! you, Great and Supreme King of the Universe, let thanks and praises be given to you in the Name of Our Lord Jesus Christ, Amen.*

*Thank you Father, because you have descended your heavenly hosts to join your children on the earth below to sing praises and glorify your Name just as it is done in heaven above. By songs of praises your glorious Name has been raised; through songs, there is no more war in Nigeria, Africa and the entire four corners of the inhabited earth. Through songs, the dead is raised; through songs, the chronic sinners are converted and transformed unto God. By songs of praises all those who died in the Lord are resurrecting daily, and through songs also the sick are healed. Through songs, those who always deliver still-born babies now bear living children. Similarly the barren now have children through songs. Through songs you have wiped away tears from our eyes. Through songs, death and hades are removed and put into fiery furnace. Through songs, division, brawl, and wars are taken away - in the Name of Our Lord Jesus Christ, Amen.*

*Through songs, the kingdom of this world has now become the Kingdom of Jehovah God and His Christ, let you Father, in the Name of Our Lord Jesus Christ, let thanks, praises, dominion and power be given to you Father in the name of our Lord Jesus Christ, Amen. Through songs, those who have no husbands or wives have now been given; and through songs those who need passports, visas and scholarships, are given. We thank you because your children are no longer hungry and thirsty. The sun and moon no longer scorch your children because you have spread your wings of protection over them. And you have successfully piloted them to the stream of living waters. You have wiped away tears from our eyes; let thanks, praises and adoration be given to the Father in the Name of Our Lord Jesus Christ, Amen. We thank you for there is no more crying, wailing or lamentation, in the Name of Our Lord Jesus Christ, Amen. The tabernacle of God is now crowded with men, He is our Father, and we are His children. And neighbour shall not teach his neighbour to know God, for all shall know Him, from the least to the greatest. He shall remember our iniquities no more, in the Name of Our Lord Jesus Christ, Amen.*

*The first heaven and earth had passed away, and the oceans and the Atlantis are no more - in the Name and Blood of Our Lord Jesus Christ, Amen. For you have said, except Jehovah builds a house, they that labour are doing so in vain. And except Jehovah watches over a city, the watchmen stays awake for nothing. He has taken dominion in the sun, moon and the stars. He has taken dominion in the heavens, on earth, in the high seas and in waters below the soil. He has taken dominion in our bones, marrow, blood-stream and in our entire flesh, in the Name of Our Lord Jesus Christ, Amen. We thank you oh! Father, for what belongs to the Father, belongs to us, and what belongs to us, belongs to the Father, let glory be to the Father in the Name of Our Lord Jesus Christ, Amen. In all the places where the sun and the moon shine, your glory and power engulf the four corners of the universe. And by this, we are united as one fold under one Shepherd, now and forever more - Amen; let thanks, praises, dominion and power be given to you, in the Name of Our Lord Jesus Christ, let thanks, praises, adoration be given to God, in the Blood of Our Lord Jesus Christ, Amen; let thanks, praises, adoration and supremacy be given to our Father now and forever, Amen."*

This Prayer is the Greatest of all Prayers. It clearly reveals that JEHOVAH GOD and His heavenly hosts are now on earth.

"Prayer is the most powerful force in the universe. It is stronger than the armies, and more terrifying than automic and nuclear weapons in the world. In these perilous and dark days of fear of nuclear annihilation, famine, terrorism, alcoholism, drug abuse, sexual perversion, herpes and 'Aids,' the only silver lining is prayer. Prayer is our only hope of victory in everything, and the promoter of holiness. Prayer is the remover of all obstacles and adjuster of all disputes. It is only prayer that can reveal the Holy Spirit and His mission to you. Prayer changes people, things and circumstances. But yet, it is the greatest force in the world that is so seldomly used....."
*Excerpts from Leader O.O. Obu's sermon entitled* **"Prayer is the Greatest Key to Success."**

# CHAPTER 20

# "THE POWER OF THE SPOKEN WORD"

Everlasting Gospel delivered by Leader Olumba Olumba Obu

Sole Spiritual Head of the Universe

**1st Lesson: Ephesians 4: 29**

"Let no corrupt communication proceed out of your mouth, but that which is good to the use of edifying, that it may minister grace unto the hearers."

**2nd Lesson: Colossians 4: 6**

'Let your speech be always with grace, seasoned with salt, that ye may know how ye ought to answer every man."

**Golden Text James 3: 2**

"For in many things we offend all. If any man offend not in word, the same is a perfect man, and able also to bridle the whole *body*",

## Beware of what you speak

The texts form the indices for the identification of a child of God. In the world, a person who gives you some money, no matter what he does to you not even if he curses or disgraces you, would still be regarded as a very good man. Does it mean that once a person gives you money, that automatically makes him a man of God? Are these the things that identify a person as a man of God? Through Paul, did Christ not say that even if a man should sell all that he has, distribute the proceeds to the poor or even offer himself to be burnt, would gain nothing without having love? 1 Corinthians 13:3.

What is responsible for the downfall and destruction of the whole world? It is evil communication. What the world refers to as juju, apparition, witchcraft, death or ghost is none other than evil communication. All the superstitious beliefs and fetishism are founded on evil word. Who is the "Creator" of these evil things? It is the evil man himself. When God made the first day, He blessed it. He also blessed the second day, third, up to the seventh day. He equally declared the world and the fullness thereof as good and perfect. The question is where do the evil things come from? This explains the reason why we are enjoined not to allow evil communication to proceed out of our mouth. If everyone should from now cease to speak evil, evil will also cease to exist.

## The Real Meaning of Satan Explained

The sower of the good seed in the vineyard did a good work by planting a good seed. But at night, the evil one (an enemy) went into the field and planted bad seeds along with the good ones. The bad seeds here represent evil communications. The real meaning of Satan is evil communication or vain words which does not give glory to God. Our greatest salvation is to avoid vain words to proceed out of our mouths. If we abide by the word of God, which we hear daily in the form of gospels, testimonies, songs, visions, dreams and prophecies, we would be saved. If we hearken to God's injunctions that come in these forms, then the evil route shall have been sealed. If we speak only edifying words then evil will cease to have a place in the world. Our Lord Jesus Christ made it clear when He said that, you have been made holy by the words He gives to you. What changes a man? What prospers a person? What gives a person good health, peace, love, happiness and joy; it is the word of God; edifying words.
A local adage has it that; good words prevent quarrels, whereas evil and provocative words fuel animosity. If you observe closely, the source of all problems in the world is traceable to evil words. When you hear of sowing a bad seed, it is nothing other than vain words. Satan himself is none other thing than evil communication. The bad seeds sown by the enemy, are the evil words, abuses and curses, which ultimately are responsible for the sickness, starvation, poverty, war, mishaps and deaths It is responsible for all the problems in the world.

## The Genesis of Human Problems

Jacob had 12 (twelve) sons and Reuben was his first born. Others include Levi, Simeon, Judah and the last born, Benjamin. When he was about to die, he invited all of them for blessing. When they had assembled, he called Reuben and emphasised his position as first born and then cursed him for defiling his father's bed. He stated clearly that even if all the wealth in the world were given to him, he would not prosper. That curse explains the source of poverty in the world today, which indicates the fact that, this group of people come from the stock of Reuben. If Jacob were to come round and see the manifestation of his spoken words he would not fail to weep. Consequently, if Reuben were to be present to know the root cause of his penury he would vow never to touch a woman, even if such a woman were to be offered to him free. If he had not defiled his father's bed, he would not have been under a curse. That is why it is said that "a wise man sees an evil far off and takes precautions; but a foolish man waits tor the evil to overcome him."

It is also said "a child that walks circumspectly, will kill that which killed his father, but a child, who is careless, would be killed by the same thing that killed his father. Is the world today not mature enough to know itself and walk circumspectly? Jacob did not stop his curse on Reuben; he extended it to Levi and Simeon. To these two sons of his, he cursed that the sword shall not depart from them, for the part they played in the destruction of both human and material resources. He vowed that his soul would have nothing to do with them. That is why no matter what good thing you would do to a person of the likes of Levi and Simeon, they would end up chopping off your head. This is the fulfillment of the curse upon them. The descendants of Levi and Simeon thus produce warriors, violent and heartless murderers.

The twelve stars signify the twelve tribes of Israel, which also give the source of the twelve months of the year and the twelve Zodiac signs. Therefore, any person who is born in the same month in which Levi and Simeon were born, will be violent, destructive and murderers, depicting the stock they rightly come from. When Jacob was on his way home, he tarried in a certain city with Levi, Simeon and their sister. Incidentally, the son of the King of the city happened to meet Jacob's daughter, and they fell in love. The prince slept with her, and she conceived, and gave birth to a baby boy. When investigations fully proved that it was the king's son that was responsible for the pregnancy, the king apologized and promised to do whatever he was asked to do, in order to marry the daughter of Jacob to his son. Jacob gave the king the condition of being circumcised with his household.

Circumcision was at that time a mark of the children of God, the descendants of Abraham, according to God's promise to him. Circumcision was to the Israelites what baptism is to christians today. Both Jacob and the king's families were assembled to settle the matter. But Levi and Simeon, whose sister was involved in the incident, were not happy with the affair in the first place and therefore did not accept the settlement. Under normal circumstances, Levi and Simeon were not expected to make any contribution towards the settlement, therefore, their opinions were not necessary and were not sought for. Although the case was amicably settled, these two brothers were still dissatisfied.

Their father who would have been considered to have the last say in the matter was brushed aside only for the two sons to take the law into their hands. Thus, they went ahead and destroyed the indigenes of the place and their properties. This singular act of his sons caused Jacob to escape for his dear life. It was because of this, that when it was time to bless his sons, Jacob cursed Levi and Simeon that the sword shall never depart from them. He also vowed that his soul would have nothing to do with them. This also separated them from Jacob. You would now realise that if the murderers of today were to be aware of this historical background, they would refrain from such acts.

Unfortunately, the whole world is taking delight in killing. God distances Himself from all murderers. Even though some of these people go to church claiming to enjoy God's protection and guidance, they are merely making false claims. It is said that, come what may. no sinner will ever be saved. Whoever kills another person shall be killed. Whoever commits adultery and fornication shall not go unpunished. The lesson however, that you should hold fast to, is that you should not allow evil communication to proceed out of your mouth.

Whenever the word of God falls to the ground, it breaks mighty rocks and rises up to accomplish the intended purpose. The whole world is replete with sins, as individuals and groups continue to wallow in abominable acts. The stock in trade of the inhabitants of the world is to curse, to maim and to kill. The husband would curse the wife and the wife would also curse the husband. The parents curse their children and vice versa. That is what has kept the world in the position it fmds itself. All these go to prove that the source of evil to the world is evil words. If I should enumerate all the areas of your aftlictions, you would realise that your problems are from evil communications.

## The Source of African (Blacks) Sufferings

Now, if Isaac were to know the efficacy of the word, he would have been quite objective that he was not misdirecting his love. Isaac called Esau, his beloved son, and asked him to prepare him some food with fresh meat. The mother, Rebecca, when she heard this, immediately directed Jacob to bring a ram. The ram was slaughtered and Rebecca used the meat to prepare a delicious meal for Isaac. When he asked his mother how he would go about the differences in his voice and skin, she told him not to bother. Jacob had a deep voice, and in order to deceive his father, his mother advised him to intorm his father that he (Jacob claiming to be Esau) lost his voice while he was returning from the bush in search of animal. Esau was naturally hairy and to successfully deceive the old man, Rebecca covered Jacob's arms with the skin of the ram to impersonate Esau.

While Esau was still in the bush hunting, Rebecca had prepared the food, which Jacob served his father Isaac. On presentation of the food, Isaac observed that the voice he was hearing resembled that of Jacob, when he felt Jacob's body coupled with the excuse he gave as regards his voice, Isaac was convinced that it was Esau kneeling before him and so he blessed him. Immediately Isaac had finished showering blessings upon blessings on Jacob, Esau appeared and went to his father to inform him of his return from the hunting. Isaac was most disturbed when he realised that he had been tricked because he was blind. When Esau insisted that Isaac should bless him, he said that he had no blessing left.

In our present age, unlike Isaac, the blessing of our Father is inexhaustible. If Isaac were to come around to see the consequences of his action on the blacks, their predicament today, he would have wept. The source of the suffering of Africans is traceable to the statement, which says that, the elder shall serve the younger. Out of anger for being triicked, Esau decided to kill Jacob. But because Rebecca loved Jacob more than Esau, she advised him to escape to another land. On the other hand, Isaac their father loved Esau more than Jacob, because of taking very good care of him.

## Why the Whites are blessed

The whites are so abundantly blessed and they prosper a great deal because of Isaac's blessing upon Jacob. Nevertheless, Esau's predicament could not entirely be blamed on Isaac. In fact, to a greater extent, Esau is to blame for the whole situation. One day when he (Esau) came back from hunting he was so hungry that he went and asked Jacob for food. On his part, Jacob told him to decide between food and his birthright. Esau being so hungry decided to sell his birthright in exchange for the food. This can prove to you the efficacy of word. It also confirms the nomination in the bible that, through the words of your mouth you will be justified or condemned. Esau, therefore, was responsible for his predicament, so each one of you is responsible for your misfortune or predicament. Esau did not think of the slightest implication of his verbal transfer of birthright to his younger brother. He thought after the meal everything would end there. Little did he know that it was stamped and sealed, it finally came to pass as he had spoken.

**God Remembered Esau (Blacks)**

The word is God Right from the beginning, the word had been with God. Everything that exists is a manifestation of the word. Whether it is death or life, prosperity or lack, peace or war, good health or sickness, good or evil and even man, are all the manifestation of the spoken word. It is for this reason, that you are enjoined not to allow evil communication to proceed out of your mouth, but that you should utter only words that are edifying.

When all else had failed, the word was still there on the lips of Isaac for him to speak. In spite of the disappointment, Isaac finally prayed to God to **'remember'** Esau in the scheme of things. That word alone remember is what has restored Esau to his rightful place today. This, also confirms the scriptural nomination that Ethiopia shall rise.

The goodness and prosperity enjoyed by the whites are the birthright of the blacks they had cheated. Whatever advantages the whites have, belong to the blacks. All the human and material resources abroad, in America and in Europe came from, and belong to the black race. The Africans have really been exploited and cheated by the whites.

Africa is so richly blessed. Fortunately tor the blacks, it was only their birthright that was sold and not their land. Since Isaac had prayed God to remember Esau the manifestation of that plea is taking place now in Afiica. Civilization is said to have originated from Africa, in Egypt. During the 2nd world war, there was acute scarcity of salt. One of the reasons for the scarcity was because Egypt, the chief producer of the commodity then rescinded its conflict with the foreign firms that undertook to produce it. All the good things you can think of, such as gold, oil and the rest of the minerals, both materials and human resources are derived from Africa. The wealth that abounds in Africa is inexhaustible. The **whites will surely bow for the blacks** in **this world.**

## The Coming of the Holy Spirit

The former USSR outlawed Christian religion calling it a religion for the lazy. In 1917, the Russian government dealt a devastating blow to Christianity in the region and put it to rest. That same year, three nuns revealed the descension of the Holy Spirit in Africa. The whites started from that time to search for the Holy Spirit for the purpose of discovering or locating Him. God has done that in remembrance of Isaac's prayer that He should remember *Esau,* representing the blacks. These things are happening now because this is the close of age. All these things further confirm the efficacy of the spoken word. You are the architect of your own fate.

A local adage has it that "the death of the monkey is caused by its own mouth." Nobody is mindful of the spoken words; instead, many people are after physical features, such as the hand, eyes, legs, head and other parts of the body. All these parts of the body are not as important as the spoken word with positive or negative effect. The sun, sky, mountains and valleys, human beings, fishes in the water, birds of the air, trees and animals in the forest are all manifestations of the spoken word. God declared: let there be light (day), night (darkness), air, and all the things that were created and they all came into existence. The word is the Father and the creator of everything. Instead of man to worship the Creator, he has gone astray to worship what is created. This explained why Job refused to blaspheme against God even when he was badly afflicted and his wife asked him to denounce God. He said that instead of blaspheming against his God he would rather curse the month he was conceived and the day he was born. He said so because he considered himself to originate from the stock of Reuben, born on first April. Levi and Simeon were born in May and June respectively. That is the system that astrologers use in foretelling events. Therefore, the words you toy with could be destructive or constructive.

## With the Word Everything is Possible

Initially, God created everything in the world except man. Man came into being through the spoken word. It was pronounced, let us make man in our own image.

Zacharias's wife was barren, but Angel Gabriel came to him and told him that his wife would bring forth a male child and his name will be John. Those words came to pass and Elizabeth delivered a baby boy. If the words had said she would bring forth a baby girl, the same would have taken effect.

## The Source of your Problems

Your problem is that you do not know what the word is, and therefore do not listen to it and take it seriously. The word is spirit; it is life, God and power. Everything that you see was through the word, and what is yet to come into existence shall be through the word. Many do not worry about the effects of the word, yet they claim to worship God. Is God not the word? If you fail to honour the word, would you honour God? This explains why you are enjoined not to allow evil communication to proceed out of your mouth. From now henceforth, you should only speak edifying words. Speak only the words that will bring peace, prosperity, love and all the good things. You are very careless and reckless with what you speak.

Every prophecy foretold by Angel Gabriel about John the Baptist; all came to pass one after the other. Also, everything that was spoken about Christ was equally fulfilled accordingly. After God had created man, He commanded him to go into the world and multiply and replenish the earth. These words have now come to pass so much that countries are now applying various family planning methods to check their population. Read the first lesson once again:

**lst Lesson: Ephesians 4: 29**

*"Let no corrupt canmunication proceed out of your mouth, but that which is good to the use of edifying, that it may minister grace unto the hearers."*

**The Word - the Creator of all**

To reveal to you how foolish the world is, human beings have failed to note the fact that in the beginning was the word and the word was with God, and the same was God. Man therefore is an embodiment of the word.

In your ignorance, you claim that man is not God. If man is not God what is he? Once there is stoppage of the word in you, it means your life is finished. The world claims to know only God and nothing else. Whoever does not recognise the word does not recognise God. The whole world needs to be pitied. Human beings are dissipating their energies and wasting their time praying for money, husband, wife, children and all the material things. Many complain of problems from evil powers and so on. These people do not realise that it happens to one according to his belief and faith. The words that you speak act accordingly in you. This is why you are enjoined to speak only positive words. You should at all times endeavour to speak only edifying words, words that are capable of bringing about spiritual upliftment. I will now prove to you why there is need to divorce yourself of evil words, and to speak only words that are capable of bringing love, peace, good health, prosperity and all the good things. Untortunately, even the Bible itself is filled with evil words. If you utter positive words about yourself or another person the same will come to pass.

The words of Satan bring about trouble, nothing good or useful. Evil words bring about hatred, distrust, division, war, poverty and death. There are some words that can be spoken and a group of people would be thrown into confusion and would hold each other on the throat. The same confirms the fact that a city without a prophet is perished. And a city that is without a speaker of edifying words of progress, peace, love, unity and wisdom is doomed. Once there was a particular city with one particular family that considered themselves created to be poor. The family was however blessed with educated, knowledgeable, handsome and beautiful people. In terms of human resources, it was blessed greatly, but one thing they lacked was prosperity in material things. It was their belief that God created them to be perpetually poor. Each time a member of that family went out to marry or was to be married, the members of that family would firstly inform the suitor or intended bride that theirs were poor family from God. They believed and lived in that notion., and were even satisfied with the situation.

The situation could be compared to the encounter between the Ethiopian Eunuch and Philip. When Philip inquired of him whether he knew what he was reading, he simply answered by questioning Philip about the possibility without being led by someone. Except he was taught, he would not know. But for Philip, the Ethiopian Eunuch would not have been converted.

On his way from a certain Jewish feast, Philip met the Ethiopian Eunuch trying to read the book of Isaiah. When he accepted ignorance of the nominations therein, Philip sat him on his horse and began to teach him as they travelled along. When they reached where there was water, he demanded that he should be baptised there. Philip agreed to baptise him so long as he believed that Jesus Christ is the Son of God. He accepted this immediately and was consequently baptised. This goes to prove to you that any city without a prophet is doomed. Therefore, a city that is without a speaker and a practitioner of truth is doomed. You have been told daily that God the Father is in our midst Yet you do not know Him, the world is still searching for Him in the moon, sky, and sea, on top of a mountain as if He is bound to a particular spot. Is there anyone in your midst who understands the things that are seen every day? (Romans 10: 6-9). God's position with men has been clarified in the above text.

One day a certain prophet came to the city where the self-acclaimed poor family lived to preach. As he was preaching, the wife of one of the members of the family told the story of their poverty to the prophet. The prophet laughed and asked the woman to repeat the story, and she did feeling so concerned. The prophet immediately began to preach to her the words of the Bible as regards such belief. He pointed to her where it is said in the Bible that by a man's words he would be justified or condemned. He explained to her that the family members were responsible for their fate. He then asked the woman to declare and believe fervently that from that moment their family was blessed with riches and prosperity. The prophet also asked the woman to tell her husband and children to make the same declaration and believe same. The woman, her husband and the children believed fervently and began to say as the prophet had directed. Others, who watched them behave as the prophet had directed, laughed them to scorn. The prophet did not charge the woman any money for that knowledge. He left after that. The family continued to believe and say as they were directed. Before that week ran out the husband was promoted in his place of work and his children who had finished schooling were gainfully employed. During the second week, the woman won a contract to supply food to the prison service. Within a short space of time that family became the richest in the community and has remained so even till this day. Such is the efficacy of the word. That explains how profitable it is to think and speak positive words always.

Our Lord Jesus Christ stated that whoever believe in Him would not taste of death. He said that He is the bread of life and whosoever eats of Him shall have everlasting life. All these are words of life, peace, and prosperity. Whoever believes in them shall neither die nor be confronted with any problem. You can now realise that the poor family that became rich did not resort to juju or sacrificed to idol to be rich. They believed in the spoken word.

## Man is the Architect of his Woes

Whatever predicament you find yourself in you are responsible. Your inability to practice the gospel comes from you. If you are fond of saying that you are unlucky, that people do not appreciate your good works and so on, the same will happen to you according to your belief and faith. You are always sighing and complaining of being worried by juju, mermaid, wizard and so on. This is because you believe in such things, so they fulfill in you according to your faith. But if you do not believe in such they will also not be effective in you. If you believe only in God, you will see and have nothing other than God. There was another case of a certain Queen who lived in a city that was so terrorised by armed robbers both in the day and at night. She felt so concerned. One night as she went into her room to sleep, she knelt down and prayed to God to change the robbers, give them employment and bless them. She said that the robbers were stealing out of despair as a result of lack, and that they would not love to do so if they were gainfully employed. She committed all of them and their souls into God's hands. As the Queen was praying inside her room, she did not know that the robbers had already surrounded her premises, and some of them were even hiding under her bed. But as she echoed Amen, one of them emerged from under her bed, and asked her whether she was aware that he was hiding under her bed, she said no. The robber made it known to her that they had planned to rob her that night but because of her prayer God had aborted their plans. The robbers came out one after the other confessing to the Queen about their plights and problems. They complained that they were married with children, some up to ten children. As such, they had problems to make both ends meet. They all confessed their wrong doings and expressed their belief in the Queen's prayer that God would definitely help them and the Queen too. The Queen gave them some money but they would not take it because her prayer was sufficient. All the robbers quietly left. Before that week ran out, behold the robbers were gainfully employed and robbery ceased in that community instantly. Can you realise now the effect of speaking words that are edifying? God is here with you, yet you do not know Him. He continues to do His will but none understands. Read our Second Lesson again:

### 2nd Lesson: Colossians 4: 6

*"Let your speech be always with grace, seasoned with salt that ye may know how ye ought to answer every man."*

If from now you season your words with salt your problems will surely cease. Now that you know that the word is life, power, good health, God, Son of God, angels, wisdom, peace, joy and all the virtues, if you continue to speak only edifying words you will have no problem.

You will also realise that, it is God that kills, and He gives life. He exalts and debases and does everything. That is so because He is the word and the word is the origin of everything. If you say, ' it looks as if I am going to be sick', you will surely be sick. If you say, 'it appears as if I will fall and die, you will surely fall and die. If you say that people do not love you and do not reward you positively for the good things you do to them, the same will come to pass. You should even draw a lesson from the case of Our Lord Jesus Christ when He said, 'I shall go to Jerusalem and there I will be tortured and killed but shall resurrect on the third day'. The same words came to pass as He had spoken. He also stated clearly that, nobody was responsible for His predicament that He offered His life voluntarily and could secure it back at will. If He did not give His life nobody would have been able to take it. Moreover, if He had not stated that God would make Him to resurrect on the third day, He would not have resurrected. It is said that the word is so close to your mouth and heart, and this is the word of faith, which we preach. Ever since you came to Brotherhood, have you heard any evil word spoken by the Holy Father? In as much as you do not know the power of the spoken words, then your claim to know God is false. That is why it is said that, none can see God's face, but that we can only hear His voice. It is said: (Hebrew 3: 7-8) No person is capable of causing what is not in existence to come into being and what is existing to cease to exist, except the word of God. There is nothing the word cannot do. Our Lord Jesus Christ healed the sick, raised the dead and performed many other miracles. All these were manifestations of the word. It was the same word He pronounced on the barren fig tree to wither away.

Lazarus died and on the fourth day Christ went to the graveside, spoke the same word to the Father in prayer and Lazarus resurrected. Before He did the miracle, when Christ was told that His friend Lazarus was dead, He told them that he was not dead. That was the word that sustained Lazarus. To the leper and the rest of the afflicted who came to Him, He did nothing but merely asked them what they wanted Him to do for them? It was fulfilled to each and every one of them according to their faith. With all these wonderful things done, do you still believe in Him,? On the contrary, you are watching and waiting for a huge person with a long beard to come and tell you behold I am the one expected. He is right here with you very close to you. So also are death, sickness and other problems close to you on your lips. This is why you are warned not to allow evil communication to proceed out of your mouth. Allow only words that are edifying, to come out of your mouths.

I give you all these examples, and take enough time to fully expatiate on these facts, so that you will know and believe that the word is God, life, power, prosperity and everything. That is why it is said that in everything a man offends, but that any person who is able to bridle his tongue is perfect. <u>Therefore a Perfect man. is the one who does not speak evil words. and who believes in God. and believes that everything originated from the word:</u> That was why Christ did not speak evil words but uttered only positive words. Christ knew that whatever word He uttered would come to pass. Even where people were starving, sick and dying, whenever Christ arrived there and uttered a positive statement, the situation became normal.

The occultists and metaphysicians rely on the spoken word as their weapon and not on leaves or any other thing. Equally if you go to a person's house and speak only positive words, that God should bless him, protect, give him long life and so on, the same will manifest for the man. Even the necromancer or juju doctor involves only the spoken words into the leaves, water or whatever materials they use. In the court, the judge relies purely on the words to decide a case. In the war front, except the commander speaks the word by way of command, would his troops open fire? The answer is no! Before a policeman would set out to arrest a person he has to be authorised to do so. All these explain the power of the word.

**Words Identify a Person**

It is the Father, therefore, that does the work here and not you. It is for this reason that whoever you discharge of his problems stand so discharged. The gospel 'What is Brotherhood' explains that the trees, the ants, the grass, the fish, the birds, animals, human beings and everything created are Brotherhood. It is therefore very ridiculous when some of you would say that you are the only member of Brotherhood in your family. There is nothing positive the word cannot achieve. It can change black into white, imperfection into perfection, death into life and so on. A local adage has it that a cow uses its tongue to clean its young one newly delivered.

I have lots of things to teach you. This has prompted Me to desire that I should be wifh you every time of the day to teach you. I have not even open My bag yet to bring out My course contents. Good words constitute the Holy Spirit while evil words are evil spirit. Good words is God while evil words is Satan. So long as you continue to speak good words you identify with God and all good things will follow you.

If you speak the words of love, mercy, kindness and words filled with peace, patience, progress, togetherness and prosperity, all will surely happen accordingly. The truth, love, humility, peace and righteousness have now taken dominion all over the world. Time has since passed and gone when evil overwhelmed the world. Whoever is able to bridle his tongue, and does not allow evil words to proceed out of his mouth, is perfect and capable of ruling the world. Such is the person who knows the truth and has it. Whoever speaks the truth would know quite well that there is no impossibility with God.

That is why the Father constantly, pronounced positive words, words that are edifying. Soon you will realise that it is through these positive utterances that evil is conquered. Any person who gives you money, car, house, food and all the material things, but has no good words in his mouth is satanic. A person who does not utter evil communication is perfect.

## An illustration

The third illustration, to confirm the efficacy of words concerns a king who was exiled. One day a certain prophet went to that village to preach and there he met with a son of the exiled king. When the prophet asked him of his father, the young man said that he had been exiled. And when he inquired from him why they could not do something to prevent the king from being exiled, the young man said that, they had engaged the services of two hundred lawyers, prepared some juju, sacrificed human beings, bribed the council all to no avail.

The prophet asked the young man whether they offered prayer? Then he told the prophet that, the problem that took place did not call for prayer and that prayer could not solve it. The prophet asked the young man if he was still in need that his father should return and be restored to his throne. In his reaction the young man expressed the impossibility of that. The prophet directed him to persistently say "Thank you Father for making my father to return". He did not ask him to burn any candle, incense nor to sacrifice anything. The young man continued to say this time and again until one day the village council rescinded its decision and recalled the king home. The ways in which God does His own things and perform His miracles confound human knowledge. This is because He does not follow conventional methods. That is why God's way cannot be understood by men. But if a human being does something, men easily believe it because his means is familiar and conventional.

If prayer cannot solve a problem, what else would solve it? Of the three, the word, money and conventional weapons, which is most powerful? In reality, there is nothing which money or man can do. Read the golden text once more:

**Golden Text: James 3: 2**

"For in many things we offend all. If any man offend not in word, the sane is a perfect man, and able also to bridle the whole body".

## The Distinction between Prayers

There is a prayer of faith and the prayer of faithlessness. This is a big lesson on its own. There are vain words and also the words of God. There are words, which you can speak from morning till night and will not yield any good fruit. But a person can utter a word and it will be so effective and powerful even if it is a jot, as little as the mustard seed. That is why it is said that, the word of God is like the mustard seed that is so minute but when it grows, all the birds in the air make their nests on it and animals in the bush take shelter under it.

This explains the reason why Christ told the Samaritan woman that, they worshipped what they knew not. That is to say it was quite unnecessary for them to go to the mountains or to Jerusalem to worship God. He is not limited to these places. You can stay wherever you like but speak just the word and it will come to pass. Be positive always and endeavour to bid people the peace of God and it will surely come to pass. The prayer of faithlessness is offered when a person requests of God to give him money, wife, husband, food and other material things. This means that such a person has only succeeded in piling his requests before God and left. Such will never be answered. But if you pray saying, thank you Father, for giving me food or money or whatever you desire, it will be done accordingly. That is the prayer of faith. You have to continue to thank God for everything. But if you say to God, that if He could give you a wife, husband, or money etc, you would praise Him exceedingly. Such a prayer is a manifestation of disbelief in God.

I know that, what I am teaching you, is greater than you; it is advance for you. Even so, this is the time of truth, the fullness of time for all to practice the word of God. From today, do not utter evil words again, do not condemn, curse or abuse anybody.

Be steadfast in pronouncing only good words by the power of the spoken words. Whatever situation you find yourself, whether a sick person is brought before you, or you are in a precarious position, if you utter good and edifying words the situation will be changed from bad to good.

Beloved, a stroke of a cane is sufficient unto the wise. Those who have ears to hear let them hear. May the Lord bless His Holy Words. Amen.

# CHAPTER 21

# ONE GOVERNMENT ONE CURRENCY

Everlasting Gospel delivered by Leader Olumba Olumba Obu

Sole Spiritual Head of the Universe

**First Lesson: Matthew 6: 9-10**

"*After this manner therefore pray ye: Our Father which art in heaven, Hallowed be thy name. thy Kingdom come. Thy will be done in earth, as it is in heaven.*"

**Second Lesson: Revelation 21: 1-3**

"*And I saw a new heaven and a new earth: for the first heaven and the first earlh were passed away: and there was no more sea And I John saw the holy city, new Jerusalem, coming down from God out of heaven, prepared as a bride adorned for her husband. And I heard a great voice out of heaven saying, behold; the tabernacle of God is with man, and he will dwell with them. and they shall be his people, and God himself shall be with them, and be their God.*"

**Golden Text: Matthew 21: 33-43**

"*Hear another parable: there was a certain householder, which planted a vineyard; and hedged it roound about, and digged a winepress in it, and built a tower, and let it out to husbandmen, and went into a far country, and when the time of the fiuit drew near, he sent his servants to the husband men, that they might receive the fruits of it. And the husbandmen took his servants, and beat one, and killed another, and stoned another. Again, he sent other servants more than the first: and they did unto them likewise. But last of all he sent unto them his son, saying, They will reverence my son. But when the husbandmen saw the son, they said among themselves, This is the heir; come, let us kill him, and let us seize on his inheritance. And they caught him, and cast him out of the vineyard: and slew him.*

*When the lord therefore of the vineyard cometh, what will he do unto those husbandmen? They say unto him, He will miserably destroy those wicked men, and will let out his vineyard unto other husbandmen, which shall render him the fruits in their seasons, Jesus saith unto them, Did ye never read in the scriptures, The stone which the builders rejected, the same is become the head of the corner: this is the Lord's doing, and it is marvelous in our eyes?"*

*Therefore say I unto you, The kingdom of God shall be taken from you, and given to a nation bringingforth the fruits thereof.*"

## The Prophecy of Christ Fulfilled

Beloved, this gospel is a discourse on the fulfillment of the words spoken by Our Lord Jesus Christ many years ago. This is by way of reminding the entire world and declaring as a witness, the manifestation of the portions of the scriptme.

The salient questions arising from the parable in the golden text are who were the husbandmen, the fanners? Who cultivated the soil and fenced the fann? Is the fanner not the householder who fenced round his fann? Who also sent out the servants to carry out the harvest? Who sent the prophets and angels, who were beaten, chased out of the fann and even killed? Was it not the owner of the fann who sent in messengers to work for him? The first group, were victimised and so were the next. Finally, He sent His only begotten son who was equally maltreated and killed. Even when the Lord told them that He was sent by His Father, the people did not believe Him. God sent down His begotten son, in the belief that the husbandmen would recognise and respect Him, yet they did not:

"*But last of all he sent unto them his son, saying, they will reverence my son. But when the husbandsmen saw the son they said among themselves this is the heir; come let us kill him and let us seize on his inheritance.*"

## The Lord of Harvest

Who was that son? Was he not Our Lord Jesus Christ? Who sent Him? Was it not God the Father? Why did He send Him? The answer is found in His statement, which He said" .... they will reverence my Son... . For what reason did the husbandmen chase away the heir?

Their ambition was to claim the vineyard. Who do you think God should have sent after such torture, humiliation and even further threats? A local adage says, when the battle is fierce, the King takes over the command. There lies the answer. This means that the King Himself has now taken over the command having seen that the battle is really fierce. He is the commander-in-chief of the Armed Forces. He has come by Himself.

Now is not the time for anybody to ascribe the glory and praises of God to any human being present or past. It is an act of foolishness for a man to thank Olumba Olumba Obu, Joseph, Moses, or indeed any of the prophets of old for anything. What were the prophets of old to do? Recall the question Our Lord Jesus Christ asked His disciples after the parable. He asked them, when the Lord therefore of the vineyard cometh, what will he do unto those husbandmen? The disciples in one accord replied that he, the owner of the vineyard would miserably destroy those wicked men, and would take away his vineyard from these wicked men and entrust it to other servants who would accurately render the farm yields to him in their seasons. That is exactly what is happening now on earth.

Which other person or being is capable of destroying this earth and re-organising or reconstructing it than the creator Himself.

**CHORUS**: "*I have come by myself sending no one. I will reveal myself to the world. I have not come to die again as people think. My people sing* and *rejoice, for I, the Lord have assumed glory.*"

**An Everlasting Reigning Monarch**

Beloved, this gospel centres on the fact that this is the reign and glory of the Holy Spirit. Give not this glory to any man or angel but to the Owner, God, the Father who has come by Himself, sending no one. He would not have repeated the same mistake over and over again, sending messengers only to be chased and killed. This explains the reason why He has come by Himself. We should, therefore give Him His due glory and honour. We should call a spade a spade.

## A Time for God's children to harvest freely

All along people have been calling Jesus, Jesus, repeatedly, yet violence, hunger, diseases and death have not ceased. Our Lord Jesus came and was arrested by the same husbandmen and nailed to the cross. Our Lord Jesus Christ asked His disciples what the Lord of the vineyard would do to those husbandmen when He comes. By this question, the Lord was invariably informing the world of the coming of the Father who Himself is the Lord of the vineyard.

**Leave Vengeance to The Lord**

Christ once said that even though God may be slow in His response, yet He never forgets. Therefore, He has this day, hearkened to the prayers of the faithful ones. In another instance also, Our Lord Jesus Christ prayed the Father to let His kingdom come. . . (MATTHEW 6: 10). This is the exact time He pre-arranged to avenge for His children. This is the reason why Christ advised us to leave vengeance to God. Thus, He advised that if you are slapped on the right cheek, you should turn the left one for the same purpose. He also advised that if a man wants your inner wear, you should give him also your cloak, and if he should desire that you go a mile with him, go two instead. By so doing, the Father will not fail to give vengeance, despite His long suffering.

**On evil deeds**

God made it categorically clear that no evildoer will be saved. This explains why He teaches us to refrain from stealing, killing, idolatry, fornication, hatred, division, and falsehood and from all ungodly acts. He has rather advised that we should be meek, prompt in tithe payments, kind, and obedient. He has promised to take vengeance on your behalf and to destroy the husbandmen and their likes.

## On Oath Taking

He has warned you against swearing neither upon the heaven, for it is His throne, nor upon the earth for it is His footstool. No man should swear even upon Jerusalem, for it is the city of the great King. Let your Yes be Yes and your No, No. Anything short of this, the Lord says, it comes from the wicked one. Today, even Christians swear upon the name of God as a matter of routine.

**Total Power of the Father**

Pilate put Our Lord Jesus Christ in the dock and asked Him several questions, but He never responded at all. Out of anger, Pilate asked Christ whether He did not know that he had power to either release or condemn Him? What was Christ's reply? Christ told Pilate that if His Father did not give him the power from above, he could do nothing. By that statement, Our Lord

Jesus Christ bore eloquent testimony about the power of the Father. But today, whom do people testify about? On what do you base your testimony? The Father has come by Himself. Our Lord Jesus Christ did not relent in calling on the Father. Always, He would mention the Father either at the beginning of His statement or at the end. He made sure He glorified His Father and attributed everything to Him.

### The Creation of Heaven and Earth

It is said that if the housemaid were to know at what hour the thief would come, he would have kept watch. This means that you have to keep watch at all times in the morning, afternoon, evening, night and midnight. Who in the world is aware of the arrival of the Father as promised? The same God who sent Elijah of old. and other prophets of old,. who created heaven and earth and the fullness therein,. He who sent Our Lord Jesus Christ is now here on earth.

Is there anyone, who knows this fact? Do the rogues, drunkards, smokers, murderers, idolaters, the unfaithful and unbelievers know this? He has come to straighten all the crooked paths and put things aright.

**CHRIST SAID**:

*"Nevertheless I tell you the truth; it is expedient for you that I go away; for if I go not away; the Comforter will not come unto you; but if I depart, I will send him unto you. And when he is come, he will reprove the world of sin, and of righteousness, and of judgement. Of sin because they believe not on me: Of righteousness, because I go to my Father, and ye see me no more; Of judgement, because the prince of this world is judged."* JOHN 16: 7-11.

### The time of Judgement

Now is that time of judgement. He has come to address all the wrongs perpetrated by men. Our Lord Jesus Christ explained to the people that His Father sent Him but they did not believe Him. The Jews contended that it was written in their laws that the genealogy of the Messiah could not be traced. Here was a man whose parents was not only known but were assessed and found to belong to the lowest class in their society. For that reason, none then, and even now, believed in the Lord and His words. Phillip, one of the disciples, also demonstrated this act of unfaithfulness when he sought the Lord to show them the Father who He so frequently mentioned and they would be satisfied. That was when the Father came through the Son. Now, He has personally come down, using no intermediary. But who knows Him?

### Magnify His Name

Our duty is to glorify Him, be of good conduct, and refrain from all sinful acts. Disputers of the word of God should refrain from unecessary argument and behave well, because this is the judgement time for all. Evildoers should pray fervently for themselves. Now is not the time to continue to pray God to give you money, food, husband, wife, children and other material things. We should rather be relentless in thanking Him and praising His name, for His Kingdom is here. The kingdoms of this world have become the Kingdom of Jehovah God and His Christ and He shall reign forever and ever. This forms the good news of great joy.

**He Has Come**

He has come in His power, might and wisdom. None should feel proud of his or her material wealth and knowledge for these are nothing in the sight of God. After all is He not the Creator and Owner of all things that man claimed to own? He is the Lord and King of wisdom, power, health, wealth, and all things. Ours is to bow to him, sing to His praises, glorify His name and call upon Him every time. Whether in bed, at table, on the road, in your conversations, in and out of season, we are to praise Him at all times. In times of joy and trouble, continue to call upon His name. It is blasphemous for anybody to arrogate to himself the ability to see vision, heal or do anything. It is an offence of a gross proportion for any person to trade in visions, prayer or any service in this kingdom. Members of Brotherhood of the Cross and Star are the more guiltiable in this wise. Who on earth has power to do anything? It is God who has healed a person or opened your eyes to see visions. These visionaries and so-called healers are so faithless and full of unbelief that if left on their own; they cannot move a fly.

### Man is empty and void

It is really funny to watch a man testifying how he has healed diverse illnesses, prayed until the dead was raised, and has done many more wonderful things. What is man in the first place, and what does he know! The doer of all things, the beginning of all things, and the last, *is* here, and we should give Him glory .

In the past, man, angels and spirits were glorified but now, is the time for God to be glorified.

Let the first lesson be read once again-

### First Lesson: Matthew 6: 9- 10

" After this manner therefore pray ye: Our Father which art in heaven, Hallowed be thy name. Thy Kingdom come. Thy will be done in earth, as it is in heaven."

### Time for God's Glory

We are indeed the luckiest generation to have God's promise fulfilled in our time. We have a Father, the Father of peace, hope, mercy, truth, and all the virtues. Time has since passed and gone when people entertained various fears. There are no more sorrows and pains. Weep not child, for the Saviour is not on His way, but is already in our midst He is the Comforter and adviser, the only way, the truth and life. Do not give God's glory to man, who is mere mortal and incapable of doing anything.

### The only ruling force

Humble yourself, and do not be proud of having power or anything. Submit to Him and give Him His due glory. In the whole of Cross River State and Akwa Ibom State here in Nigeria, there is no particular people as wicked and adventurous as those of Akwa Ibom in Cross River State or Achara Okpo in Abia State. But it should interest you to know that, the Father has come into their midst and subdued them. They were at daggers drawn with each other and not even the government; State and Federal could successfully intervene in their inter-communal boundary conflict. They have now laid down their arms because they have seen this glory. The same rancour prevailed between Adim and Agwaguna in Cross River State. The squabble defied every human solution, but by celebrating a full feast, peace has been restored in their midst and they are united as one.

### Listen to God

This is not the time to establish churches, healing homes or prayer houses. Tell even the government to listen to God and obey His rules. It is time we should love one another, humble ourselves and become merciful and meek.

We are God's vineyard, His temple, city, kingdom and His Christ. We should rise in concert and glorify Him as Christ testified of His glory in every statement that he made. Our duty is to chorus that His words are true. None should consult his fellow man, angel or spirit for anything. There should be no ritual sacrifice of any sort and for any reason whatsoever. The Father is in perfect control of all affairs. His glory He shares with only those He pleases. Go and advise all to desist from carnal thoughts. Tell the sorcerers, prostitutes, deceivers and swindlers to refrain from such devilish acts. People who are power-thirsty and egoistic should bow down to God and give every glory to Him. The owner of heaven and earth and the fullness therein is now here on earth Personified.

It is God's wish that none should perish. This is why He has come by Himself. Therefore, go and inform all those who are claiming ownership of one thing or the other, to desist from such claims; tell those who struggle for land, house and positions, to stop it, for the real owner and creator of everything is here. The Owner of cities, human beings, banks, governments and their agencies, children, husbands, wives, water, air, mountain, and all things has come. Our only duty is to show complete obedience and loyalty to Him. Let us all carry the banner of Christ and His truth to the entire inhabitants of the world to follow. No matter how little the service you render to God without fee, His divine blessing to you is a hundred-fold

### The World is empty and void

We have no reason to consult physicians, herbalists, sorcerers, healers or soothsayers. The whole world is empty, and human beings are also blank, without any knowledge. Man's only hope is in the Father. What is written in the book of **Isaiah** 2, is here fulfilled. Let us now turn away from evil and pursue peace, love, truth, and all the virtues, which form the component parts of the kingdom. He cares, teaches, and guides us all daily. No man is capable of changing, caring for or tolerating his fellow man.

### A Message to the World

His appearance now is a clear indication that His Spirit flourishes the earth. He has come with His host of angels, children of God and His long-awaited Kingdom. Let us now leap for joy, and sing His praises. Let all those who are still at war lay down their arms. Tell litigants to withdraw all their cases from the court. The judges should desist from judging others. Let all evildoers and whoremongers refrain from their evil ways. Now is the time to obey the voice of God and turn a new leaf, for destruction is at the doorstep of every man, for the destruction of disobedient people. Tell all politicians who form the habit of deceiving the people and looting the public treasury, to desist from such. Tell the troublemakers, coup plotters, usurpers of govenunents and all evil doers to refrain from these.

**Second Lesson: Revelation 21: 1-3**

*" And I saw a new heaven and a new earth: for the first heaven ard the first earth were passed away; ard there was no more sea. And I Jolm saw the holy city, New Jerusalem, coming dawn from God out of heaven, prepared as a bride adorned for her husband. And I heard a great voice out of heaven saying, behold, the tabernacle of God is with men, ard he will dwell with them, ard they shall be his people, and God himself shall be with them, ard be their God."*

How many of those who have been reading this passsage believe in what is written in it? Who in the world today believes that God is here on earth? Christ is here with us, and so is the Holy Spirit and angels. We are all God's children and by that His messengers and servants.

We are now in a New World. The old one has given way with its old things. Now, ask yourself why the attention of the world is focused on Nigeria in particular, and Africa in general. Has anyone read the present events in the world in books, seen in a vision or dream? He has come to reign in heaven and on earth. He is neither Olumba nor any prophet. He is not an angel either. His glory has no beginning or an end. His reign has no limit at all.

**America should be careful**

Tell America that claims to be the world's police to put its sword into its place. The same warning goes to China, Spain, Britain, France and all the troublesome countries, the world over . Now is the time for peace, love, truth, and glory of God. God abhors disobedience. A local adage says that, a cock that is stubborn and recalcitrant hears very clearly only in a pot of soup. No person should take vengeance. God has promised that vengeance is His, He will repay. Members of the various secret societies should resign their membership and follow God. He is with us everywhere and at all times. We are very fortunate to be called the children of God, and given the right of sonship.

## There will be One Currency under One Government.

Time has since passed and gone when anger, division, war, cheating, swindling, oppression, occultism and other evil practices rule over man. There is no distinction as to colour, age, race, sex or status in life in the kingdom of God, for we are one in the Lord. This is a completely new world in which peace, love, co-operation, economic integration under one universal umbrella prevail. **It is one currency under one government.**

This gospel is to be disseminated to all parts of the world. He that perishes has himself to blame, as his soul shall also perish with him. No man has ever contested with the Holy Spirit. Therefore, you have to submit to Him and live in peace. Do not seek for salvation and solution to your problems from any man. Let your hope and trust be centered on your creator. Go to Him on bended knees and He would surely give you rest.

He has said that this generation will not pass away until every word that He spoke shall be made consumate. 'This generation', refers to this twentieth century. The end of the twentieth century will mark the end of all hostilities, diseases, illnesses and all sinful acts. Division, hunger, and all forms of problems will be over with the turn of the century.

**Transition Period**

We are now in a transitional period into oneness, unity, love, peace, and all goodness. Now is the time to get the kingdom from the disobedient and wicked (husbandmen) and give to those who keep His commandments. In this Kingdom, there is no place for divided loyalty, falsehood and self- projection. He has accomplished His will.

**Prophecy of the Three Nuns Fulfilled**

The First World War of 1914 came with a revelation in 1917, to three Roman Catholic Nuns, that the Holy Spirit shall appear in Africa. He has since taken His advent and is actively working. The Catholic Church, when it heard the revelation by the nuns, concealed it on the orders of the then Pope. Tell me for how long can the truth be concealed? Like the mustard seed He has germinated in Africa and all the countries in the world. The inhabitants of the world have seen Him.

This explains why the whites are rushing to Africa and many are tracing their roots to Nigeria. He is a quickening Spirit.

## The end of vice

He said in the scripture that all those who seek to save their lives would lose it, but those who forsake their lives for the sake of the gospel shall gain them. All those who continue to indulge in diabolism, fetish and membership in secret societies shall be destroyed.

What we are witnessing now is the dream of Nebuchadnezzar as interpreted by Daniel. It is now fulfilled. He saw many kingdoms coming and going until a particular one that was to be resolute and strong, overcoming every other kingdom. This dream is fulfilled in Brotherhood of the Cross and Star. This is the kingdom established by the Father Himself. He has come now as the Holy Spirit, having been before as the Father and the Son. The Trinity God is here with His heavenly hosts. He has come to put an end to prejudice based on colour, language, and economic, religious, political, or social factors. That is the final prophecy of Our Lord Jesus Christ, which has equally fulfilled. This is the reason for charging that we should go into the world and make all nations His disciples. Baptising them in the Name of the Father, The Son, and the Holy Ghost, and teaching them all He has taught us, for He is with us always, even to the end of the world - See Matthew 28: 19- 20.

Read the golden text again:

### Golden Text: Matthew 21: 33-43

*"Hear another parable: There was a certain householder, which planted a vineyard, and hedged it round about, and digged a winepress in it, and built a tower, and let it out to husbandmen, and went into a far country. And when the time of the fruit drew near, he sent his servants to the husbandmen, that they might receive the fruits of it.* And *the husbandmen took the servants and beat one, and killed another, and stoned another. Again, he sent other servants more than the first: and they did unto them likewise. But last of all he sent unto them his son, saying, They will reverence my son. But when the husbandmen saw the son, they said among themselves, This is the heir; come, let us kill him, and let us seize on his inheritance. And they caught him, and cast him out of the vineyard, and slew him.*

*When the lord therefore of the vineyard cometh, what will he do unto those husbandmen?* They *say unto him, He will miserably destroy those wicked men, and will let out his vineyard unto other husbandmen, which shall render him the fruits in their seasons. Jesus saith unto them, Did ye never read in the scriptures,* The *stone which the builders rejected, the same is become the head of the corner: this is the Lord's doing, and it is marvellous in our eyes* ?

*Therefore say I unto you, The kingdom of God shall be taken from you, and given to a nation bringing forth the fruits thereof."*

## A Reward for the Righteous

Beloved brethren, all those who are kind, loving, obedient, merciful, truthful, humble, faithful and righteous shall inherit the Kingdom of God. But the disobedient and faithless ones shall be damned. Remember the case of a certain widow in the Bible who attended a fund raising. While others donated in thousands, out of her generosity she donated her widow's mite. That was all the money she had, and with this action she stood distinct from every other person because of her generosity. In that congregation were chiefs, kings, millionaires, and great men, but the woman's donation attracted a blessing. So would the so-called great men of this world, the scientists, the royal highnesses and all disobedient and faithless people be destroyed and swept off. Only the children of God shall inherit the earth.

A stroke of a cane is sufficient unto the wise. Let those who have ears, hear what the Holy Spirit has imparted to the world.

May God bless His Holy Words, Amen.

# CHAPTER 22

# "MY WORDS; YOUR WATCHWORDS"

## A Farewell Message To The Universe

**SPIRITUAL FOOD: ST. JOHN 12: 40-50.**

*"He hath blinded their eyes and hardened their heart; that they should not see with their eyes, nor understand with their heart, and be converted, and I should heal them.*

*These things said Esaias, when he saw his glory and spoke of him. Nevertheless among the chief rulers also many believed on him; but because of the Pharisees they did not confess him, lest they should be put out of the synagogue: For they loved the praise of men more than the praise of God. Jesus cried and said, He that believeth on me, believeth not on me, but on him that sent me. And he that seeth me seeth him that sent me. I am come a light into the world, that whosoever believeth on me should not abide in darkness. And if any man hear my words, and believe not, I judge him not: for I came not to judge the world, but to save the world. He that rejected me, and receiveth not my words, hath one that judgeth him: the word that I have spoken, the same shall judge him in the last day. For I have not spoken of myself, but the Father which sent me, he gave me a commandment, what I should say, and what I should speak. And I know that his commandment is life everlasting: whatsoever I speak therefore, even as the Father said unto me, so I speak."*

### Spiritual Blindness and its Adversities

Beloved, that is the farewell message. It is the spiritual food that will suffice you till eternity and you would no longer need any other preaching. Though blindness is said to be a bad sickness, spiritual blindness is the worst. Why the world is in this deplorable state is because of her spiritual blindness. You have heard Christ said thus: I did not come to judge you but to save you. I do not want money from you neither do I need your wisdom, praises, nor recognition. The truth is that if I did not come, the world would have perished completely. And with My coming, I have transformed you from depravity to eternal life. My words are such that when you put them into practice they give you eternal life. To this end, you need to imbibe all My words and practice them, My words should be your watchwords at all times. From today it is expected that you all love Me and My words because these constitute the sure way to salvation. Practice My words immediately without depreciation for they constitute eternal life. If the world had loved Christ and His words, by now everything would have been streamlined.

Even the Israelites, if they had accepted Christ, they would have obtained salvation from Him. After all it is said, "light attracts light. As I have come, if there was even one person who possessed love, everyihing would have been streamlined in the whole world. I do not need a multitude of people to work with; just one is enough for Me to use in salvaging the entire community. Jolm the Baptist bore testimony about Christ but Our Lord Jesus Christ bore testimony about My coming into the world, that is why He enjoined you to have love. What has hitherto tied you down is your lack of love, nobody in the whole world has love, that is why the spiritual food has it that God has blinded their eyes and hardened their hearts so that they will not repent. Everything has been fulfilled as spoken by Christ. Today I want to assure you that there is no more spiritual blindness and deafness. Those who were hitherto blinded spiritually, their spiritual eyes have been opened and those who were deaf have equally been made to hear so that you will be able to appreciate this love so that all may be well with you.

### An Illustration

I have given you an illustration about a man, his children and the eaglet. The man caught the eaglet, tended it and had it to be among his children. Then came a trader who saw the eaglet among the chicken and said to the man, that is an eaglet but the man denied and said it was an ordinary chick. But the trader insisted, saying he recognised the eaglet. And so the trader turned to the eaglet and said you are eaglet the king of the birds, you need to go up high in the heaven and what are you doing here among the chickens? Then the trader asked the owner to throw the eaglet into the air to set it *free* and let it be at liberty. The owner laughed and said he will not be able to accomplish that and so he handed over the eaglet to the trader to try what he requested. The trader abandoned his luggage and picked up the eaglet and said, 'thou eaglet; king of the birds, your abode is above'. And thereafter, he let the eaglet off and it jumped down and perched again on the ground.

The owner was laughing at the trader because he thought the eaglet could not go up again. The trader repeated his feat the next day and told the eaglet that you are the king of all birds, including the fowls of the earth and when he let go the eaglet it went back to the ground. Realise that six days are for the thief while one day is for the trader. The trader went on with this exercise for some days and on one fateful day, as he was saying everything and letting the eaglet down as in other days, it flew off into the air and never returned to the earth.

## God's Most Treasured Asset

The above illustration refers to the children of God. God does not have any other thing apart from man but now you do not regard man as anything, hence, you kill man, and eat as food, insult man and treat him with all amount of disdain. As I watch the way you treat your fellowman, My eyes are filled with tears, if you will allow the light of God to shine on you, then your eyes will be opened. I need one person who will practice the injunction of love so as to work with him, to perfect everything in the whole world. Man is the treasure of God but the way you treat your fellow human being is very pathetic. I am looking forward to seeing the day the scales will fall off your eyes, so that you will fully appreciate My teachings so that all will be well with you. Have you bought any idea from the point so far made? Read Hebrew I: 1-6:

The Father has opened your eyes and ears and as well broadened your intellects for you to be able to practice His words. You will no more be foolish because up till now you were deaf and blind as a result of focusing all your concentration on the earthly things. This great light was hidden from all the inhabitants of the world. Who is man that all the angels have been commanded to worship him? All the angels are under his superintendence. Angels are messengers of God and not his children; as such they have to minister to man who is His son. All the hosts of heaven comprise angels, death, sickness, wind, sun and everything is under the supremacy of man who is the only begotten Son of God. Read Hebrews 2: 1-10.3: 1-6. And 4: 4-10.

## The Efficacy of The Spoken Word

As you are, do you know that just one spoken word from Me can stop all the things you are doing here which are inimical to the Holy Spirit? At No.8 Eton Street, Calabar, because of the rate at which members were committing fornication, I declared that right from that day anyone who indulged in fornication would see what would happen. A sister who went and indulged in the said act died on the spot, and the man ran away. The members all came and appealed to Me to repeal the statement and so I accepted and told them to limit the rate of fornication. Even now if you cause Me to make any pronouncements you will see what will happen. All these little sins you are committing now only one spoken word by Me will just take them away completely. Do you hear Me speak on all these things you have been committing? You regard Me as a periwinkle which you can pick up easily. You even regard Me as your equal. You do not have any fear of God because of the love I have for you. Just one spoken word will stop all these things. If you say something should happen and I say no, can such a thing happen? If I say man should stop to exist. he will not exist any more. As you regard Me as your mate, do you know the Being in your midst? Do you think I am of this world, do you see anything in Me which is a replica of yours? Why are you so stubborn? Do you want to be damned? A local adage has it that you cannot splash water on your enemies. Right now if I issue orders that action should be taken against offenders, the same shall be effected. Even the animals are on the alert; they have dangerous swords ready to carry out My orders.

In 1974, during August Pentecostal Assembly like this, because of your deeds, I decided to show you the judgement equipment. When I showed the said things to you, what happened in this house? I only showed the equipment, not judging the world and you saw what happened. I had intended to display them for three days, but pity made Me to take them back. Darkness engulfed the whole place. Vision was even given that if the sword were taken out of the sheath, something disastrous would have happened. Now, who would have been left in the entire world? You do not believe in God and do not want to stop committing sins. What do you think I came to do apart from to judge the world? I have to start the judgement with you. Therefore, brethren, practice the word of God because the time is up, otherwise, you will perish. No one ever confronts God and goes home scot-free. Many people are ready to inherit this Kingdom, this I know. You have been made clean from the spoken words even as you are here.

## The Divine Order

And when you fail to heed My instructions, do you think you have obeyed God? You have to be mindful of the spoken words of God because they are of significance. Watch all My pronouncements for they must all be consumed. The time is nigh for everything to be accomplished but things are still stagnant because I have not issued orders. That is why, from today you have to abide by all My words so that you will be saved. It is said that 'today when you hear His voice do not harden your hearts'. You are told not to eat fish and meat, not to be angry, steal and commit fornication.

Love one another and stop behaving unseemingly because all unseeming things incur the wrath of God on you.

This is when the key to your salvation has arrived, even if you want to go to the moon to do anything, if I do not consent to it you will crash land. Anything you want to do behind Me is bound to meet with failure, therefore from today abide by My instructions so that you will not perish. I know all your problems and I am gradually taking them away. There is a saying: 'Rome was not built in a day'. Anything I tell you to do, when you do it you will not have any problems. Stop doing things according to your dictates because this has been the source of your problems. By obeying the instructions of God you receive blessing from Him. This love I am talking about daily, do you know the benefit you will derive in putting it into practice?

## The Key

Obedience is the key to salvation and if any of you were to be obedient to My injunctions, all would have been well with you. Do not do anything according to your heart's desire because your heart will only end up misleading you but only abide by God's injunctions. When Adam had eaten the forbidden fruit and Eve gave birth to the twins, Adam did not want to meet her again and so he went up on the roof. Satan came and called Adam and he did not answer but when God called him, he answered and when God asked what he was doing on top of the roof he said he was avoiding meeting the woman who was with him, so God asked Adam why he did not request for the desire to be taken away from him. When Adam then requested for it, God granted it to him. From that day they stayed as brother and sister in the house, so also it is with you here.

Anything you do not want which is troubling you put the request before Me, and it will be taken away from you forthwith. It is not My intention to take anything away from you forcefully but when you are fed up with anything then communicate wth the Father and He will grant your request. Why I do not take away these things forcefully, is that it will result into some other things.

God has time for everything. When you request Me to make pronouncement so as to accomplish a particular thing, when it is not yet time, I will not speak the word. When you are told to forsake sins do not harden your heart. If you fail to abide by all that I have taught you, then you will be known as a rebel. When you are told to walk in spirit it means you should abide in God's instructions. Brother Essien Umoh on coming here to read the Bible started searching his bag for his eyeglasses and so I shunned him and told him to go on reading the Bible without the lenses and since that time did he not see clearly? Is he still using the lenses? No matter how thin the letters are he sees them clearly now, so also it was with Brother S.I.U. Etuk, and M. Akwang. Your main sickness is because you do not believe in God; right from the day you believe in God, all your problems will be taken away from you. Nothing is impossible with God.

The moment I say go all is well it is so accomplished, because the flesh is leading you that is why you have been given this little message.

May My peace and blessing abide with the entire universe now and forever more. Amen.

# CHAPTER 23

# THEOLOGY, HYPOCRISY AND OUR LORD JESUS CHRIST

Everlasting Gospel Delivered By:
Leader Olumba Olumba Obu
Sole Spiritual Head of the Universe.

**First Lesson: St Matthew 7 v 21**
"Not everyone that saith unto me, Lord, Lord shall enter into the kingdom of heaven; but he that doeth the will of my Father which is in heaven."

**Second Lesson: St Luke 6 v 46**
"And why call ye me Lord, Lord, and do not the things which I say?"

**Golden Text: St John 14 v 21**
"He that hath my commandments, and keepeth them, he it is that loveth me: and he that loveth me shall be loved of my Father, and I will love him, and will manifest myself in him."

### Those Who Chase The Shadows:

It is excellent to be called a child of God. How about what it takes? You have read the words of our Lord Jesus Christ as outlined above. You will notice from your readings that disobedience is not a new arrangement. Furthermore, you may grasped fast what it takes to qualify as a child of God. Take note also that, the intrique of the flesh is not new. The shouting of 'Jesus' endlessly and frivolously is one of such carnal expressions, and hypocrisy which does not start from now. If the mere expression of that great name of our Lord Jesus Christ is not a pretence, why do you indulge in terrible and unwholesome acts? You hate and even destroy many. How can we reconcile this 'double back'? On one hand you are a master in fornication, idolatry and gossips; on the other hand, you are proclaiming profoundly and rebuking sternly with the name of our Lord Jesus Christ. Oh man! my heart bleeds for you. It bleeds the more because, in the midst of ignorance, you claim wisdom, power and righteousness. Where do you think you could go to, to acquire the knowledge of God? Who told you that there is a 'Bible college' and where is it? Our Lord Jesus Christ said: *"Neither be ye called masters; for one is your Master, even Christ."* ( St Matthew 23 v 10 )

Somebody would claim to have graduated out of the university and that he read Religious Studies but he still drinks, steals, fornicates, worship idols and indulges in all forms of immoralities. If I may ask, what were you taught in the university? If your course content is devoid of how to transform yourself and man, then, what is the difference between you and the heathens? What have you to show as a major in Theology? Churches have sprang up with different names. The truth is that whether you establish numerous churches or not, you must practice the injunctions of God otherwise you have ear-marked your person for condemnation. This had been lucidly explained in this passage of the scripture: *"Not everyone that saith unto me, Lord, Lord, shall enter into the kingdom of heaven; but he that doeth the will of my Father which is in heaven."* ( St Matthew 7 v 21 )

### Why These Hues And Cries?

The teachings of our Lord Jesus Christ are so direct that its comprehension, interpretation and implementation are supposedly not cumbersome. I liken same to a teacher who sets a test on one hand and provides the answers with the other. The test being the ultimate aim of every man, which is eternal life with God, the answer He has simply provided by urging all and sundry to practice the injunctions of God. So, why launch all these campaign of calumny against that Leader of others, what are all these churches meant for?

Of what use are all these empty boasts about strength of the churches or fellowships, bank balances of individual preachers and churches? Let it be known to you that, if you had sponsored the building of all the churches and personally call on the name of our Lord Jesus Christ a million times a day, it profits you nothing, except you accept and implement the directives of our Lord Jesus Christ to the letter.

If you wish, go around all the streets with megaphone and a lorry load of Bibles; preach day and night unceasingly; if you do not practice these words, it is of no gain to you. It is indeed, awful to see the whole world, black and white, young and old deceiving themselves and thinking that they are deceiving God. In the past, those that gave themselves up for the services of God were few, hence, they called Him the God of Abraham, Isaac and Jacob; but now, everybody claims to be His servant. The thieves, fornicators, idolaters, necromancers, murderers, etc, are all inclusive. Everybody now shouts at the top of his voice 'Jesus! Jesus! Jesus!' day and night, what a colossal waste of energy! What a deceit! However, He had taken personal note of this when He was quoted as saying: *'And why call ye me, Lord, Lord, and do not the things which I say?'* (Luke 6 v46).

He knows too well that, right from the foundation of the world was laid, nobody has ever practiced the word of God. Most of us believe that God has no eyes, ears or concience. Who told you? He has all organs and capabilities irrespective of His meekness, patience and tolerance. So brethren, stop deceiving yourselves, God cannot be mocked. He sees and notes all your activities. Read His scriptural expressions: **"Be not deceived; God is not mocked; for whatsoever a man soweth, that shall he also reap."** ( Galation 6 v 7 ). The placard-carrying 'disciples' of our Lord Jesus Christ; the 'praise singers,' the religious fanatics; 'the sticker sellers, buyers and users;' the numerous university graduates who merely pay lip services to the teachings of our Lord Jesus Christ, are labouring in vain. The way to salvation is short; that is, practise the injunctions of God.

### The Second Chance:
Our Lord Jesus Christ did His utmost best. He Loves man. He cherishes him, his recalcitrance notwithstanding. Consequently, before His ascension, He made yet another promise. He created a second chance for man. He urged man to utilise the expected opportunity effectively .
in order to obtain salvation.. That promise was effectively recorded in the scripture: *"And I will pray the Father, and He shall give you another Comforter, that He may abide with you forever." (St John 14 v 16).* The emergence of the Comforter was obvious because He would have enough time to teach and lead men to the accurate knowledge of truth. Salvation then, will be made easy. Yet, how many are prepared to receive this Comforter? Who believes in Him? It is a generally acceptable fact that, flesh and blood cannot practise the injunctions of God. Hence, we require the Comforter to see us through; the Holy Spirit to keep the zeal in us functioning and stem out our interest from inordinate acts. Who on earth is prepared for this? The situation has remained the same since the fall of Adam. The Queen Mother who gave birth to this male child shared in His aspiration. She urged all through her child to turn a new leaf. She is here to bless you tremendously.

You worship idols and mermaids, build shrines here and there, at the foot of trees, mountain tops, at the river side, inside the room, forest, etc, but no one has ever put the word of God in practice. What do you expect? This gospel is not addressed to the christians alone; it is universal. Let the Jews repent. Let the entire world repent, that the anger of God may not be rekindled, or else it shall be worst for this generation.

*"But when ye shall hear of wars and comotions, be not terrified, for these things must first come to pass; but the end is not by and by. Then said He unto them, nation shall rise against nation, and kingdom against kingdom. And great earthquakes shall be in divers places, and famines and pestilences, and fearful sights and great signs shall there be from heaven. But before all these, they shall lay their hands on you, and persecute you, delivering you up to the synagogues, and into prisons, being brought before kings and rulers for my name's sake.*

*And it shall turn to you for a testimony. Settle it therefore in your hearts, not to meditate before what ye shall answer: for I will give you a mouth and wisdom, which all your adversaries shall not be able to gainsay nor resist. And ye shall be betrayed both by parents, and brethren, and kinsfolks, and friends; and some of you shall they cause to be put to death. And ye shall be hated of all men for my name's sake. But there shall not a hair of your head perish. In your patience possess ye your souls.*

*And when ye shall see Jerusalem compassed with armies, then know that the desolation thereof is nigh. Then let them which are in Judea flee to the mountains; and let them which are in the midst of it depart out; and let not them that are in the countries enter thereinto."* (St Luke 21 v 9 - 21).

The excerpt above is a clear evidence of the signs of time, the tribulation and rapture. Take this as a last warning and turn a new leaf, that your second chance may be properly utilised. This is a simple and straightforward appeal. He speaks no more in parables. The mere belief in the name of our Lord Jesus Christ will not save you, because one question still stands unanswered; have you practised His teachings? Parading in long white apparels will not save you. In the previous generation, many had worn garments, sang beautiful songs, played drums and danced dexterously but this did not fetch them the kingdom. The repentance is the prerequisite for this kingdom. Hence, our Redeemer rightly stated: *" I tell you nay; but except you repent, ye shall all likewise perish." (St Luke 13 v 5).* He further added: *"For I say unto you, that except your righteousness shall exceed the rightiousness of the Scribes and Pharisees, ye shall in no case enter into the kingdom of heaven." (St Matt. 5 v 20).*

This gospel clearly points out the fact that, our salvation lies in our practising the word of God. Do not deceive yourself by claiming to be Jesus, Jehovah or Lord. All these and many more will not save you. Do have it in mind that, there is no other approach to salvation except you keep the instructions of God. My teachings and injunctions constitute the heavenly bread; whoever 'eats of it' will live forever. My teachings are true. They constitute wealth, peace and power. I exhort you to put same into practice. Do not be deceived by the mere assertion that your father is a Bishop or your mother is a Deaconess or that you have built a church etc. All these and many more claims will not give you salvation. He had said that, the Comforter will come; and now truly the Comforter has come. Our Queen Mother is hailed today because the man-child passed through her. He also promised that, He would lead us to the perfect knowledge of truth. This He has done. He said that He would not speak of Himself. Have you not realised that He does not speak of Himself? See reference below:-
*" Howbeit when He, the Spirit of Truth, is come, He will guide you into all truth: for He shall not speak of Himself, but whatsoever He shall hear, that shall He speak; and He will show you things to come. "* (St John 16 v 7). He has revealed to us through the three texts that, except we practise the word of God, we shall not enter the kingdom of God. Go through this gospel thoroughly and practice same. I have briefed you in honesty and in love.

If after all these exposure, you refuse to hearken and keep His instructions, you shall have yourself to blame and the labour of the Queen Mother shall be in vain. I exhort you to re-examine these things. He teaches and demonstrates righteousness seven days a week, four weeks a month and twelve months a year. Ponder over this self-exertion. What shall be your excuse on the judgement day? I urge you to turn a new leaf.

All the churches built around the world today are empty and vain. All the big names: founders, bishops, cardinals, etc, tantamount to nothing. 'I came before you, I started it all' will not fetch you salvation. You build a church but cannot practice the word of God; the preacher preaches the word of God but he does not practise it; salvation shall elude you. The question now is, what stops you from practising the word of God? Men of yester-years failed to practise the word of God and perished. Do you think you will be spared?

God has appointed our Lord Jesus Christ as His Mouthpiece and Source of salvation, power, wisdom, light, truth and love. And as many that would hear and practise His words will be saved. First and foremost, it is an offence for one to put aside our Lord Jesus Christ and employ another teacher to teach him. You have committed a grievious offence by putting aside the teachings of our Lord Jesus Christ.

Any leader that does not lead in line with the teachings of Christ has neither Christ nor God the Father. But any leader who leads by the examples of our Lord Jesus Christ has both the Father and the Son. Do not have anything in common with anybody that imbibes teachings other than that of our Lord Jesus Christ. Do not eat with him or allow him to enter your house; for if you admit him or allow him to enter your house, it implies that you are encouraging him to sin. Finally I exhort you, sin not that you might be saved. May the Lord bless His Holy Words, Amen.

# CHAPTER 24

## THE CREATOR IS ON EARTH

Everlasting Gospel Delivered by Leader Olumba Olumba Obu
Sole Spiritual Head of the Universe.

**1st Lesson: St John 5: 30**

"I can of mine own self do nothing: as I hear, I judge: and my judgement is just, because I seek not mine own will, but the will of the Father, which hath sent me"

**2nd Lesson: Sf John 12: 49- 50**

"For I have not spoken of myself, but the Father which sent me, he gave me a commandment, what I should say, and what I should speak. And I know that his commandment is life everlasting: whatsoever I speak therefore, even as the Father said unto me, so I speak."

**Golden Text: St John 6: 45**

"It is written in the prophets, AND THEY SHALL BE ALL TAUGHT OF GOD. Every man therefore, that hath heard and hath learned of the Father, cometh unto me."

**THE GLORY OF GOD IS REVEALED**

Beloved, this is the glory of God revealed in your midst for your benefit. This is in fulfilment of the scriptures - that in the days ahead, God would teach you everything. Today the Holy Spirit is in our midst, teaching us all things. A righteous one was sought after in heaven and earth, to open the seal; and to teach everyone written words in the book of God, but no one was worthy to open the book. It was for this reason, that our Lord Jesus Christ openly declared, that the Holy Spirit of truth would come and lead mankind to the accurate knowledge of truth. It is believed by all that there is no righteous person on earth.
God commissioned the prophets to come and teach human beings but when they arrived, they discovered that everyone derailed from the path of rectitude. Other sets of people went out, but they also found the world in that state of sinfulness. At the end of it all, He sent His only begotten son who declared to the world saying:

"*1 have yet many things to say unto you, but ye cannot bear them now. Howbeit when he, the Spirit of truth, is come, he will guide you into all truth: for he shall not speak of himself; but whatsoever he shall hear, that shall he speak: and he will shew you things to come. He will glorify me: for he shall receive of mine, and shall shew it unto you. All things that the Father has are mine: therefore said* I, *that he shall take of mine, and shall show it unto you."* - St. John 16:12-15
This is not the time to emulate your fellow man. Rather, it is time we all should

follow the Holy Spirit who is in our midst. He had stated:

***"FOR THIS IS THE COVENANT THAT I WILL MAKE WITH THE HOUSE OF ISRAEL AFTER THOSE DAYS, SAITH THE LORD, I WILL PUT MY LAWS INTO THEIR MIND, AND WRITE THEM IN THEIR HEARTS. AND I WILL BE TO THEM A GOD, AND THEY SHALL BE TO ME A PEOPLE. AND THEY SHALL NOT TEACH EVERY MAN HIS NEIGHBOUR, AND EVERY MAN HIS BROTHER, SAYING, KNOW THE LORD: FOR ALL SHALL KNOW ME, FROM THE LEAST TO THE GREATEST."*** - Hebrews 8: 10-11

That period mentioned is our present age. The Holy Spirit is now dwelling in us. He is our instructor, teacher, Leader and the doer of all things. So, do not allow anyone to make you derail from the path of rectitude. Rather, be led by the Holy Spirit in you. As the heaven is higher than the earth, so also is the wisdom of God much greater than man. At times you would hear some church leaders asking their followers, to practise what they preach but not what they themselves do.

Some leaders advise their followers to refrain from eating the flesh, fornication, theft, falsehood etc., yet they are seriously indulging in those sins. Some of them advise their flock to forsake fornication, but at the same time they are committing the act. They would even term such an act, holy. For now, God trusts no one. Hence, the Holy Spirit decides to come personally into the world to dwell in each and everyone. Our Lord Jesus Christ was a leader, taught by the Holy Spirit and for this reason, He was able to bring salvation to us. Our main problem is contingent on the fact that we are following individuals and not abiding by whatever advice the Holy Spirit gives us.

You have come into the Kingdom today, so that you should hear words from the horse's mouth. It is your failure to do most of the things He advises you to do that account for your inexplicable problems in life. If it were not for the Father's coming into this world at this end of time, the world would have perished. Whenever someone tells you something, before you react, listen to the spirit. By so doing, the Holy Spirit in you will discern whether the information is true or false. You will hear preaching, but the Holy Spirit in you will inform you that the word is not correct. At times, you may plan to do something and He tells you that plan is bad. Therefore, we have to abide by every piece of advice given us by the Holy Spirit at the expense of man's advice. He is the one who sees things within and beyond.

The Holy Spirit does not only exist in 34 Ambo Street but He is in the body of all His children wherever they are. He is our Leader and Teacher. Many that keep His teachings and instructions will He save. So the only person you have to emulate is the Holy Spirit.

You can find a person who was through the help of Brotherhood of the Cross and Star, discharged and acquitted in the law courts returning to his former church. At the time, advises anyone who has problems to come to Brotherhood. You would also find such a person reviling and condemning Brotherhood of the Cross and Star . You need not look at such a person; rather you have to listen to the Holy Spirit in you and do all that He directs you to do. This is so because your salvation is contingent on His words.

The Father commissioned the angels and the prophets to come and teach mankind and salvage them. Unfortunately, not until He sent His only son to die, for the effective accomplishment of the task. Now, He has come by Himself to dwell with human beings and lead them in the right way. The golden text of this sermon has explicitly stated that the Holy Spirit will teach people and those who will keep His teachings will follow Him. We are really the luckiest of all the generations. Had it not been for the love of God, humbly accepting to dwell with us, we would all have perished. Therefore you should follow and emulate no other person other than the Holy Spirit. His teachings are wholesome, worthy of emulation. If you are given a vision for instance, all you need do is to listen to the Holy Spirit in you. By so doing, He informs you if the vision is correct or incorrect. Stop doing things out of your volition, as you have been doing in the days gone by, for God has now come to dwell with human beings on earth, though they do not know him. At times you do say that your heart tells you not to tell lies, commit fornication and indulge in the like sins. Note however, that it is not your heart that so directs you but the Spirit of God in you.

Christ was in the Spirit. He was the first person that God lived in; that is why He did everything according to the dictate of the Holy Spirit. Hence, He conquered. You are a witness to the fact, that on different occasions our Lord Jesus Christ was asked to heal the sick. He would wait for a while, to receive directives from the Holy Spirit, on how to go about healing the sickness. Thereafter, He would either place His hands on the patient's head or take him by the hand or instruct him to take bath in a river depending on the Holy Spirit's directives. Christ did nothing out of His own volition; therefore it is imperative that you do nothing out of your volition. A great number of you do make mistake by claiming that you are not being taught by anybody. If you are not being taught by anybody, how then do you have this wonderful knowledge? Always inform people that God is teaching you.

When preaching to people, they must have the assurance, that you only say what the Holy Spirit directs you to, notwithstanding the reaction of the listener. There is a saying that "an errand boy has never died for responding positively to his master's instructions".

Here in the Kingdom, it is the only one God existing that teaches all the people - Choristers, Pastors, Students, Christ Servants, or Children of God. You have but one God. Since it was destiny, that He would come and lead humanity, He has in earnest come to accomplish the set task.

If any person instructs you to fornicate or commit adultery with them, and claims, that the instructions are from God, no matter who the person is, or the position they occupy in the Kingdom; it is a woeful lie. God cannot, and will not instruct anybody to indulge in any sinful act. Also make the person to be conscious of the fact that God cannot instruct anybody to indulge in sins.

If a person tells you that God instructed him to tell you that you should embrace righteousness and be virtuous, you should keep to such instruction religiously because it is from God. In whatever fellowship and group you find yourself, always abide by any instruction given which is from God irrespective of the age, status, position and educational attainment of the person.

Here in this Kingdom, no one has the authorisation to do things out of their free volition. Nobody has a right to flout what the gospels ask us to do; instead, we should follow the Holy Spirit without resistance! Your problems emanate from the fact that you do not listen to the Holy Spirit in you. This is why you see most chairpersons, secretaries and other executive members of different organisations in this Kingdom not agreeing with one another. The reason is that, when this person tries to listen to the spirit, the other listens to the flesh. Consequently, their decision became conflicting. I am telling you the veritable truth that Brotherhood of the Cross and Star is not of this world but from God.

If someone from another church informs you of instructions they received from God, and continue to advise you to fast and celebrate a love feast. Do exactly that, for it is from God. Never you shun the advice by claiming that he is not a member of Brotherhood of the Cross and Star. In the same vein, if a member of Presbyterian church advises you, that God says, you should refrain from keeping the boyfriend you have been keeping. You will have to refrain from such an act, because the instruction is from God.

## CRUSADERS ARE THE SOLDIERS OF GOD

Many of you here long ago were asked to come here by the Father, but you refused. So your coming here today is not the work of the flesh and blood, but it is the will of God. However, having come here, your problems have been solved. We are those who worship God in Spirit and in Truth. Many of you reject vision, regarding it as false. That is why you become annoyed and regret ever going on a ministry work to another place if a vision directs you to do so, and you will remark that such vision is a false one. You will then go on to quote that; "the Father has never been at the Village Square yet masquerade beats up his child at the same place". Nothing would harm you in this Kingdom if you were obedient to the Father yet it is your act of disobedience that deprives you of the Father's protection and blessings.

It is advisable to be in the spirit, and by so doing we would not do what pleases the flesh. There is a saying that anyone who lives according to the dictate of the flesh shall die, while someone who lives according to the dictate of the spirit shall live forever. We do not have any business in segregating against non-members and embracing our members. Rather we should love everybody equally. Your coming here this week depicts that you are all crusaders. You are all soldiers of God. You have all been commissioned by the Father to come into the Kingdom this week.

Before now, when the Father used to call you, you would resist the call into this Kingdom and imbibe the gospel from the horse's mouth. You would attribute your inability to respond to the call to financial problem. <u>It is high time you all come into the Kingdom from all parts of the world to imbibe gospels from the horse's mouth.</u>
Believe fervently that by your coming to 34 Ambo Street, your testimonies are on the way, and all your problems are no more. Here in the Kingdom, there is no sickness, healthy, poor or rich, beautiful or ugly, person. For we are all one in the Lord.

Some of you lament that you do not hold any position of responsibility in this Kingdom. I would love to ask you whether you are not a Brotherhood? Never allow such thought to disturb you, instead, always listen to the spirit and abide by the instructions He gives you. By so doing, you are all right. He is the Father who sends one on an errand and goes along to accomplish the task by Him. He does everything. So it is insignificant for you to claim that you are illiterate, inexperienced, wretched, etc. As such you cannot do anything. He has even told you not to be anxious of what you would speak. When you are faced with any difficulty, the Holy Spirit will deliver you, it is not you who speak, but the spirit of the Father in you. This is a proof that He is the one who does all things for us.

God knows what is good and would always enjoin you to do only what is good. He knows that respecting the leaders is good hence, He admonishes you to be obedient to them. Therefore, if a person tells you that God says you should disobey your leader, you should discard such advice and make it clear to him that such advice does not come from God. Let no person stop you from being charitable to the needy, orphans, destitute, widows, etc., for it is God's instruction that such people should receive care. He has also enjoined you not to begrudge anyone or to be recalcitrant in your matrimonial homes. He has also enjoined us not to behave as if we were hopeless and comfortless, but to put everythmg into prayer . In addition, we have to practise the word of God. As many that have received baptism into this Kingdom, are the soldiers of God. Their assignment is to serve God every day of their lives. Read the fIrst lesson again:

**Ist Lesson: St John 5: 30**

" I can of mine own self do nothing: as I hear, I judge: and my judgement is just, because I seek not mine own will, but the will of the Father which hath sent me."

**GOD OWN YOU**

As a sequel to the above excerpt, you are not the owner of yourself. Rather, it is God who owns you. He is also the one to instruct and lead you, and so, you, should refrain from speaking and doing things out of your free volition. In the compound where you live, there are virgins, even though the Father has been requesting virgins, to be brought here to serve Him. Although they are yet to come, whenever the spirit in them persuade them to come, they would all be here because this is not the time that people do things out of their free volition. The Father is often talking to us and directing us on what to do.

As the international chairperson of this Fellowship testified, there was a child of God in Lagos whom the Father commissioned to go to the prison and preach to people there. At the completion of the assignment, about thirty prisoners received baptism into this Kingdom. So this is a proof that it is the Father who directs all to accomplish every task. Anyone who does things out of his or her free volition cannot please God. Hence, they will surely die, whereas a person, who works according to the Holy Spirit's directive, would live.

The Holy Spirit who is in our heart is jealous and desirous of our service. He needs us so seriously to avert being condemned along with other people of the world. We are God's temples, but the people of the world are not aware of this fact. However, the Holy Spirit reveals it that we are His temples. Hence, we should not defile ourselves with sin, particularly fornication. We should live according to the dictate of the Holy Spirit. Therefore, if there is something you vowed not to resolve in your life, but the Holy Spirit directs you to resolve the situation, be sure you abide by that directive.

There is a brother in Warri - Delta State, who was given a vision by a small boy, to go on a ministry work to three stations. At the end of it, he should celebrate Feast. This brother who is a Pastor, instead of abiding by the vision, decided to scold the boy, and saw the boy as an inconsequential person. The boy reiterated to the Pastor, that the vision was from God. That non-compliance with it would result in his dismissal from office, divorce by his spouse, selling of his car and house, and that he would not have a place to shelter his children.

Despite the emphasis, the Pastor scoffed at the vision because it came from a poor small boy. In a characteristic way, the Pastor refused to obey the vision. By then, he was a boss in his place of work and had many houses and properties. After one year, the Pastor was dismissed from work. His wife left him. He sold all his property and did not have refuge for his children. Finally, he came here and testified, advising other members that no one should scoff at the Holy Spirit's directives. So many people are disobedient and stubborn.

**The scripture says:**

*"If we would judge ourselves, we would not be judged. But when we are judged we are chastened of the Lord that we should not be condemned with the world"* (Corinthians 11:31-32).

A true child of this Kingdom does not belong to any particular Bethel. Instead, they go into every nook and cranny of the world, serving the Father according to the instructions from the Holy Spirit. This explains why we have the song, 'My disciples be ever ready by day and by night'. Do not give directives to people out of your free volition. Instead, instruct people as the Holy Spirit in you directs. Make sure you direct according to the Holy Spirit's directive, irrespective of the position of the person you are sent to, so that you might be justified for being obedient. The receiver of the message may receive judgement accordingly, depending on his response to the instruction.

Since we have knowledge of the fact that His advice is life everlasting. We should be obedient to Him and make sure we do not resist an evil doer. The contentment of all couples with their partners is essential. On no account should you commit adultery with someone's husband or wife. On no account must you be harsh with your children. Never segregate against any person or group of persons but accept every one. Husbands and wives should respect each other: because as a couple you need to endure each other. God is not lazy and He is not an idle Being.

That was why Christ said that His Father worketh hitherto and He works. Therefore God cannot instruct anybody to be a parasite. Instead, He gives everyone the ability to fmd his daily bread. Read the second lesson again:

**2nd Lesson: St. John 12: 49-50**

*"For I have not spoken of myself, but the Father which sent me, he gave me a commandment, what I should say, and what I should speak. And I know that his commandment is life everlasting: whatsoever I speak therefore, even as the Father said unto me, so I speak."*

**LIFE ETERNAL**

Make sure you refrain from adding to or subtracting from the Father's instructions, and do not ever do what the Father does not ask you to do. In short, whenever you wish to put any message that is from God across to the listeners, tell the people the message as you receive from God as His advice constitutes life eternal.

Here in this Kingdom, it is the dictates of the Holy Spirit that everyone adheres. Besides, it is not the knowledge of education, or wealth acquisition, or beauty that is used to accomplish many spiritual assignments. Rather, it is the Father's directives, which are used as inputs to accomplish every spiritual work in this Kingdom. The knowledge, power, and doctrine that are here in the Kingdom are not of this world, but from God.

There lived a woman who was revealed to go and minister prayers on a pregnant woman, but she refused. As a result of that, the pregnant woman gave birth to a premature child. The woman ( a visioner) became lame, a price she paid for her negligence of duty . This is the cause of most problems of many people in this Kingdom.

There was also another person asked to undertake ministry work to three stations, but he refused. As a consequence, his plague was hernia. He took the sickness to hospital, it was not an easy thing to be identifying, but each time he came back home, and the hernia would re-appear . One day, he decided to go on the ministry work as was directed. Where he went, the demarcation was a river. Hence, he crossed the river to the place. While on his way to the place he felt like defecating and as he went into a nearby bush to defecate, he observed at that spot, that the hernia disappeared to date.

There are many stories here in the Kingdom for you. Moreover, your disobedience deprives you of such joy and glory . There are some people here in the Kingdom who have stayed for up to three decades, without consulting medical doctor for any sickness. Rather, what they do when they are sick, is knock their heads on the ground, fast, pay tithe, give free will offering, etc., healing them of their sickness. So there is no sickness, fear, deceit, loneliness, etc., here in the Kingdom.

Your problem emanates from the fact that you have failed to understand that the words imparted to you are from God; hence, you act contrary to them. Here in the Kingdom all the things done and words spoken are from God. You should therefore discard the habit of treating the word of God with levity. The shoe that we do not put on, and all other doctrines practices here in the Kingdom, are not pronounced by Me to be practised. Rather, it is the Father who pronounced such practices. The word of the Father is efficacious and that is why I do not toy with it and do not wish any of you to toy with it. Always be charitable to the needy and widows, for these people are Brotherhood. Never impute sin to anyone. Do not hate and begrudge anyone, for these are the words of God.

Always listen to the Holy Spirit at every time, and make sure you abide by His injunctions. Whatever He directs you to do, you must. Never allow financial problem to debar you from doing whatever God advises you to do. Any time you set off to do whatever God directs you, He is ever ready to accomplish such assignment for you by himself. The scripture has it that, as many as hear God's word would follow Him. So always listen to Him and do not doubt His instructions, for by so doing you would be His, and salvation is yours. Do not fail to relate God's message to whoever it is meant for, and do not claim to be a visioner. You are all visioners of God, and His mouthpiece.

**HOPE IN GOD**

Submit yourself to Him always, and make sure your hope and boast is in Him. In so doing, He would lead you to the accurate knowledge of truth. Establish your faith and hope in Him. Do all that He directs you to do for his directives are true and wholesome. When the angel of God advised Joseph to flee with our Lord Jesus Christ, so that He would escape being killed by Herod, there was no trouble in the city. Joseph did not raise an objection to the instruction. In the same vein, you have to emulate what Joseph did by always keeping to whatever advice God gives you without asking questions. Read the Golden text again:

**GOLDEN TEXT: St. John 6: 45**

*"It is written in the Prophets, and they shall be all taught of God. Every man therefore, that hath heard, and hath learned of the Father, cometh unto me."*

**WHO ARE THE REAL CRUSADERS:**

Beloved, following the excerpt above, it is a veritable truth, that as many as imbibe God's words and practice them, would follow Him. While those who do not imbibe His words, and refuse to practice them, He would condemn. The many that do things out of their free volition, at the expense of God's directive, would receive perdition as their reward. Let us be the set of Crusaders who imbibe and practise His words, so that we are called Crusaders by example.

When Saul attempted to kill David, David went and hid in a certain bush. Then God made it clear to David, that should he continue to hide there, Saul would kill him. He should therefore flee from the place. Immediately, David fled the place. You always sing that the spirit of the living God should come and lead you, as it is written, that He shall lead. There is no statement that neither a person nor an angel shall lead. Instead, it is the Holy Spirit who is to lead. Therefore, shun all other people's leadership and subject yourself to His leadership alone.

The children of God are often informed of what would happen, before such event takes place, so that there is nothing happening in the world, which surprises them.

If you have not been taking the word of God seriously before, you should start now to practise them seriously. Whenever you are faced with one tribulation or the other, He is always there to tell you that the tribulation is a price for your disobedience, or is to test your faith in God. So always listen to Him so that you will be able to face any tribulation that befalls you with confidence.

If God instructs you not to board nor drive any vehicle throughout a certain interval of time, make sure you do just that. This is because there is a reason for giving you such instruction.

During Men's Fellowship with the Father last week, the international chainnan of the Fellowship testified, that when he came here last April, he knew that the Father would not fail to wash his feet among the twelve apostles. Hence, he decided to stay on till that night. Now a day to that day, one of the brethren who came with him that time, wanted him to accompany him home. The brother did not remember what he resolved to do and so he accompanied the brother home. On their way, they had a motor accident. During the time the Father performed the washing of the feet, the Father asked about this brother only to be informed that he had left for home. This brother blamed himself for being disobedient to the Father's advice. This constitutes the problem we have in this Kingdom.

Disobedience brings diverse problems to human beings. That is why those whom the Father reveals Himself to and they refuse to recognise and embrace Him often have problems, as testified by many of our brethren. Let those who have ears hear. May God bless His Holy Words. Amen.

# CHAPTER 25

# THE LAST COMMANDMENT

## WHAT YOU SOW IS WHAT YOU REAP

Everlasting Gospel delivered by Leader Olumba Olumba Obu
Sole Spiritual Head of the Universe

*First Lesson* : 11 *Timothy* 3: 13

"But evil men and seducers shall wax worse and worse, deceiving, and being deceived".

*Second Lesson* : *Colossians* 3: 23-25

"And whatsoever ye do, do it heartily, as to the Lord; and not unto men; Knowing that of the Lord ye shall receive the reward of the inheritance: For ye serve the Lord Christ. But he that doeth wrong shall receive for the wrong which he hath done: and there is no respector of persons."

*Golden Text* : *Galatians* 6: 7-8

"Be not deceived; God is not mocked: for whatsoever a man soweth, that shall he also reap. For he that soweth to his flesh shall of the flesh reap corruption; but he that soweth to the Spirit shall of the Spirit reap life everlasting".

## THE LAW OF RETRIBUTION

Murderers, dupes, armed robbers, thieves, fornicators, adulterers, the wicked, arrogant and saucy ones, gossips, prostitutes, liars, quick-tempered and all categories of men should listen with rapt attention because something serious is about to happen. I want you to know that giving is synonymous with receiving. We are now harvesting all what we sowed for there is nothing we do without receiving our due recompense. I am not saying that your father, mother, brother or sister will receive your reward, you will receive your reward personally, both good and bad as the case may be. If you sowed bad seeds, same shall you reap. Hence, whatever happens to you is the compensation for your deeds. You will say, "I am very regular in the church, yet I am being afflicted" and I ask, have you ever done something good and benefiting? You cannot reap what you did not sow. You keep saying that you cannot abstain from sin because you are not Christ, that you are only of flesh and blood. Be aware that if you are inclined to the flesh you will perish, and if you are committed to the Spirit, you will reap eternal life.

To you deceivers and dupes, are you not aware that if you con somebody and obtain N20 that another person will do same or even worse to you? If you deceive another person, and elope with his wife, the same recompense would you receive. If you tell one lie against somebody, another person will tell five lies against you. So brethren, whatever evil somebody speaks of you, do not respond because some other person will speak even worse evil of him or her, else, you will share in the ill fate that is befalling the worldly people presently. That is the law of retribution.

## MISSION ACCOMPLISHED

This lesson denotes the fulfillment of all the scriptures, which means that I have accomplished my work. So, take note, because we have finally come to our berthing point. This is the last of the scriptures. Let our first lesson be re-examined:

### FIRST LESSON: 11 TIMOTHY 3: 13

"But evil men and seducers shall wax worse and worse, deceiving, and being deceived".

## YOUR REWARD

Murderers, tricksters, con-artists, liars, dupes, thieves, armed robbers, have you heard what is being read? If you dupe somebody of N20 (Naira) and another person dupes you of N40, what is your gain? You are granted loan in a bank to help you finance a business but you refuse to repay the loan, at the same time, you have contracted somebody to build a house for you but after building that house, he claims it to himself, what is your gain? Or if you grant another person a loan and he refuse to pay you back, what is your reward? Know from now that there is no evil committed which reward you will not receive irrespective of prayers and fasting, or your charitable tendencies.

## ILLUSTRATION

For instance, there was a young man who seduced his father's wife and the father summoned him before the village council. According to the norms and values of this village, he was to pay a specified fine for that offence. There was one old man in that village who on hearing the case and the penalty the young man was to pay interfered. He saw no reason the young man should be penalized. According to him, the young man committed no offence because he was simply taking after the father's precedence that also had seduced his father's wife. At this point, the case ended itself as people immediately scattered and went back to their houses; they quickly reasoned with that old man. So, the message here is that for anything you do, you will be rewarded in your own coin.

Brethren, you are aware that whenever I cite instances, I make them three. Here is another one: There was a certain man in a certain village who had a son. This man took ill and was taken to all the hospitals both orthodox and native but to no avail. At a point, the son was fed up and discouraged. He now tricked the father saying that he was taking him to another town to meet another specialist whom he was sure would cure him of the sickness. He drove the father in his car to a very remote village and into a forest. There, he dumped him. When he got home, people asked him, "where is your father?" He lied that he was being hospitalized.

As he grew up, he picked a wife and begot a son. At his old age, he developed the same sickness of his father. As it were, his son struggled and took him to almost every hospital of repute including native homes but to no avail until he was fed-up. This son deceived him that he was taking him to a specialist hospital in another town and drove him in his car to exactly the forest and spot he dumped his father. As he was about going back, the father called him saying, "my son, come, I have something to tell you. I am not saying that you should take me back or leave me here but I want to tell you a story so that this curse will leave our family. Because if you leave me here, your son will also bring you here and so on from generation to generation. I want to tell you the story. This place you have dumped me was my father's grave. He had the same sickness I am having and all the hospitals you have taken me to, I had taken him to. Everything you have gone through, I had also gone through with my father. Therefore, I want this curse to stop in our family because if you leave me here, it will go on unabated; your son will bring you here."

So beloved brethren, when the son heard that confession, he took him back home and eventually, he recovered. Realise therefore that whatever you do to somebody, another person will also do to you. Let the second lesson be reviewed.

### Second Lesson: Colossians 3: 23 - 25

*"And whatsoever ye do, do it heartily, as to the Lord, and not unto men; Knowing that of the Lord ye shall receive the reward of inheritance: for ye serve the Lord Jesus. But he that doeth wrong shall receive for the wrong, which he hath done: and there is no respecter of persons."*

## DISSEMINATE THE GOSPEL

Brethren, know that there is nothing that is done in the world today that has never been done before and there is nothing in particular that is done to you that has never been done but right now, that spirit of deceit has been taken away from you. Such thing should end now because this lesson marks my last advice to you. Register this lesson in your memory, publish and disseminate for others to read without discrimination. If they like, they take and if they do not like, it is their business for anybody who derails from the truth is perished from this generation and generations to come.

Is it not baffling that from the time of Adam, we are still prey to offensive styles and thus inheriting problems? This is the last injunction I am giving to you. If you do not practise it, you will have to suffer for it. Personally, since I was born, I have not associated with anybody who is of the flesh because I know the repercussion of it. I know also that right from the foundation of the world there is not one honest person. We are not truthful. A child is not truthful to the parents, the husband is not truthful to the wife, a brother is not truthful to a sister, friends are not truthful to friends, kith and kin, the whites, the blacks are not truthful and nobody is truthful.

But remember that every evil you commit shall find you out: you must pay for it. If you did not know, know it now. Even if you go to the sky, the abyss or ocean to perpetrate evil, you will pay for it because the scripture stipulates that your sin shall find you out. If you do not adhere to this instruction, till eternity, you are doomed.

## WHO IS TRUTHFUL

Brethren, I do not intend to belabour you. But know that God is a respecter of no person. If you do not forgive, you will not be forgiven and any sin you commit lives with you and, whatever you do unto others will be done unto you. Take a cue from the whites. They are truthful. Reference here is made to the late King George of England. He had three children, two males and one female. When he died, the first son was called upon to inherit his throne but he declined and ran away to Germany. That throne was vacant until the second son came of age and then inherited it. He ruled and later died. The question I am asking is, were there no other men in England when this throne was vacant? There were men but nobody struggled for that position. If it were in Africa, heads would have rolled between greedy aspirants. But there, the whites will rather preserve it for the family with the bonafide and exclusive right irrespective of the time somebody would emerge.

In Africa, some greedy prominent men would have gone there and offer money to take over the position and rob that family of their right. It is the struggle for power and positions that claim the lives of many people in Africa. If it is not the struggle for position, it is the struggle for the acquisition of land. My advice to you therefore is that, if you are in possession of somebody's land, quietly relinquish it to the owner until it please him to dash it to you. Any other thing you are keeping, hand it over, because anything you obtain by force or out of your influence will be collected from you by a more powerful and influential person. If you capitalize on one's weak position or limited power to hurt him or her, another person will do the same to you. Therefore, anything we embark on we should do it with a truthful, kind, merciful and pure heart so that we may not regret at last because God is a respector of no persons. That is why it is often said that as far as you cannot forgive your brethren for his wrong, God too cannot forgive your sins because He is the Chief judge.

You are familiar with that story of one master who was owed ten thousand pounds by one of his servants and when he asked for it, the servant prostrated on the ground pleading that he did not have the money yet. The master had mercy on him and forgave him the debt. But as soon as this servant got to the street, he saw somebody who owed him only one hundred pennies. He held the person on the shirt and said, until his debt was paid, he would not be released. Inspite of the person's persuasions that he had not the money as yet, he refused to let him go.

On seeing the attitude of this man with his debtor, the other servants of the rich man went and reported him to their master saying that the debtor whom he just pardoned was holding another debtor of his to ransom. The rich man ordered that he be brought immediately. He asked him, you owed me ten thousand pounds and I forgave you, why then could you not pardon another person? He ordered him to be locked up in prison until he paid his debt. The question is how is he going to repay the loan? Had he pardoned his debtor, would he have been involved in such a problem? That is what you all are doing today but this is the last advice and if you do not heed it, you will have yourself to blame. Let our golden text be read again.

### Golden Text: Galatians 6: 6 - 8

*"Be not deceived: God is not mocked: for whatsoever a man soweth, that shall he also reap. For he that soweth to his flesh shall of the flesh reap corruption; but he that soweth to the Spirit shall of the Spirit reap life everlasting."*

## BE FAITHFUL

Brethren do not blame your mother, father, and brother, sister, friend, relatives, child or any other person, let the blame be on you because you are the architect of your fate. Any good thing you do will accompany you and any evil you commit lives with you. You are rewarded according to your deeds. Even if you live for one thousand years and you continue to dabble in evil, corruption shall be your lot all the days of your life. If you do good your days will be glorious.

The scripture has already stipulated that deceivers will equally be deceived, therefore, for everything you do, do it faithfully and with a pure heart, do it as if you are doing it unto God because in due season, you shall receive your reward. If you perpetrate evil, your reward will equally not be in doubt.

Why you do not receive anything good is because of your evil ways. Do you know why our Lord Jesus Christ was able to open the seal spoken of in the bible? And do you know why it is said that those who believe in him have everlasting life? The reason is that he is the only truthful and righteous person, he believes in His Father and does only His will. Besides, He voluntarily shed His blood for our salvation. Consequently, we are now walking majestically without fear, and through Him the Kingdom of God is here on earth. As our last commandment, I say, do unto others what you wish others to do to you. Brethren, a word is sufficient unto the wise. Let those who have ears hear what the Holy Spirit has imparted to the whole world. May God bless His Holy Words, Amen.

# CHAPTER 26

# THE REIGN OF LOVE BY 2000 AD

Everlasting Gospel delivered by Leader Olumba Olumba Obu
Sole Spiritual Head of the Universe

**FIRST LESSON: JOHN 15: 5-6**

*"I am the vine, ye are the branches. He that abideth in me, and I in him, the same bringeth forth much fruit: for without me ye can do nothing. If a man abide not in me, he is cast forth as a branch, and is withered; and men gather them, and cast them into the fire, and they are burned."*

**SECOND LESSON: JOHN 14: 9-10**

*"Jesus saith unto him, Have I been so long time with you, and yet hast thou not known me, Philip? he that hath seen me hath seen the Father; and how sayest thou then, Shew us the Father? Believest thou not that I am in the Father, and the Father in me? The words that I speak unto you I speak not of myself but the Father that dwelleth in me, he doeth the works."*

**GOLDEN TEXT: JOHN 13:34 - 35**

*"A new commandment I give unto you, That ye love one another; as I have loved you, that ye also love one another. By this shall all men know that ye are my disciples, if ye have love one to another."*

## THE WEIGHT OF LOVE

Beloved, this message has a lot to do with the Kingdom of Brotherhood. When it is said that the Kingdoms of the world have become the kingdom of God and His Christ, it means that love has engulfed the entire universe. The importance of love cannot be over-emphasised. It is so important that even if somebody should sell all his possession and give the proceeds to the poor, such display of charity would be worthless and meaningless, if he does not possess love. Similarly, even if somebody surrenders himself to be burnt in a furnace of fire when he does not have love, it is equally meaningless and unprofitable. Further emphasis is still laid on this issue of love even if a person gives his life as a ransom for others but does not have love; such an exercise would also be unprofitable to him.

The greatest thing as far as the present dispensation is concerned is love. Love is the greatest thing in the whole world. Subsequent generations would not be known without love. The interpretation of King Nebuchadnezzar's dream about a certain kingdom that would emerge, tower over and swallow up all other existing kingdoms referred directly to love. What it implies is that love would be the only covenant and ruler of the whole world. Therefore it would be meaningless to have mercy, be truthful and honest if you do not have love. Even if you are the most eloquent and astute preacher in the world, your eloquence would amount to nothing and would not be appreciated if you do not possess love. This time is meant for you to realise that love is God, Christ, man and every good thing that exist in heaven and on earth.

## THE DEADLINE FOR THE MANIFESTATION OF LOVE

Your claims to love God are false if you do not love man. If you love man, your love for God and Christ would be profound. Christ unequivocally stated that, whoever loves his brother is the one that adheres to His commandments and His Father would make His abode in him. You are living witnesses to the fact that since the time of creation, love had never before existed in this magnitude in the world. You are considered most lucky because the Holy Spirit has descended to earth, and by the close of the century, that is, 2000 AD, you would witness the profuse and full manifestation of love. The activities going on now are preparations for the enthronement of love by 2000.

From then love will reign till eternity. This happening will be an affirmation of the scriptural statement that the kingdoms of the world have become the kingdom of God and His Christ, and He shall reign eternally.

## THE ORIGIN OF THE CONCEPT OF LOVE

Recall the statement that was made during the baptism of Christ by John at the River Jordan. John heard a voice, which said, "Thou my beloved son, in whom I am well pleased. This statement was referring to love, for Christ is love. Any person who has love has obeyed God. Our Lord Jesus Christ first introduced the concept of love into the world. And as the one who introduced it, He as well practically demonstrated it to the fullest. It is therefore imperative that everybody follows the path paved by Christ by demonstrating love. Certainly, if you practise love, you will have eternal life. Our Lord Jesus Christ is love. God is love and in order to resemble Him, you must demonstrate love.

## THE ONLY EXISTING LAW

The only existing law in the kingdom of God is brotherly love. Everybody co-exists in oneness and love. So all you are required to do is to express love for one another. If there is anything worthy of human consideration, it should be love. The most precious and worthiest thing in life is love. There is no doubt that all of us are familiar with the teachings of Our Lord Jesus Christ on love. In His teachings, Christ thoroughly expatiated the concept of love so that nobody would feign ignorance of its paramount importance in our daily lives.

Christ's unique ability to practically demonstrate love was the only overwhelming achievement that conferred on Him the divine title of King of Kings and Lord of Lords. It would not be an exaggeration if we accord love the greatest glory much more than anything else in the whole world. There was no other thing apart from love that prompted Christ to stoop so low as to accept the shameful death on the cross for the remission of the sins of humanity. So it was Christ who revealed love to the world. What we are enjoined to do is to closely follow His footsteps. Although love was never practised until the advent of our Lord Jesus Christ, but it had been in existence even before the foundation of the world was laid.

## CONTINUE IN LOVE

Everything in heaven and on earth is ruled by love. We are advised to continue in love, especially now that we have the understanding that God and Christ are love. Undeniably, it is better to dwell in love than cause confusion, engage in quarrelling, falsehood and other unwholesome acts. Love does not rejoice in evil. Love constitutes mercy, meekness, humility, kindness and the rest of the virtues.

Summarily, love entails everything; that is why it is said, 'love covers iniquities.' It is the fulfilment of all the laws. Any person who has love is not boastful and does not hate his fellow man. There is no pride in anybody who possesses love, and such a person can never hurt his brother. The signs that are found in somebody who embodies love are humility, temperance, mercy, endurance, patience, long suffering, and the ability to live peacefully with one another. But the reverse is the case with someone who lacks love; he is always surrounded by one kind of problem or the other, quarrelsome, impatient, intolerant, merciless and always in an aggressive mood.

Christ is love, and because of that, He declared that He is the vine while we are the branches; and whoever does not abide in Him cannot accomplish any work. All the problems that befall man emanate from his lack of love. A sower of a seed of discord indulges in falsehood, stealing, nurtures the spirit of disunity, stinginess and malice. There is an iota of love in everything visible and invisible. Love is immeasurable.

Re-examine the First lesson:

**FIRST LESSON: JOHN 15: 5-6**

"I am the vine, ye are the branches. He that abideth in me, and I in him, the same bringeth forth much fruit: for without me ye can do nothing. If a man abide not in me, he is cast forth as a branch, and is withered; and men gather them, and cast them into the fire, and they are burned."

## THE CHARACTERISTICS OF LOVE

Brethren, this is the plain truth: Love is like an egg; fragile and delicate, whenever it falls on the ground, it gets broken and useless. Love is light; without it, you cannot see. You become decomposed and useless anytime you indulge in falsehood and all your efforts to progress in life will be futile.

Each time you keep malice or get angry, you break the law, nothing can amend it. Love could be likened to a needle that cannot be mended once it is broken. That is the reason why you are to have love, for it constitutes eternal life. You can only be an heir to the kingdom and a permanent dweller of the kingdom when you possess Love. And on the other hand, if you lack love in you, you shall be destroyed from the earth surface.

Love is the only key to the Kingdom of God. Anybody who does not have love cannot see the gates of God's kingdom. In the kingdom of God, love constitutes everything to everybody. Division, hatred, fighting and quarrelling does not have any place in the kingdom. There is no sex, age, or race distinction in the kingdom. To God, everything is masterminded and controlled by love. So, we do not have any problem whatever since love constitutes everything to us.

## THE CONSEQUENCE OF LACK OF LOVE

Any person who indulges in falsehood does not have love in him, and the only alternative is to cast him into a lake of fire burning with brimstone. Love is the supreme commander of heaven and earth. Whenever reference is made to the New Kingdom we are referring to love. The stipulated punishment for whoever contravenes the dictates of love is condemnation to a lake of fire. The time is ripe for everybody to demonstrate love because if you do not practise love, you will be shown the way out of the kingdom. Even though you surrender all your possession to the poor, it would not benefit you anything if you do not have love.

## LOVE: ANOTHER NAME OF GOD

Love is God, and it is everlasting; it neither deteriorates nor can be diluted. God does not have another name apart from love. Love is perfection. God has been in existence before the foundation of the world was laid. He has been from the 'everlasting of the Past' and shall be till eternity. What we call the world is an overflow of the love of God arranged in artistic perfection. And because the world is not aware of this truth, it becomes inevitable that the people of the world must experience inexplicable problems as a way of making them recognise Him. There would have been no more problems if everybody had surrendered to love.

## THE FULFILMENT OF LOVE BY THE HOLY SPIRIT

This gospel is serving as a final warning to the entire dwellers of the world. Whoever refuses to love his brother by deviating from the path of love will be doomed. Christ was the first to introduce the doctrine of love, however, He did not ensure its full manifestation, He merely laid its foundation. And in the present dispensation, the Holy Spirit has come down to the earth to bring everything to full manifestation.

That is why you are enjoined not to ascribe the title of teacher to any other person other than the Holy Spirit, for He is the Sole Instructor and only Teacher.

The problems in the whole world became compounded because of the absence of a righteous man who could lead mankind. However, in the present dispensation, the Holy Spirit has come down on earth to lead everybody. It is therefore expedient for us to look up to Him as a model, for the scriptures had revealed that we shall emulate Him when He makes his appearance in the world. God has one truth, which reveals His steadfastness and omnipotence: indeed, when He sends you on an errand, He goes along with you to accomplish it. Presently, He has manifested on earth to get rid of the wrong conceptions that had before now been associated with love.

The present generations will not pass away until everything that was ordained to happen comes to manifestation. The Father has come to establish love in the entire world. This is the first time since creation that love has manifested physically in the world. When He came as Christ in His last advent, He could not demonstrate perfect love hence, He said,

*"I have yet many things to say unto you, but ye cannot bear them now. Howbeit when he, the Spirit of truth, is come, he will guide you into all truth: for he shall not speak of himself; but whatsoever he shall hear, that shall he speak: and he will shew you things to come."* (John 16: 12- 13)

This is the time prophesied about. Evidently, He has come to you to lead you to the accurate knowledge of the truth. He has also come to establish love in the whole world. All the people who do not possess love are not worthy to enter into the kingdom of God. And if you are not in the kingdom of God, you will be eliminated from the surface of earth.

## AVOID THE MISTAKES OF YOUR PREDECESSORS

It is not possible to adulterate love; love is unique and vibrant. As popularly said, when one finger touches oil, it soils the other finger. Also, bad habit corrupts good manners. Imagine what will happen if a person who was elected into an office of the Prime Minister embezzles an enormous sum of money from the government's coffer during his tenure in office, indisputably, whoever succeeds him will be regarded as an embezzler. This is the ugly situation prevalent in the world. One evil deed multiplies or produces many more evil.

The reason why Abraham cannot be regarded as a completely righteous man is because he waged series of wars against his neighbouring people. Paul's belated righteousness cannot also be accepted because he consented to Stephen's death. Moreso, Matthew a tax collector and later disciple of our Lord Jesus Christ cannot be rated as good, because of the nature of his job before his apostleship; he was considered a cheat and an enemy of the public. All these problems and situations are commonplace in Nigerian society in particular and the whole world in general. Re-examine the Second Lesson:

### SECOND LESSON: JOHN 14: 9-10

"Jesus saith unto him, Have I been so long time with you, and yet hast thou not known me, Philip? He that hath seen me hath seen the Father; and how sayest thou then, Shew us the Father? Believest thou not that 1 am in the Father, and the Father in me? The words that I speak unto you I speak not of myself, but the Father that dwelleth in me, he doeth the works."

## DIRECTIVES OF THE ALMIGHTY GOD

Since the disciples of Christ were not aware that Christ was the Father Himself, Philip demanded that Christ should show them the Father. The entire teachings of Christ to His disciples came from the Father. This gospel you are reading equally comes from the Father who is the Almighty God. No other being apart from the Almighty God will advise you to desist from stealing, fornication, hate, and other malicious acts. The Almighty God is love. He has now manifested physically on earth for the whole world to see Him. If you are lucky to find yourself in the kingdom, it is advisable that you hearken to the injunctions, which I give to you. In the nearest future, all will constitute a shining example of a nation led by the Mighty hand of God. Indisputably, it is only a nation led by God that can achieve what is only obtainable in a utopian state.

Your refusal to practically demonstrate the injunctions of God as I impart to you has a great deal hindered the manifestation of the love of God in you and in the whole world. The reason why you have not begun to emulate God is that He is not yet revealed. I know you would certainly do so when He is revealed. God does not demand anything from you apart from you practising all the teachings given you in the kingdom of God now among men.

Having come into the kingdom, you have utterly been transformed into a new being. While many people are wallowing in sins in the world, you are enjoying in the kingdom. At present you may not be able to see the differences, but in future when the scales that are preventing you from seeing clearly shall have fallen off your eyes, you will then behold the glory of God. It is impossible for you to see the love of God when you are still neck-deep in sin.

## THE BENEFITS OF BEING IN BROTHERHOOD OF THE CROSS AND STAR

Various church denominations still regard Brotherhood as an organisation that is opposing the practice of the injunctions of God. Others say it is not a church. Of course, this group that says Brotherhood is not a church, is right because Brotherhood is no church but the kingdom of God on earth, where righteousness reigns. It is where all the injunctions of God are practised. The world is expecting the coming of Christ but fortunately, you have the Promised Comforter in your midst and you are also lucky to be by Him.

As many as would put into practice His teachings would have salvation. It is worthy to mention that many of the members have, through the teachings of the Holy Spirit, abstain from the eating of fish, meat, refrained from fornication, indulging in diabolism and other vices. You have now been born anew; you have become a child of God. Vision and prophecy cannot confer on anybody the title of child of God. The childhood of God can only be acquired through practising the injunctions of God.

Love is the embodiment of all things. So it is imperative that everybody in the world, irrespective of church, age, sex and racial differences possesses love. Whether you are a churchgoer or pagan all you are required to do is to possess and demonstrate love in all your dealings in life. The reason why you are asked to show love is that if you have love, you automatically, are a child of God.

## BCS THE NEW KINGDOM OF GOD:

In order to have good preservation, new wine should be put in a new wineskin. Brotherhood of the Cross and Star is the New Kingdom of God and the only known law is love. Everybody is implored to express love to one another. If you do not have love and express it to others, you would not have share in the kingdom. Should you take a critical look at the entire situation in the world and her inhabitants, you would discover that there is nobody who loves his brother. But God has now come with His kingdom to supplant all other worldly kingdoms. So the consequence for those who do not have love is complete extermination from the surface of the earth. When this mass elimination would be carried out, no consideration will be given to the Catholics, Presbyterians, Methodist, Buddhists, Eckists or Muslims. As a matter of fact, religious affiliation is not a criterion for salvation. The only key to salvation is love. If you possess love, the gate of the kingdom lies ever open to you.

Re-examine the Golden Text:

## GOLDEN TEXT: JOHN 13:34-35

"A new commandment I give unto you, that ye love one another; as I have loved you, that ye also love one another. By this shall all men know that ye are my disciples, if ye have love one to another."

## SPIRITUAL CHORUSES:

**I have brought a new commandment:**

**Dwell in love**

**The covenant of Moses has gone,**

**Love is the new covenant**

## THE ESTABLISHMENT OF THE NEW COVENANT

Beloved, God has come into the world to reform mankind. You should count yourself most fortunate to be taught by Him. So you do not have time to waste, you should at once start expressing love to one another. Where you fail to do so, you will certainly face damnation. Let this sink into your marrow, blood and mind, the covenant of Moses is now obsolete and no more relevant to the new system; love is now the covenant. Therefore, if you refuse to exhibit love to everybody, you would not exist in the world by 2000 AD. The divine assurance is that love will permeate all realms, and control all planes of manifest by the close of this century. Let me resound this warning: whoever do not turn a new leaf by practising love shall be destroyed. There is no other law that shall exist at that time in the world apart from love. The deadline meant for everybody to possess love is 2000 AD. Anybody who has no love by this time shall face destruction. Love is the only law for all the children of God. It is only through love that you can be identified as a true child of God.

Do not rejoice because you are holding any ecclesiastical office such as Pope, Bishop, Archbishop or Pastor; God is no respecter of persons. If you hold any of these offices but do not have love, it will amount to complete waste of time. Brethren, a stroke of the cane is enough for the wise. Let those who have ears hear what the Holy Spirit has imparted to the whole world. May God bless His Holy Words, Amen.

# APPENDIX 1

# ADDRESSES OF MAIN BCS BETHELS ( Places of Worship )

## AFRICA

**NIGERIA**: World Headquarters & Everlasting Gospel Centre: 34 Ambo Street, Calabar, C.R.S., Nigeria, Tel. +234 87 225 423;  Uyo Pentecostal Centre, AKWA IBOM 25 Ekpenyong Street, Uyo.

**CAMEROON**:  Douala Central Bethel, P.O. Box 131290, Douala.; Buca in Faco Division, Southwest Province, Cameroon.

**GHANA;**  Odokor Central Bethel, P.O. Box 2853, Off Kwashicman Road, House No. B2120, Odoroko, Accra.  Old Tafo Central Bethel, P.O. Box 799, Behind Methodist Church, Old Tafo, Kumasi.

**LIBERIA**:  Lower Cald Bethel, H/Q, P.O. Box 2089, Monrovia.

**GAMBIA:**   Lamin Central Bethel, PMB 294 ( Along Madinary Road Lamin, Sierrekanda. National Headquarters Bethel, Behind Kololi Clinic, Kololi PMB 148 Banjul, The Gambia.

**SIERRA LEONE**: Peacock Farm Bethel, 22 Peacock Farm, Wellington, Freetown.

**COTE D'VOIRE:**   De Taskhville Bethel, De Taskhville Avenue 22, R15 Lot 513 16 BP, 1365, Abidjam 16, Cote D'Voire.

## EUROPE

**UNITED KINGDOM:**   BCS Information Centre & Elephant and Castle Bethel, 5 Falmouth Road, London SE1 5AE, Tel. +044 0171 403 9048. Mill Hill Bethel, Angel Pond, The Ridgeway, Mill Hill Village, London NW7 1QG, Tel. +044 0181 959 6606. Forest Gate Bethel, 72 Cemetry Road, London E.7, Tel. +044 0181 555 1903. Luton Bethel, 92 Hampton Road, Luton, Beds, LU4 8AR, Tel. +044 01582 611883. Manchester Bethel, 151 Raby Street, Manchester 14, Tel. +044 0161 226 0330. Liverpool Bethel, 40 Princess Road, Liverpool 8, Tel. +044 0151 709 0268. BCS Leaders Representative's Office, 12 Keere Street, Lewes, East Sussex, Tel. +044 01273 477795.

**WEST GERMANY**: Stutgart Bethel, Wumensteintrabe 42, 70186 Stutgart, W. Germany, Tel. 0711 48 47 98. Sabruncken Bethel, Dredsner St, 9, 6600 Saarbruken, W. Germany.

**BELGIUM**: Brussels Bethel, Rue De Flandre 160, 1000 Bruxells, Tel. 02 223 4483.

**ISRAEL**: Tel Aviv Bethel, 15 Neve Sha'nan, Tel Aviv, Tel. 03 972 687 3766.

**ITALY**: Brescia Bethel, Via Solferino 55, 25013 Carpendolo, Brescia, Italy, Tel. 030 969 8276.

**FRANCE**: Paris Bethel, 80 Rue Macardet 75018, Paris, Tel. 0033 148333350.

**UKRAINE**: Kharkov Bethel, Kloch Kouskaya St, House 307, Kharkov 31005, Tel. 380 572 383786.

## UNITED STATES OF AMERICA

Blue Grass Bethel, 4207 Marseille Drive, Louisville, Kentucky 40272, Tel. 502 372 2331 (Digital Pager), E-Mail: bcslove@gte.net. Chicago Bethel, 1544 West Jarvis, Chicago, Illinois 60626, Tel. 773 381 1629. Dallas Bethel, 411 Ledbetter Drive, Dallas TX75216, Tel. 214 372 0001. Washington DC Bethel, 916 Rittenhouse Street, NW Washington DC 20011, Tel. 202 291 5245. Atlanta Bethel, 345 Blairvilla Drive, Atlanta, Georgia 30354, Tel. 404 361 3238. Oakland Bethel, 2014 San Pablo Avenue, Oakland, CA94612, California, Tel. 510 986 8665. Los Angeles Bethel, 1850 W. Slauson Avenue, Los Angeles, CA90042, California, Tel. 213 298 9510. New Jersey Bethel, 88/94 Boylam Street, Newark NJ07106, Tel. 973 373 6679.

## REST OF THE WORLD

**WEST INDIES**: TRINIDAD: Prizgar Lands Bethel, Laventile, Port of Spain. **GRENADA**: Faith Bethel, Springs P.O., St. Georges, Tel. 443 2867.

**SOUTH AMERICA**: GUYANA BETHEL: 73 Victoria Road, Plaisance East Coast, Demerara, Guyana, Tel. 001 868 623 5843.

**INDIA**: Delhi Bethel, H.NO 380, Gagan Vihar, I. Delhi - 110051.

**CANADA**: Ontario Bethel, 1232 Woodbine, Toronto, Ontario MAC 4E4.

---

BCS INTERNET WEBSITE: WWW.OOO.ORG.UK
E-MAILS: KOK@BETA.LINKSERVE.COM
OOO.BCS@VIRGIN.NET

**NOTE**: Some address details may change after going to press.

# APPENDIX 2

# GOD AND THE INTERNET

**By Elder W.B. Smith** - *( Circulated Electronically Worldwide 1995 - 1997 ).*

The Internet is the handy work of the Almighty God. It comes into existence mainly as a means of uniting the Nations of the world through the New Information and Communication Technology. All the Internet Backbone and Access Providers from the Greatest to the Smallest are Chosen by God for executing His Will, i.e. bringing the peoples of the world closer together. The entire world must change from sins and vices to righteousness or perish. It is not the wish of God that human beings should continue to suffer; that is why Jehovah God and His Christ have now come down to earth to unite all the Nations of the world as 'ONE' and to judge any Nation, Community or Individual that resist this change ( those with pure hearts and Spiritual eyes and ears are already aware of this Truth ). The Commonwealth of Nations, U.N., O.A.U., E.U., N.A.T.O., World Council of Churches, etc. are also God's handy works for World's Unity, but the Brotherhood of the Cross and Star is the ultimate Divine Universal Force for unity, oneness, love, peace and salvation.

Human Beings fail to realise that God works through man. Man is only God's Tool, but man takes all the praise and glory of his achievements for himself and ignore and disgrace God Who is the Architect and Doer of everything. Without God there is nothing any human being can do. Who designed Electricity, Telephone, Radio, Television, Computers, Aeroplanes, Ships, etc? It is God. Who is responsible for the ending of Communism in the U.S.S.R. and Apartheid in South Africa? It is God. Who is responsible for the Peace Process in the Middle East, Yugoslavia, Northern Ireland, etc? It is God. Who is disabling and preventing the use of Chemical and Nuclear weapons of mass destruction? It is Jehovah God at work. There is no other power at work apart from God. Angels, human beings and other creatures are His Servants and Messengers and He uses them as He likes, i.e. for Constructive and Destructive assignments. All the inhabitants of the world must become 'ONE' in order to escape the wrath of God. There must be One People, One Love, One Religion, One Faith, One Spirit and One God. <u>The Internet is designed by God for human beings to communicate and share informations that will establish Oneness, Love, Understanding, Peace and Unity.</u> There must be no division and hatred, but man always misuse and abuse God's handy work for devious and selfish reasons. The Internet is our golden opportunity to unite and share Technical, Social and Spiritual information and make the world a better and peaceful place. Let us not abuse it and suffer the consequences.

**OBSERVATIONS IN YEAR 2000:**

*Computer Hackers are creating havoc on the Internet; Pornography and paedophilia has multiplied in alarming proportions.*

# APPENDIX 3

# FATHER'S PHONE NUMBER

Everlasting Gospel delivered by Leader Olumba Olumba Obu

Sole Spiritual Head of the Universe

(*Summarized by Elder W. Smith*)

<u>First Lesson</u>: St John 14 v 13  <u>Second Lesson</u>: Matthew 18 v 19  <u>Golden Text</u>: St John 16 v 26 - 27

Now is the time to worship God in Spirit and in Truth. There is no need for anyone to go to Jerusalem, or Mecca, or to the Mountain, or 34 Ambo Street, or the Bethel or Church or Secret Society in order to worship God: nor ask a Prophet, Priest or Pastor or anyone to pray for you. Freedom, authority, liberty and entitlement are now given to everyone to ask the Father directly for whatsoever you want via the name of our Lord Jesus Christ and your request will be granted. This is the New Covenant of the Father at this fullness of time. This Promise is now consumated. It is given to everyone in the New Kingdom of God. Anywhere you are, just kneel down, knock your head and ask the Father for whatever you require, in the name of our Lord Jesus Christ and HE will not fail to give you your desire. The Father has given this Power to ALL and not only to the Ordained Ones; that is why I do not ordain anyone again.. Even if you are a Necromancer, just carry out this instruction and you will receive whatever you have requested. I give this Key to ALL; it is not restricted to a selected few, but to all who believe and call on the name of our Lord Jesus Christ, and separate themselves from all manner of sins and vices.

Confess your sins and repent. Even a small child in this New Kingdom is given that Power and Freedom. If anyone request prayer from you, just tell him or her that the Father has given him or her the power and freedom to ask God himself or herself, as long as he or she is baptised in the New Kingdom of Brotherhood of the Cross and Star. If you do not put this Gospel into practise it means that you do not believe in God and your blood shall be upon your head, because this power and freedom comes to you directly from God our Father. All other Gospel is second to this one; this is the first and foremost of all the Gospels. You have got the mouth to ask God yourself; do not go to anyone or to any place; do not ask questions; do not doubt; just ask the Father directly for whatever you want.

The Phone Number straight to your Father is: **OUR LORD JESUS CHRIST**. Just ask the Father via this number and your request will be granted straight away. The Father is in you and with you, to solve all your problems, just ask. This power and freedom was the Key that was given to Peter, it is now given to you. Whenever you have problems, just fast from 6 A.M. to 12 Noon or 6 A.M. to 6 P.M; then pray to your Father and make your request via that name - **OUR LORD JESUS CHRIST**, and your request will surely be granted. No matter what service you do to the Father, or, what you give to the Father, these will not solve your problems. God is a God of equality; that is why He has given this power, freedom and promise to all generations until eternity. Going to the Bethels is just for Fellowship, not for solving your problems; you have to pray to the Father for yourself, via that Name - **OUR LORD JESUS CHRIST**, to solve your problems. Many people come to 34 Ambo Street for Ordination, for their means of living; then when they go back to the Bethel, they flash their turbans about and say that they now have the power. Now the Father has given that power to ALL. That is why some Ordained Ones are annoyed of this, because All and Sundry now have the power. You dont even have to go and see the Father again at 34 Ambo Street, because He has given you the Power, Freedom, and Liberty. Just speak the Word, call on that Name - **OUR LORD JESUS CHRIST**, and the WORD will get into action immediately. THANK YOU FATHER.

# Index

**A**

ADAM'S ASSIGNMENT, 93   93
AFTER 1999 ?   97 - 104   97
ASSIGNMENT OF THE HOLY SPIRIT, 95 - 96   95

**B**

BCS BETHELS, 183 - 184   183
BROTHERHOOD, 12   12

**C**

CELIBACY, 27 - 29   27
CHRIST CRUCIFIED THURSDAY, 17 - 19   17
CHRIST'S ASSIGNMENT, 95   95
CREATOR IS ON EARTH, 166 - 174   166
CROSS, 13   12

**D**

DECARNATION, 89 - 90   88

**E**

ELIJAH'S ASSIGNMENT, 94   94
ENOCH'S ASSIGNMENT, 93   93

**F**

FIRST STEP TO GOD, 39   39
FOURTH STEP TO GOD, 43 - 44   43

**G**

GOD AND THE INTERNET, 185   185
GOVERNMENT of BCS, 154 - 159   154

**H**

HOLY TRINITY, 5 - 11   5
HUMAN BEINGS, 1 - 3   1

**I**

INCARNATION, 88   88

**L**

LETTER TO THE WORLD, 141 - 143   141

**M**

MAN FIGHTS AGAINST GOD, 32 - 33   32
MELCHIZEDEK'S ASSIGNMENT, 94   94
MISSION OF JOHN THE BAPTIST, 95   95
MOSES'S ASSIGNMENT, 94   94
MURDER, 135 - 140   135
MY WORDS; YOUR WATCHWORDS, 160 - 162   160

## N

NOAH'S ASSIGNMENT, 94    94

## P

Paradise Lost, 1    1
Paradise Regained, 3    1
PHONE NUMBER GOSPEL, 186    186
PRAYER FOR THE WORLD, 144 - 146    144

## R

RE-INCARNATION., 91 - 94    88
REIGN OF LOVE BY 2000 AD, 178 - 182    178

## S

SECOND STEP TO GOD, 40 - 42    40
SERVANTS ARE GREAT, 125 - 134    125
Smith's Recipe From Above, 26    26
STAR, 14    12
STEPS TO GOD, 34 - 46
   Worship God, How to 36    34

## T

THE LAST COMMANDMENT, 175 - 177    175
THEOLOGY AND CHRIST, 163 - 165    163
THIRD STEP TO GOD, 42 - 43    42

## U

UNIVERSAL LEADER IN 2001, 105 - 115    105

## V

VEGANISM , 20 - 25    20

## W

WHEN GOD BECOMES MAN, 116 - 124    116
Where are we going?, 2    1
Where are we now?, 2    1
WHO WILL GO TO HEAVEN, 47 - 64    47
WHO WILL GO TO HELL, 65 - 87    65
WOMAN MUST NOT RULE, 20 - 21    30
WORD, Power of 147 - 153    147